The Edge of Enchantment

Sovereignty and Ceremony in Huatulco, México

BY ALICIA M. GONZÁLEZ

PHOTOS BY ROBERTO YSÁIS

NATIONAL MUSEUM OF THE AMERICAN INDIAN
SMITHSONIAN INSTITUTION
WASHINGTON AND NEW YORK

Head of Publications, NMAI: Terence Winch
Editor: Holly Stewart
Designer: Steve Bell
Photography © 2002 Roberto Ysáis and
National Museum of the American Indian,
Smithsonian Institution. Text © 2002 NMAI,
Smithsonian Institution.
All rights reserved
under international copyright conventions.
No part of this book may be reproduced or uti-
lized in any form or by any means, electronic
or mechanical, including photocopying,
recording, or by any information storage and
retrieval system, without permission in writing
from the National Museum of the American
Indian, Smithsonian Institution.

For information about the National Museum
of the American Indian, visit the NMAI Website at www.nmai.si.edu.

First edition
10 9 8 7 6 5 4 3 2 1

Distributed by Fulcrum Press,
Golden, Colorado

Publication of The Edge of Enchantment was made
possible in part through the generous support
of the Latino Initiatives Fund, administered by
the Smithsonian Center for Latino Initiatives.

The exhibition Edge of Enchantment, on view at
the National Museum of the American Indian's
George Gustav Heye Center in New York, was
supported in part by the Latino Initiatives Fund
and by the Rockefeller Foundation.

Library of Congress Cataloging-in-Publication
Data
González, Alicia María.
The edge of enchantment : sovereignty and
ceremony in Huatulco, México / by Alicia
María González ; photographs by Roberto
Ysáis.
    p. cm.
"Published in conjunction with the exhibition
The Edge of Enchantment, on view at the
National Museum of the American Indian,
George Gustav Heye Center, Alexander Hamil-
ton U.S. Custom House, New York City, winter
2002 through August 2003"—Verso t.p.
Includes index.
ISBN 0-9719163-0-6 (softcover : alk. paper)
1. Indians of Mexico—Land tenure—Mex-
ico—Santa María Huatulco—Exhibitions. 2.
Indians of Mexico—Mexico—Santa María
Huatulco—Religion. 3. Indians of Mexico—
Mexico—Santa María Huatulco—Government
relations—Exhibitions. 4. Santa María Huat-
ulco (Mexico)—History—Exhibitions. 5. Indians of Mexico—Mexico—Oaxaca
(State)—Exhibitions. I. National Museum of
the American Indian (U.S.).
George Gustav Heye Center. II. Title.
    F1219.1.O11 G655 2002
    972'.74—dc21
                              2002008332

The National Museum of the American Indian,
Smithsonian Institution, is dedicated to
working in collaboration with the indigenous
peoples of the Americas to protect and foster
Native cultures throughout the Western Hemisphere. The museum's publishing program
seeks to augment awareness of Native American beliefs and lifeways, and to educate the
public about the history and significance of
Native cultures.

Photo credits: P. 8, ceramic trumpet (22.5717),
photo by Katherine Fogden (NMAI); shell
chest ornament (22.5275), photo by Ernest
Amoroso (NMAI). P. 9, gold labret (18.0756),
photo by Pam Dewey (NMAI). Pp. 12-13, map
by Jaime Quintero. P. 20, painting reprinted
with the permission of INAH Oaxaca. P. 21,
reprinted with the permission of the Pinacoteca Virreinal de San Diego, Mexico City. P.
24, derrotero courtesy of the Henry E. Huntington Library, San Marino, California. P. 175,
family photo. Cover flap: Photo of Roberto
Ysáis by Peter Brill (NMAI).

Cover: Preparing for the Feast of San Pedro, San Pedro
Huamelula, 1999. Back cover: Alligator, dressed to
play the central role in the Feast of San Pedro, San
Pedro Huamelula, 1999. P. 1: Palms, Bajos del Are-
nal, 1997. Pp. 2–3: Fireworks for Cuarto Viernes (the
Fourth Friday of Lent), Santa María Huatulco, 1998.

972.74
GON
2002

Contents

FOREWORD

7   W. Richard West, Director,
National Museum of the American Indian

INTRODUCTION

15   The Place at the Edge of the Sea

BAHÍAS | BAYS

27   Bahía de Santa Cruz | Bay of the Holy Cross
38   El Pedimento
40   Bajos de Coyula | Lowlands of Coyula
49   Bajos del Arenal | Sandy Lowlands
52   Cacaluta (Cacalotepec) | The Hill of the Crows
55   Bahía Chahue | The Place that Floods
55   Arrocito | Little Rice
57   Punta Arena | Sandy Point
57   Tangolunda | Beautiful Woman
59   Barra de la Cruz | The Sandbar of the Cross

RÍOS | RIVERS

63   Río Copalita — The River of Incense — and La Bocana
66   Río Seco | The Dry River
70   Zimatan (Cimatlan) | The Root of the Mountain

MONTES | MOUNTAINS

73   Xadani |Foothills
75   San Miguel del Puerto, the Wingless Saint
81   Cerro Lobo | Wolf Mountain
81   Cuajinicuil | The Place of the Cuil Tree
82   Xuchitl | Flower Mountain
84   Benito Juárez

POBLADOS | VILLAGES

93   Santa María Huatulco (Coatulco)
104   Erradura and the Footprint of Santo Tomás
106   On the Way to San Mateo Piñas
113   Piedra de Moros | Rock of the Moors
118   Paso de los Robles
125   San Isidro Chacalapa | The Place of the Sweetwater Shrimp
126   Santiago Astata | The Place of the Storks
136   San Pedro Huamelula | The Place of the Seeded Trees
150   Feast of San Pedro: The Path of the Alligator

EL ENCANTO DEL NORTE | THE ENCHANTMENT OF THE NORTH

167   Baja California: The Peninsula and the Border
169   Baja California Norte
170   California
173   New Jersey
175   Epilogue

178   END NOTES
185   BIBLIOGRAPHY
190   INDEX

Numinous Landscapes

COMMUNITY LIES AT THE HEART OF NATIVE LIFE. By community, I mean the shared histories, practices, and beliefs that sustain our sense of identity and the specific places we call home, to which we remain rooted. What delights me most about this marvelous book, and makes me particularly proud of its publication by the Smithsonian's National Museum of the American Indian, is the way in which, through the voices of the people themselves, *The Edge of Enchantment* invites us into the Native communities of coastal Oaxaca.

Native scholar Jace Weaver has written of the "numinous landscapes that are central to [Native] faith and . . . identity," but rarely have those landscapes been so rapturously portrayed as they are in *The Edge of Enchantment*. For the better part of the last decade, anthropologist and folklorist Alicia González, a senior curator at the Museum, and photographic artist Roberto Ysáis have visited the towns and hamlets of the Huatulco–Huamelula region of México, speaking with and photographing many of the people who live there. Over time, the scholar, the photographer, and the people of coastal Oaxaca became a greater part of each other's lives. The trust that grew up among them pervades this book, as it does the exhibition of the same name on view at the Museum's George Gustav Heye Center in New York. Dr. González, whose writing captures enduring modes of memory and expression, has structured her book to reflect boundaries the people of Huatulco and Huamelula use to define their communal sovereignty. By printing many of his photographs on old cloth and paper, or as antique postcards, Roberto Ysáis has created an imagery that pays homage to traditional forms of photography in México, as well as to the beauty of the people and landscapes of this part of the world. Together, this culturally empathic photography and narrative create a powerful new vocabulary through which the histories of these nearly hidden communities are related.

In *The Edge of Enchantment*, people speak intimately about work, family, property, history, religion, and dreams. Edmundo Cruz Martínez describes what it was like to fish the ocean by night from a dugout canoe, using only a lamp, harpoon, and trident spear. Two elderly women remember their initial unhappiness with the men chosen for them to marry. On the eve of the Day of the Dead, doña Celia Piñon talks about the observances to follow as she prepares her special *mole poblano*. Indeed, several holidays are celebrated in these pages, including the Feast of Saint Peter, when the town of San Pedro Huamelula reenacts its history and, through a communal, ritual marriage to an alligator (shown in the

El Morro (the Lookout), Bahía de Santa Cruz, 1999

Shell chest ornament with stone inlay. Maya region, C.E. 900–1200. Merida, Yucatán, México. (22.5275)

Ceramic trumpet in the shape of a conch shell, with frog design. West Mexican style, C.E. 200–600. Colima, México. (22.5717)

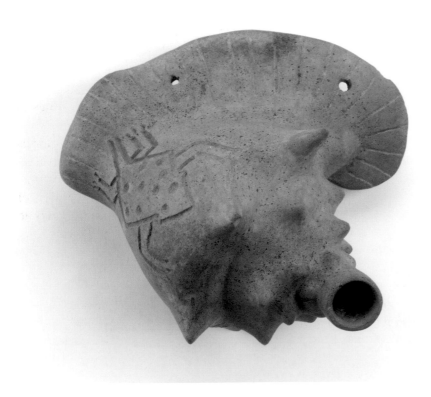

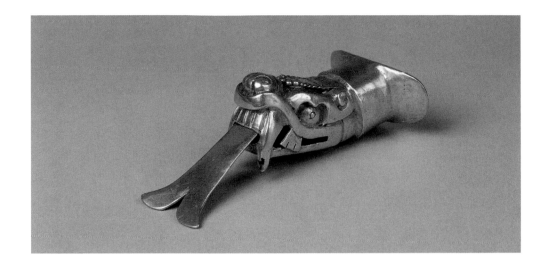

Gold labret representing a serpent's head. Mixtec style, C.E. 900–1521. Ejutla, State of Oaxaca, México. (18.0756)

extraordinary photograph on the back cover), reaffirms its ties to the land.

Some of what is described in this book strikes me as particularly illuminating of the Indian cultures of México and Central and South America, and wonderfully so—the specific syncretism of Mesoamerican and Catholic beliefs, for example, and the fondness (one I confess I share) for legal language and documents. Other issues—including the importance of sustaining our cultures, languages, and lands—will resonate with indigenous peoples throughout the world. The loss of lands, the disruption of communities, and the struggle for survival have long marked our experience.

The kind of profound intellectual exchange with Native communities that characterizes *The Edge of Enchantment* is crucial to the work of the Museum. Indeed, nothing is more important to me, as founding Director of NMAI, than the Museum's relationship with the Native peoples of the Western Hemisphere who form our constituency. In 2004, we will open our Museum on the National Mall in Washington, D.C., the culmination of many years' work, generously supported by the U.S. Congress and Native and non-Native individuals and families, corporations, nations, and tribes. I am committed to ensuring that the exhibitions and public programs presented on the Mall reflect our partnership with Native communities with the same substance and passion you will encounter in this book.

Finally, as an institution of living cultures, the Museum must reach beyond its walls to work with Native peoples seeking to document and preserve their own histories and cultures. During the course of Dr. González's and Mr. Ysáis's work in the region, the jurisdictions of Huatulco and Huamelula decided to move forward with plans to build their own museums. The research, historical resources, and photography developed for this book will be available to scholars and other visitors there, allowing us, in some small way, to return something to these communities, which have given us so much.

W. Richard West
(Southern Cheyenne and member of the Cheyenne and Arapaho Tribes of Oklahoma)
Director, National Museum of the American Indian

Acknowledgements

THROUGH THE YEARS, INDIVIDUALS FROM THE MUNICIPALITIES of Santa
María Huatulco, San Pedro Huamelula, Santiago Astata, San Miguel del Puerto, and many other communities mentioned in *The Edge of Enchantment* were generous and supportive, always showing great
enthusiasm for the *obra*, or work. I regret that only a fraction of the narratives and portraits they shared
can be presented here. Over time, most individuals and families, if not all, opened their homes and
hearts to me and to Roberto Ysáis, after he joined the project. Many have become dear friends. Roberto
and I are deeply indebted to them for this partnership and to the authorities within the *municipios* who
also graciously supported our work.

Roberto's ability to capture the grace and dignity of these people, and the beauty of their land, is a
gift for which I am most grateful. The warmth, intelligence, and depth of feeling that shine through in
his magnificent photography are a reflection of his character, as well as his art.

I owe special thanks to doña María Escamilla and don Manuel Zárate of Huamelula, and to their
daughter Eli, who came to Washington to work with me for a brief period. Doña Celia Piñon and her
son Armando, from Astata, were invariably gracious and generous. Roberto's and my thanks go to the
familias Cervantes, Martínez, Alderete, and Ríos; to Salvador López Toledo and Judith Juárez Sánchez;
to Luis Galguera Scherenberg and his parents, Señores Tomás Galguera and Irma Scherenberg de
Galguera, who always opened their homes to us. I thank especially, and I will miss, the late don Isidoro
Narvaez and don Ignacio García. In our last conversation, don Ignacio asked for a pair of "ninety-two
eyeglasses." I asked, "What size is ninety-two?" His answer: "For a ninety-two-year-old, like me." I have
faith that he now has better vision than I can ever hope to have.

We are indebted to Beto Avendaño and his family, who always served tamales when we visited them.
Abdías Vasquez and Dr. Gonzalo were in on this project at the beginning and joined in supporting it at
the end. Don Mónico el Sobador, the bonesetter, treated several ankles sprained during our fieldwork.
We also thank Dr. José and Sra. Lourdes Horí, and their daughter Luisa Isabel.

There is one person to whom I owe a particular debt of gratitude: the young Mexican archeologist
Adelina Suzán Morales. Adelina first came to the National Museum of the American Indian as an intern,
then continued as a research assistant, working long hours. We managed on a shoestring budget sometimes, and Adelina's dedication meant a great deal to me. Elsa Mamani, from Argentina, an earlier
intern at the Museum's Cultural Resources Center, also worked with me and was equally steadfast in
her enthusiasm.

This work would not have been possible without the support of the Latino Initiatives Fund, administered by the Smithsonian Center for Latino Initiatives. I am especially grateful to Dr. Refugio Rochín and

Judith Scott of the Center. The National Institute of Anthropology and History (INAH–México) and the Centro Regional del INAH–Oaxaca, under the direction of Arq. Alfredo López Calzada, kindly allowed us access to important documents and materials. In particular, I thank the gracious Dra. María de los Angeles Romero Fritzi, and the late Director of the Museo Regional de Oaxaca, Manuel Velasco, whom we always seemed to meet at airports. Dr. Javier Urcid traveled with us occasionally, and Dr. Marcus Winter read and critiqued the manuscript. Special thanks are also due to my colleague, the brilliant Mexican historian Dra. Guadualupe Jiménez Codinach, who was a part of this work from the beginning and whose constructive critiques were extremely valuable throughout. Likewise, I thank Louise Jeffredo Warden for spending innumerable hours comparing notes about her work and mine along the Pacific coast, and about our work as women in traditional indigenous communities. Dr. Alfredo López Austin encouraged me in my decision to approach the titles and other municipal papers as living documents. Dr. John Pohl also read this book in draft form.

Our thanks go to former Congressman and Smithsonian Regent Esteban Torres and his wife, Arcy, who hosted us in their home as we worked along the border between San Diego and Baja California Norte. Thank you also to Hugo Morales and the Morales family of Northern California. Ed Redmond and my friend Dr. John Hebert were wonderfully responsive to requests for assistance with maps from their division at the Library of Congress. Thank you, too, to Dr. Bill Frank of the Huntington Library in San Marino, California. With talent, patience, and generosity, Jaime Quintero created the first topographical map of the region of Huatulco for this book. Thank you to producer Hector Galán for his work on the video documentation of the "Path of the Alligator," and to sage Hilda Hill.

The Smithsonian's National Museum of the American Indian has been my institutional home for the most productive years of this project. Key individuals at the Museum supported my work, particularly Director Rick West, whose commitment to providing a forum for Native voices informs all the Museum's undertakings, and Assistant Director for Community Services Nicolasa Sandoval, who believed in the long-term value of my work with the people of these communities. I also thank Dr. Charlotte Heth, Diane Bird, Dr. Doug Evelyn, and Maggie Bertin for their encouragement and support. NMAI's Cynthia Smith, Rebecca Graham, Veronica Harrell, Patricia Ellington, and Glenn Burlack shouldered a heavy load administratively. The Museum is blessed in having a very talented editorial team, headed by Terence Winch. Steve Bell is responsible for the graceful and dynamic design of these pages. He and editor Holly Stewart worked long hours, enduring with me the de-selection of the wealth of materials that couldn't possibly fit between the covers of this book. Ann Kawasaki, in characteristic fashion, made things work swiftly for everyone. I thank them for their dedication and humor. A great exhibition team, led by Ann Silverman, designers Peter Brill and Gerry Breen, and videographer Dan Davis, and including Gerald McMaster, Deputy Assistant Director for Cultural Resources, Eric Satrum of the Office of Registration, Shawn Termin of the Office of Education, graphic artist Susanna Stieff, and administrative specialist Bob Mastrangelo, made the exhibition at the Heye Center a very special part of this project. Thank you to the Rockefeller Foundation for generous support of the exhibition.

Ron Smith approached his work in the photo lab for this book with patience and brilliance. Special thanks are due to Roberto's great friend and fellow photographer Steven Sakai for all his years of mentorship, and his belief in Roberto's beautiful photography. When I got the idea to follow my deepest instinct to work in Huatulco, Elsa Malvido, my colleague and friend from INAH, accompanied me. Thank you, Elsa. Roberto and I also wish to thank our families, who shared our enthusiasm for the work we were doing.

Alicia María González

The Place at the Edge of the Sea

TO THE UNKNOWING EYE, the coast of Oaxaca along México's Mar del Sur appears lush, intriguing, and temptingly unoccupied—a paradise free for the taking. Yet the land hides the heirs to titles dating back hundreds, even thousands, of years. What cannot be seen from a distance becomes clearer as you focus more closely. Then the landscape reveals a man bent over crops in the tropical forest; a shepherd herding animals on the side of a narrow dirt road; a barefoot woman carrying a load of kindling on her head, and her children doing the same, walking ahead of and behind her. For centuries, trespassers have besieged this terrain. Even now, many of its people must choose between the constant struggle to maintain their land or surrender to its forfeiture. Some have no choice. For reasons of their own, outsiders have always wished to stake their claim to all or part of this land between the Isthmus of Tehuantepec and Pochutla. Often, they have become part of its history. But this is apparent only upon closer view.

Several paths brought me to study this particular part of México. My mother was born more than eighty-five years ago in a mining town in Arizona. As a child, she moved to México, where she later met my father. He and my grandfather shared the experience of working in the United States, though my grandfather returned home, living most of his life and final days in México. My mother, too, eventually returned to the land of her birth, taking the road north with my oldest brother before my father and my other siblings followed. All this happened more than half a century ago. Mine is one of many families who have migrated north and south. For us, the roads between the United States and México lead home in both directions.

From the 1970s to the early 1980s, in Southern California, I organized cultural events in which many Mexicans from the state of Oaxaca took part, particularly native-speakers of Mixtec and Zapotec. A bit later, as a graduate student at the University of Texas at Austin, and then as a professor at the University of Southern California, when I wrote about the role wheat bread played in México, I found frequent references to the port of Huatulco. Sugar exported from Huatulco to other parts of México was used to make the popular *pan dulce*, or Mexican sweet bread. Wheat and sugar were foreign to indigenous palates before

Left: Arrocito, 2000

Above: Santa Cruz Bay, 1998

the Spanish Conquest, but they became a preoccupation and source of wealth for Cortés himself very early in the 16th century. The clothing worn by Native women of the Isthmus and their families who worked the sugar resembled the clothing worn by Moorish Iberians of the 16th century (except for the embroidery, which now had stylistic Chinese floral motifs, the result of trans-Pacific contacts), and that fact further engaged my curiosity.

I arrived in this remote coastal paradise by neither road nor sea, but in a jet filled with tourists. The wings of the plane stretched across a brilliant blue sky scattered with clouds. Here, life is governed by the wet and dry seasons, and at that time of year, the mountains of the Sierra Madre del Sur were densely covered with green. Ahead, to the south, nine bays nestled within the rocky coastline of the Mar del Sur. The jet circled inland. Large enough to be seen through the canopy of trees were two rivers, the Río Coyula and Río Copalita, some dry riverbeds, and a few pockets of settlement and small tracts of houses and hotels overlooking the crystalline water. We landed at one of the few llanos, or plains, visible in this landscape of mountains and hills, about twenty kilometers from the bays, and ten kilometers from the municipal seat of Santa María Huatulco.

Before leaving home, I had researched archives in the United States and México, and found few sources. In the 1960s, archeologist Donald Leslie Brockington worked in the region, and in the early 1970s he continued doing fieldwork with a team of archeologists throughout much of the area. His research yielded some very fine archeological material, and correlations between the material culture of coastal Oaxaca and that of other areas, but unfortunately he did not continue. I wanted to know about the people who live along the coast and their relationships with other groups. I was particularly interested in the role cyclical rituals and festivals play in pulling people back to their villages of origin. I gave myself geographic limits, based on what I had read. (Brockington noted the region's difficult terrain.) In a well-worn rented vehicle with even more worn tires, I set out on the course I had mapped. The church registry in Pochutla, the region's farthest point westward, identified baptisms, marriages, and deaths dating to the 1700s. In Huamelula, the easternmost community, hidden away behind mountains, a clerk gave me a copy of summaries of the town's holdings, and showed me an old letter from the historian Peter Gerhard, about the historical geography of the region.

In Santa María Huatulco, the municipal president and authorities said that there were no records in the town hall, though something might be found in some storage space they had taken elsewhere while that building was renovated. And indeed, there, among piles of paper, old and new, we uncovered a stack of documents, carefully wrapped in bright turquoise plastic, dating from the 1600s to the 1900s. An index, typed in 1949 and bundled together with the documents, listed forty-nine entries. Over the following days, the municipality was kind enough to make copies of these papers for me, and I noticed that one of the documents listed was missing from the stack we had found. On further inquiry, the authorities learned that it had been sent, along with other papers and records, to be conserved in Oaxaca City. When we located it there, it turned out to be the "primordial title" that delineated, by name and landmark, the boundaries of the region. The people of the community knew this important document existed—several mentioned it in interviews—but they had lost track of it. Together, these papers represent hundreds of years of contested space. Ironically, helping the municipality recover them opened communities to me and gave impetus to this research.

In any culture, in any part of the world, identity is tied to the place where the ancestors dwell. In Huatulco and Huamelula, mojoneras or linderos—landmarks or boundary lines—

Río Copalita and the Mar del Sur, 1998

define the space claimed by individuals and groups. The ocean is one of the most obvious boundaries. Beaches next to rocky cliffs, marshes, lagoons, mountains, and rivers are other natural boundaries. These features of the landscape create special places and sometimes fortress communities from the world outside. Families intermarry with people whose territory is adjacent, until family and place take on nearly the same meaning.

Over several years, I came to work closely with mestizo, Zapotec, Chontal, Mixtec, and Huave peoples, and with other groups whose ancestors helped draw the map of this place. I learned that almost every town and hamlet in Huatulco and Huamulela has its *encanto*, a physical space where a fissure or chasm leads to an unknown, metaphysical world. The origin story of each village is integrally woven into its enchanted place. Most villagers are familiar with their local encanto, but it is the elders of the region who know the stories of others. Tourism, development, emigration, conquests, plagues, and natural disasters have led to the eradication and demystification of a few encantos, bringing them to the edge, to a transformation.

In the course of this work, photographer Roberto Ysáis became my research partner. As we drove from place to place, we gave rides to everyone we could fit in the rented car. We met many people this way—and as we got to know many people, it became difficult to deny anyone a ride. Eventually, I bought a ten-year-old jeep and drove from Washington, D.C., to California. Roberto joined me there, and we went on to Baja California, then inland through the deserts all the way to Huatulco. It had been a dream of mine to retrace the path the indigenous migrants take to El Norte, although we traveled by car, while so many of them make their way on foot.

The exodus is a more recent phenomenon in Huatulco and Huamelula than in many parts of México. This once-isolated area began to change in earnest during the 1980s, when privately held and communal land along the coast was expropriated by the government of México for the development of a tourist economy. Over the last twenty years, many families have moved away from their original homes on the bays. Some have been resettled farther inland, often working in service to local developers and hoteliers. Others have joined the stream of people going north. Many never make it to the United States. They live in communities with fellow Oaxacans and other displaced Mexican Native peoples in the towns and fields of Baja California. Those who have crossed the border are lost among thousands upon thousands of migrants living in the United States, working as laborers in fields, hothouses, and vineyards, as gardeners, and as servants, until they can return home. When we traveled to New Jersey, where many young Huatulqueños now reside, we brought news of their families, and we took news back to Oaxaca as well.

By the time Roberto and I made our trek, we were well acquainted with many people who not only followed our work, but also offered suggestions for more interviews. Happily, I was trained in a scholarly tradition that recognizes the importance of working directly with people. How can we understand their history, if not through their words? A former fisherman, now a tourist guide, is the direct heir of people mentioned in two ancient land claims. Through him I first realized that I would have to abandon the approach many researchers might take, and entrust myself to the knowledge of the elders of the region. They are the people who know about the old records and about the central issue of land, identity, and history. Roberto and I owe our gratitude to them, and to all the other people we met who trusted us with their knowledge and with portraits of their lives.

There is a custom that is followed to this day, practiced among the Chontal of this region, to give reverence—*dar reverencia*—both to the civil authorities and to the power unseen, the Creator and the spirits. In all of the ceremonies performed in Huamelula, the dancers bow to the spirits, to the saints, and to the authorities. People, like Señor Jesús Avendaño, a literature professor who has written about his village, Astata; Señor Cuahtemoc Méndez of Huatulco, a local chronicler; and Señor Cástulo García García, former mayor of San Mateo Piñas and the author and publisher of his own book, are adamant to set the record straight. They have written, in many cases, for people who cannot read, but who value these books as though they were the original titles to this place. The books are written and cherished in the hope that reverence and respect will be given to this land and its special places, which continue to hold the mystery of the ancients, their ancestors.

Through my good fortune in coming to this part of the world, I've learned that the reason for doing this work is to add to the existing record of a people, or a community, especially where there is little documentation. I also know that the mirror we produce must be well polished, in order for the community to see its own reflection, and for others to admire it as well. With humility, I hope that through this book, I can show my deep appreciation for the many gifts of beauty that were given to me.

History

The title, dated January 8, 1539, contains some of the first words written by outsiders about this place: " . . . Santa María de Guatulco, town founded at the edge of the sea."[1] This beautifully painted document of twenty-nine *fojas*, or leaves—some in very poor condition, eaten by insects and illegible, others faded by time—bound together with brown thread into a book, still holds important clues about the land and its people. This is the document that was transferred to the archives in Oaxaca City for conservation and forgotten, then recovered during research on this project. An indexer's handwriting appears on the first foja of the book, an elegant blue script unlike the one used on the inside pages. Unable, perhaps, to decipher the date on the original, the indexer has described the contents as follows:

> 1528
> A very ancient title which consists of the welcome
> that the Indians of this town of Huatulco gave to Hernán Cortés.[2]

On the tenth foja there is an image in Maya blue and blackish-brown ink of a Virgin with long flowing hair, wearing a crown and standing on the quarter moon, sheltered by a

Tenth foja of the title dated 1539, showing three caciques worshipping at the shrine of the Virgin

thatched shrine. A large bell is drawn on the left side, under its own thatched roof, which supports a cross at its top. Kneeling before the Virgin are three caciques, or Native leaders, dressed in Spanish attire, hats under their arms, with their traditional staffs of authority beside them. These Spanish words are written beside the images of the three men: "Town of the Immaculate and Clean Conception of Huatulco, Don Juan de Simón, Hernán Cortés, Don Domingo Pérez, and Don Pedro García, founders of this Holy Conception."

The document of 1539 refers to this region as Guatulco, also written Aguatulco and Aguatusco. It declares that the boundaries of the properties being delivered were drawn based on the clearly stated titles of the ancestors kept in the town of Guamelula.[3] Further, it states that the limits of the settlement are "as is shown in the painting of the foundation and decree of the ancient town."[4] By the 1700s, these documents had been lost—a misfortune the people traced to several factors, including El Inglés, an Englishman, or pirate, they say ravaged the town—but clear demarcations were redrawn by interviewing witnesses from the neighboring towns of San Mateo Piñas and Huamelula.[5]

The fojas go on to say that possession of the land is turned over to the caciques, on the condition that the two towns—renamed, after the Spanish Conquest, Santa María Guatulco (more formally Santa María of the Clean, Pure, and Immaculate Conception) and San Miguel de Guatulco—retrieve and sell salt from the marshes and lagoons of Coyula, Arenal, and Mascalco in order to present the church with the proper accoutrements. It says that the people are to have cattle for the sole purpose of assisting with the celebration of the festivities of the confraternity of the "Patroness of Our Pure Conception." In addition, they should build her church and give to her according to their uses and customs. Should they fail to fulfill these obligations, the Virgin would go to Guamelula, the *cabecera*, or headquarters, of the settlement. The deed of possession also calls for the enforcement of a brotherly relationship between the port of Santa María and the town of San Miguel on the mountain.[6]

There is a series of 16th-century *Relaciones*, narratives from interviews the Spaniards conducted with the Native people, or *naturales*, of the communities they encountered in the New World.[7] These official interviews consist of fifty specific questions related to politics,

Simms Library
Albuquerque Academy
6400 Wyoming Blvd. N.E.
Albuquerque, NM 87109

religion, geography, and economy. As recorded in the *Relación de Huatulco*, the *naturales* of Guatulco, from both the port and the town, informed their interviewer that the ancient name for their village was Coatulco, which meant "the place of the snake" (*coatl* = snake, *co* = place). The residents of the port said that the place where they were standing was known by the ancients as *cerro de la petaca*, the hill of the trunk, "because the port was like a trunk, surrounded by hills." When the people were asked who they were and what language they spoke, the interviewer wrote, "These Indians say they descend from the Chichimecas, and the language they speak is Mexican, corrupt and disguised." He recorded that they also attested that their idol's name was Coatepetl, which meant "hill of the snake," and that they had: "[an] altar or shrine where they venerated the snake and offered copal incense from the copal tree . . . feathers of many colors, precious stones, and human blood that would be drained from their tongues and ears, blood from birds and animals, and that sometimes they would sacrifice some men they caught in the wars and other slaves they bought for this; and they sacrificed them in front of this idol."[8]

La Purísima, with the snake at her feet, painter and date unknown. From the collection of the Pinacoteca Virreinal de San Diego, Mexico City.

Not coincidentally, during the 16th, 17th, and 18th centuries, a snake is shown in most images of the Virgin of Immaculate Conception and Saint Michael the Archangel, patron saints of the towns of Santa María Huatulco and San Miguel. The Virgin has her feet on the snake, while Saint Michael takes his sword and slays the snake or dragon—the same snake that the ancient people of Coatulco worshiped on the hill.[9]

Another name for Guatulco is given in the *Libro de los Tributos*, or *Book of Tributes*, in the form of a glyph showing the head of an eagle holding a tree branch with a flower at its tip. Manuel Martínez Grácida, the philologist and geographer, believes that the pre-Conquest name of the region is more accurately Cuauhtxochco, which he translates as "an eagle sitting in a flowered tree" (*cuahuitl* = tree; *cuauhtli* = eagle; *xochitl* = flower; and *co* = in).[10]

Present-day Huatulqueños use the H in the spelling and center the meaning of the word Huatulco on the explanation written by the prelates and early students of Oaxaca, Fathers Francisco de Burgoa and Antonio Gay, who linked it to the cross. They say it means "the place where the wood was revered," and that it refers to the story of a cross that appeared on the shore with a white-bearded old man. But this translation relies on a relatively recent phenomenon: Father Burgoa, writing between 1671 and 1674, stated that the miraculous cross that gave the name to the port was discovered about eighty-four years earlier, in the 16th century. Others have linked the old man with the Toltec deity–king Quetzalcoatl, the religious reformer whom scholars believe lived around 700 to 900 C.E. and whose symbol is the feathered serpent.

In the later part of the 15th century, well before the time of Cortés, the "place of the snake" was conquered by Moctezuma, and became part of a Nahua stronghold that extended to Pochutla (the land of the pochote trees). This enclave of Nahua peoples lived among Zapotecs, Chontales, Mixtecs, Chatinos, Huaves, and others, who were often in competition with each other.

Situated on a current that allowed for contact up and down the coast to South America, as well as across the Pacific, Guatulco, on the Mar del Sur, was an active port, trading with other coastal communities and countries as part of a large trans-Pacific network. As early as 1522 to 1523, Pedro de Alvarado recognized the region as a strategic location and claimed it for Hernán Cortés. Alvarado—an infamous conquistador often called Tonatiuh by the Native people, after the merciless Mexica god of the sun and day[11]—conquered the area on his way from combating the Mixtec leader of the Tututepec *señorío*, or Native state, to whom Guatulco paid tribute.

The Lavariegas are one of the noteworthy families who have kept track of their family history, as well as the history of Huatulco. The following summary is taken from their notes:

> Pedro de Alvarado . . . crossed the region through the area of Huamelula on the way to the Isthmus. Two years later, in 1526, Don Juan Peláez De Barrio visited the region as a representative of the City of Antequera [Oaxaca City], with the objective of delimiting the territory which would later form part of the jurisdiction of the Archbishop of Oaxaca. Peláez found an Indigenous population of speakers of Zapotec. It is in this language that names of most geographic landmarks and boundaries of Santa María appear. According to the primordial titles, the first version of which dates to 1539, Santa María Huatulco was settled by a small group of Spaniards, among whom is Don Gabriel de Pantoja.[12] It was located in a different geographic location than the present one.[13]

Settlements in the region held off the Spaniards until their citizens, weakened by epidemics throughout the 16th century and again during the 18th, could no longer resist.[14] Guatulco, as a center of Indian government, and the people from neighboring settlements under its jurisdiction, its *sujetos*, continued to pay tribute, but now they paid it not to the Mixtecs, but to the Spanish crown. The Chontales, who spoke a language unrelated to those surrounding them,[15] controlled the important coastal towns of Guamelula, Astata, and Mazatán, to the southeast of Guatulco. They were said by the Spanish to be the most "barbarous" people.[16] Perhaps this idea persisted because the Chontales had been one of the groups most difficult to subjugate. The Chontales also had the most desirable resources, and their town of Guamelula had jurisdiction over Guatulco—in short, they had the most to lose. They were eventually made an *encomienda*, and authority over them was assigned to one person who served as their overlord, protector, and tribute collector.

Guatulco continued to be a center of trade and raids after European contact. Early Portulane maps of world ports, painted on vellum in the 1540s, show Guatulco and Guaturco on what appears to be a long peninsula.[17] By that time, Guatulco was New Spain's most important port on the Pacific, although Europe's focus centered on México's Atlantic coast.

Items of tribute, paid prior to the Spanish Conquest as well as after, include cloth dyed with cochineal or *grana cochinilla*, a red dye traditionally made from small mites that live on cacti. After the Spaniards learned about the process, dyeing became a lucrative business off and on for Native people in the mountainous parts of the region. The Red Coats of the English infantry used grana for their color. In 1787 French botanist Thiery de Menonville published the first treatise on the cochineal dye process so that it could be replicated in Europe.[18] By 1802 cochineal was the largest item of export to Europe from Veracruz, after gold and silver.[19] Cotton was grown in the region long before the arrival of the Spaniards and is still produced in the area. Woven fabrics, or *mantas*, made of ixtle (hemp) or cotton were used by Native people for their clothing, and in a quilted form as armor, and were important items of tribute among Native groups and between Natives and the Spanish. Feathers and live birds were deemed high in value. Present-day elders still talk of those whose money came from catching flocks of beautiful macaws and parrots. San Juan Alotepec (the Hill of the Parrots) is an old Chontal settlement.

The ocean, too, was a tremendous source of wealth, as well as of sustenance. Well before the arrival of the Spanish, trade took place up and down the coast, in part because the terrain inland is so mountainous. The sea provided shells that were shaped into implements and ornaments. It also yielded precious pearls, fine booty for pirates on more than one occasion. This coast offered abundant harbor for turtles, as well. Purple dye, extracted from mollusks along the rocky coasts, was considered an item of great value. Salt, so essential to the diet, was traded to inlanders from the coast of Guatulco and Guamelula further southeast. Salt was also an important element in the pre-Hispanic process for extracting and refining silver.[20]

Gold and copper were demanded for tribute wherever they were available, and the Chontal peoples were known to have a great deal of gold. Cacao, one of the most important commodities produced in the region, used as money and imported and exported throughout ancient Mesoamerica, was traded overland and through the port of Guatulco across the gulf of the Isthmus of Tehuantepec, with Soconusco, Suchitepec, and Acaxutla in Chiapas, and Guatemala and Honduras farther south.[21] In 1550, the galleon *Santandres* anchored at the Port of Guatulco, seeking permission to embark; it was on its way to Acaxutla for cacao.[22] Indeed, one of the main reasons Cortés wanted the port in the first place was because he saw how well-situated it was. As marquis of the Valley of Oaxaca, he owned lands extending well into the Isthmus of Tehuantepec, where he planted and processed sugar cane. Although Guatulco was never granted to Cortés, it did become a port where sugar from his estates could be shipped overseas or traded for other goods.

By the 1570s, most official maritime trade activity had been transferred up the coast to Acapulco, a port more easily accessible to the capital of New Spain, Mexico City. Yet trade continued to flourish in Guatulco, often clandestinely. Vessels regularly anchored at the port, on their way to or from Perú, although a document dated 1551 shows that this popular route was taken with caution. The document forbids any vessel traveling to or from Perú to embark or disembark at Huatulco, except for the ship of the viceroy Antonio de Mendoza, who is granted permission to travel there freely with four black men and one woman and others who are to accompany him.[23] Another record from the same year relates to a voyage to Perú and grants permission to take the "*Negros* . . . Francisco and Catalina and one Indian from Santiago Astata" on the voyage. Not long after, in 1554, the *navío San Jerónimo* from Perú and its captain, Francisco de Valenzuela, sought urgent permission to disembark at the same time that there was another ship in the port. The *San Jerónimo* was sailing from Guamelula with news of the death of the *corregidor*, the local governor of Guamelula. The captain of the *navío* asked to be allowed to anchor in order to fish and to supply the vessel with provisions, people, and merchandise for imminent voyage to Perú.[24] Permission was granted by the magistrate of Guatulco to navigate routinely and with no impediment from Guatulco to Guamelula and Perú with the merchandise and slaves necessary to complete the voyage.[25]

During the 16th century many ships found their way into the region's bays. The Manila galleon, known in Spanish as the *nao de China*, and other sea vessels brought goods and slaves to Guatulco—and, trailing in their wake, English, Dutch, and other privateers. As historian Peter Gerhard tells it, at that time there were at least three ships a year from Perú and many others trading with Central America, and the port "had a church, a large customhouse, warehouses, and several hundred brush and wattle huts," until it was raided by pirates.[26]

According to the Lavariega family history:

> In a 1578 request to Philip the Second, King of Spain, the deputy governor of Santa Cruz and governor of the towns of Tonameca, Pochutla,

Astata, and Huamelula, Don Gaspar de Barbas, . . . recommends the Port of Huatulco [Santa Cruz] as a safe port given the characteristics of the hills surrounding it and the configuration. . . . This port quickly attained a great amount of commercial activity, continuing the exploitation of Oaxacan textiles to Central and South America. Above all, it initiated traffic towards the Orient with the "nao de China" with such success that it attracted the attention of English pirates. The presence of the most famous English pirate Francisco [Drake] was registered in 1570 [1579], whose motives for invading Huatulco were to plunder and possess it.[27]

One incident illustrates how the coast could easily harbor activity unknown in other parts of the area. In 1591 the *alcalde* (mayor) was warned about a possible threat to safety that had been reported by a captain: the presence of "*Negros cimarrones*" (runaway black slaves), growing corn, cotton, and other crops on a hilltop of Coyula.[28]

By the 17th century, navigators had begun to document what they had learned about the ports of the world. A Spanish navigational chart, or *derrotero*, drawn in 1669, is titled *South Sea from California to the Straits of Magellan and Saint Vincent (Derrotero general de la Mar del Sur, desde las Californias hasta los Estrechos de Magallanes y San Vicente)*. Another, dated 1684—*A Description of the Sea Coasts in the South Sea of America* by William Hack—is perhaps better known as *The Buccaneers Atlas*. A third, more descriptively narrated but with few drawings, charts the course from Nicaragua northward. Each atlas rounds the coast of the region and describes its sources of fresh water; idle bays for resting, docking, and repairing boats; local islands and what they might hold. For example, sitting very close to the mouth of the Río de Coyula is the Ysla de Sacrificios, the Isle of Sacrifices.[29]

The great majority of the pirate raids along the Pacific coast took place between the latter part of the 16th century and the mid- to late 18th century. Francis Drake and Thomas Cavendish carried out the most infamous raids recorded, in 1579 and 1587, and another pirate raid took place in an undetermined year during the 1600s. These raids are still vividly commemorated by the old people and the children of Huatulco. An enactment of local history performed every year in the village of San Pedro de Huamelula includes a dozen pirates, whom they call Pichilingües or Pechelingües—a Spanish corruption of Vlissingen (the Dutch port) used by people along the Pacific coast.[30] They say that in 1579, the raid forced the entire population of the town of Huatulco to move three leagues (about fifteen kilometers) inland, the first of a series of events that eventually drove the town ten leagues (forty-eight kilometers) from the coast. During the last raid, the pirates looted and burned the people's possessions, including their documents and titles.

A document found in the archives in Santa María confirms that the people of Huatulco sought permission to settle farther inland and to have a new map drawn to show the limits of their jurisdiction. They also wished to make it clear that they were not infringing on land owned by the proprietor of the local hacienda, Bartolome de la Torre, or by other nearby towns or settlements. The authorities recorded the following statement regarding this claim:

> . . . [W]e, the Naturales of this Town Jurisdiction of the Port of Huatulco, . . . say that we do not have papers nor titles, nor instruments, and if we had we would present them to you. We are very poor, and when the Englishman came to our village, he took the papers. We were left with-

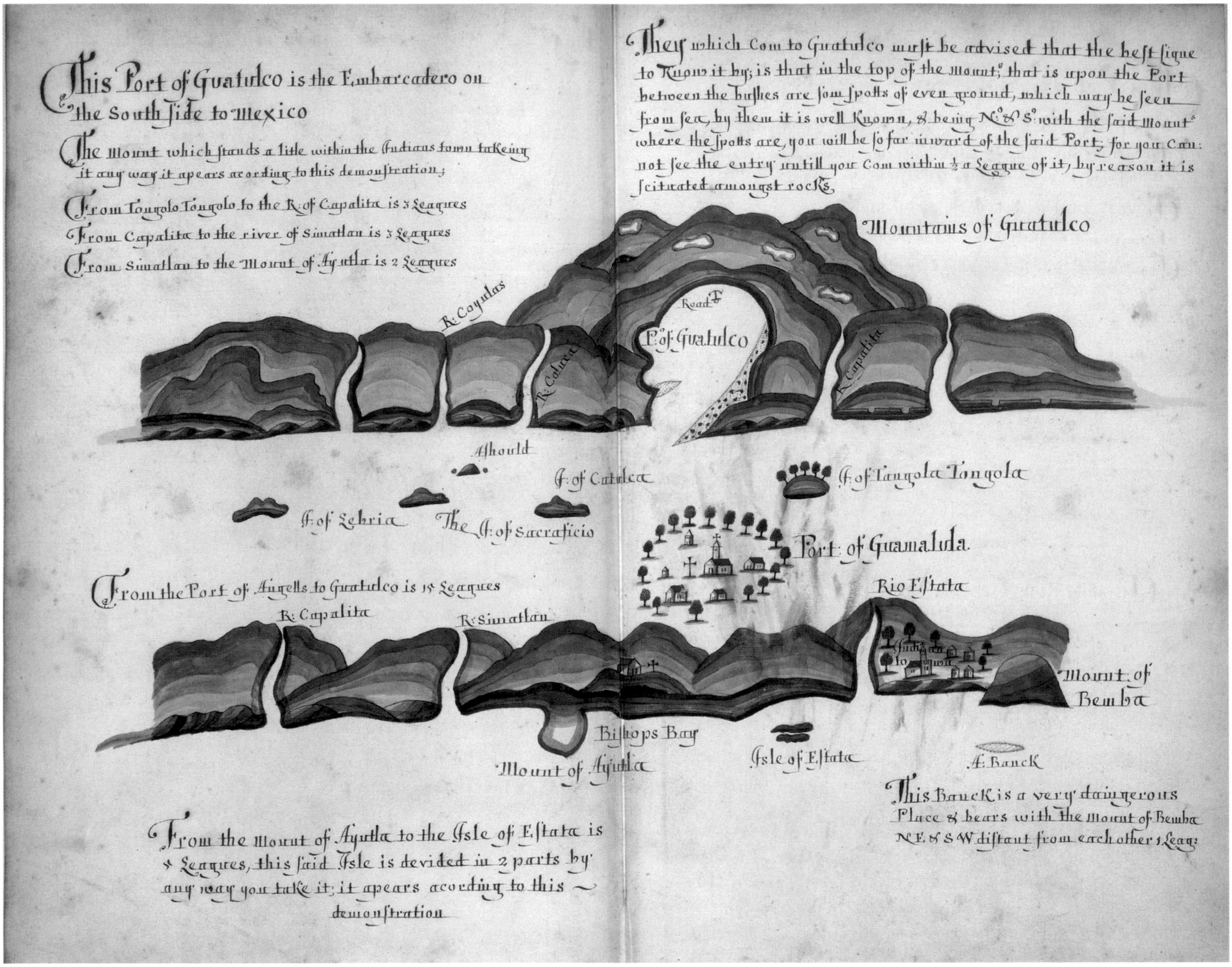
This Port of Guatulco is the Embarcadero on the South side to Mexico
The Mount which stands a litle within the Indians town takeing it any way it apears acording to this demonstration;
From Tongolo Tongolo to the R: of Capalita is 3 Leagues
From Capalita to the river of Simatlan is 3 Leagues
From Simatlan to the Mount of Ayutla is 2 Leagues
They which Com to Guatulco must be advised that the best signe to Know it by; is that in the top of the Mount; that is upon the Port between the bushes are som spotts of even ground, which may be seen from sea, by them it is well Known, & being N: & S: with the said Mount where the spotts are, you will be so far inward of the said Port; for you Can: not see the entry untill you Com within ½ a League of it, by reason it is scituated amongst rocks
Mountains of Guatulco
R: Coyulas
R: Calica
P: of Guatulco
R: Capalita
A shoald
I: of Calica
I: of Tangola Tongola
I: of Zebria
The I: of Sacraficio
Port of Guamalula
From the Port of Angells to Guatulco is 14 Leagues
R: Capalita
R: Simatlan
Rio Estata
Mount of Bemba
Bishops Bay
Mount of Ayutla
Isle of Estata
A Banck
This Banck is a very daingerous Place & bears with the Mount of Bemba N.E. & S.W. distant from each other 1 Leag:
From the Mount of Ayutla to the Isle of Estata is 4 Leagues, this said Isle is devided in 2 parts by any way you take it; it apears acording to this demonstration

Derrotero (ca. 1682–83) showing the Port of Guatulco, from The Buccaneer's Atlas by William Hack.

out any instruments whatsoever. This is what we declare before you, that you our Private Judge, look on us with mercy and charity, that you help us, poor naturales Who are tributaries to the King Our Lord. . . .[31]

Three witnesses attest to the fact that there are only ten tributaries left and that they are too poor to pay tribute, because of the losses they have suffered. Two of the witnesses state that they make some of their living from the *caracolillo*, the mollusks that provide purple dye. A third man, the son of one of the witnesses, states that he works for the man who has the hacienda. The petition was first filed in 1702 and was finally granted by the Spanish authorities in the 1790s. Almost a century passed between the raid and resolution of the claim.[32]

Throughout the 16th, 17th, and 18th centuries, the population of the region grew as more people disembarked, or escaped, from ships. Runaway slaves settled in isolated communities, as described earlier, as did Spaniards and "Chinese"—more likely, Filipinos—who came aboard the navíos. From the 18th century on, the history of Huatulco is encumbered with battles and claims about land tenure and boundary lines—with land contestation in general. As people moved into pockets of land left abandoned after earlier epidemics or forced resettlements, there appears to have been a greater need within Huatulco and among neighboring villages to redefine the original boundary markers. Often, these contests were heated. For example, both San Mateo Piñas and Huatulco claimed Cerro Leon (Lion Hill) and the prosperous business of growing cacti for cochineal there, a dispute that was resolved by dividing the mountain between the two.

Another long-standing source of conflict was cattle grazing beyond titled lands.[33] In 1551 Diego de Guinea sought permission to graze cattle on a ranch called Auscatlan and Apango, later owned by several people including an ancestor of one of the fishermen living there today. De Guinea and four "negros" were granted permission only insofar as they did not infringe on the titled land and property of the "naturales."[34] A document of the 16th century warns of the "negroes and criminals" hidden in Suchitepec, now known as Xadani, but notes that some might have gone with an *encomendero* (an overlord responsible for their conversion in exchange for their labor) to work the mines.[35] In 1723, in a dispute over Guamelula's having tied, lashed, and incarcerated people from Astata for grazing cattle on the wrong land, Juan Baldes of China (probably from the Philippines) was interrogated by the magistrate. The records show that Juan Baldes was thirty years old and leased lands adjacent to Astata. Although Baldes was not present at the incident, another "Chinese" man, whose name was Gavriel and who also leased lands, told him that a group of people had been accosted for trespassing on Astata's property.[36]

Today, the municipal archives include at least six documents that attempt to delineate the original boundaries drawn on this part of the world. Through almost 500 years' history, jurisdictional authority changed from Huamelula to Huatulco to Pochutla and back to Huatulco as the influence of each cabecera advanced or ebbed. The large neighboring settlements of San Mateo Piñas, Pochutla, and Guamelula were all given copies of the same documents in order to avoid further conflict. And with each new set of documents, more place names were translated from Zapotec, Nahua, and others languages into Spanish. Eventually Nahua and Spanish names came to predominate, although even they are sometimes difficult to recognize, altered through usage and time. Some documents call places by colloquial names unused outside the area, much less on any map. To this day, the municipal authorities and others consult the elders who know these sites and some of their stories to get a clearer understanding of what the records may refer to.

The contest over land continues in some remote parts of Huatulco and Huamelula and at the port. In other places, the expropriation of lands for tourist development has put an abrupt stop to earlier legal claims. While people in these towns still mourn the land they have lost, whether in the last twenty or 200 years, their attention has turned to retaining the land they have left. They are concerned less with boundary disputes than with supporting the communal activities in which they participate, creating a meaningful future in a place beginning to be dominated by large hotels and tourism, and sustaining their ties to their young people who migrate north to seek a better life.

Bahías | Bays

Bahía de Santa Cruz | Bay of the Holy Cross

When the Toltecs were exiled from their land, they undertook a journey along the coast, and always passing lands, they arrived at "la California," in the sea which is currently called Cortés, and they called it Hueytlapallan because it was "bermejo" [bright red]. Their arrival was in the year C.E. Tecpatl, corresponding to 387 of our era. Continuing along the coast of Xalisco [now Jalisco] and all of the rest of the south, they left by way of Huatulco and traveled through diverse lands until they reached the province of Tochtepec. . . .

— Fernando de Alva Itlilxochitl, from Historia Chichimeca, *16th century*[1]

Since ancient times people have believed that a white-bearded man was once washed ashore on a wooden cross at this place. Old fishermen like señor Fulgencio tell this story, and so do younger ones, like Mundo Cruz Martinez and Nereo Ziga, and the young teacher Higinia Alcántara Mijangos. Some say this man was Quetzalcoatl, the Toltec deity–king.

Some people believe that this land was a Chontal stronghold invaded by the Mixtecs, Zapotecs, and Nahuas. There is no doubt that it was, and still remains, a juncture, a place where at least three groups have coexisted. Archeologists surveying the land in preparation for tourist development noted extensive sites that were once inhabited, as well as architectural foundations.[2] The Chontales, Mixtecs, Zapotecs, and Nahuas have claimed all or parts of this area at different times. The Mixtecs held vast stretches of territory, from Tututepec on the mountain all the way down to the Isthmus of Tehuantepec, and received tribute from the people who lived here. Later invaders included the Nahuas and the Spaniards. Now their descendants, as well as mestizos, Chontales, Zapotecs, Mixtecs, and others, continue to populate this area and flourish here.

To explore one of many explanations for the origin of the name Guatulco, many people here say that its original meaning is "the place where the wood was revered," from the Nahua word *quauhtli*, or wood. El Madero (the Wood), now known as the Holy Cross, was the name given to the bay. It is also true that among the native flora of this area are the enormously proud ceiba, pochote, and guanacastle (guanacaste) trees. Higinia Alacántara Mijangos, the teacher, says:

Left: Beach at Cacaluta, 1999

Above: El Pedimento de la Cruz del Monte, 1999

The ceiba also has little thorns like the pochote tree. . . . The pochote and the ceiba are related. They each give cotton, but the ceiba gives more. The pods look like little bells when the cotton pops out. But there are people with bad intentions who come and destroy. They don't know what these trees signify, the value they have for our people.

Very few guanacastles and even fewer ceibas remain, survivors of the demand for boats and houses during the Viceregal period (ca. 1521–1821). The once lush jungle is more often now a parched and unmajestic landscape, as some of the people continue to slash and burn the mountainside at the end of the dry season, right before the rains.[3]

When the Spaniards arrived and heard the stories of the old man with the white beard, they consulted the notices and memoirs of the elders. Today, it has been established that the Toltec ruler Quetzalcoatl lived sometime around the Late Classic Period, from 700 to 900 C.E. But the Spanish, using the ancients' methods for computing time, assumed a correspondence with the era of the Christian apostles.[4] The mortal Quetzalcoatl was said to have worn clothing similar to that of the early Christian disciples—that is, a long mantle tied at the waist—long hair, and a beard, and to have embraced a large cross. Legends about the god–king Quetzalcoatl attribute to him the color white. From all this, the Christians came to believe that Quetzalcoatl was in fact the apostle Saint Thomas, who, after preaching in India, must have sailed to Perú and then come to México from the south.[5]

Stories abound throughout Central and South America about Saint Thomas, the man responsible for the veneration of the cross. Although scholars maintain that the apostle died in the East or Far East, for many people in Huatulco, his legend is alive. Others are more skeptical. Higinia Alacántara Mijangos says, "Saint Thomas appeared after the Holy Cross. An *abuelito* [grandfather] brought the Holy Cross long before. My grandmother would say that an abuelito arrived from the ocean and planted the Holy Cross. There, at the edge of the shore he planted the cross, and there is the Holy Cross, the place where the wood is revered."

Either way, the Huatulco legend has it that the man and his cross were first seen along the sand close to the present port, that he was kind and spoke the language of those who lived here, and that he taught the people many things. He left one day after staking the heavy cross onto the shore. Everyone agrees that this happened hundreds of years before the Spaniards arrived.

Edmundo Cruz Martínez and his family used to spend most of their days and nights fishing. His wife is from the state of Guerrero, and together they have two children, a son and daughter. (His wife has another son, as well, who lives with them.) The couple wanted to name their daughter Sabdi. The graying Mundo cradled the baby with the pride of an older man who thought he would never have a daughter. In the end, however, it is the registrar who approves the name selected—or denies it, because names in Zapotec and other languages spoken in the region do not coincide with the names on the Christian calendar. Sabdi no longer recognizes the name she answered to for a year. Now she is Carmelina. She is three and has the specialness of all the little girls from this region, winning the hearts of all around.

The Martínez family was one of the last to be moved from Santa Cruz de Huatulco. Mundo has a small open-air stall where he and his wife sell merchandise to tourists. This is what he was given in compensation for the land his family held on the bay. Now he comes every day to open his stall, which sits next to at least fifty others, by the plaza and the central kiosk of the Café Huatulco, where the coffee-growers association sells its

Edmundo Martínez Cruz, 1999

freshly picked coffee—probably one and the same place where the white-bearded man once preached. It is steps away from the site of the old fishermen's chapel and on the path to El Pedimento, the two places where Mundo's wife takes flowers and performs *limpias*, or blessings, for those closest to her, including Carmelina.

The difference these days is that the fishermen's village is a port of call for cruise ships, smaller yachts, and fiberglass motorboats, or *pangas*. The tourist season usually includes the Christmas holidays, Holy Week, and June, July, and part of August. At other times, the *lancheros*, former fishermen who now take tourists through the bays by boat, scurry about trying to make a living one way or another. But Mundo has left that life behind, he says. He is much better off than many of his fellow townspeople, he says, though he still yearns for the ocean.

At high tide the ocean dams up in places, forming deep, turbulent pools around the beach at Yerba Buena, Rincón Sabroso, and the lighthouse. A small shipwreck can be seen to one side, weathered with rust, abandoned on Yerba Buena after a hurricane. Above is the newly built, and recently vacated, naval base. This prized land was sold at a good price to the Mexican Navy. Mundo says that after the community of Santa Cruz kept growing, the old cemetery was moved from the beach there to the side of the mountain by Yerba Buena, next to an amphitheater and the former naval base. He says that some of the remains were disinterred and re-buried, while others, too old to be moved, were left in the original graves on the beach that is now a tourist resort.

Mundo's father was from San Mateo Piñas, an adjacent Zapotec municipality that has always quarreled with this area over boundaries. He often came to Santa Cruz to work and married Mundo's mother, whose family was from here. Mundo's parents fished from the old dugout canoes, rowing out at night and using a lamp, harpoon, and *sulapán*—a small trident—to catch needlefish and others fishes. The fishermen know each bay and beach for what it has to offer—lobster, crabs, or octopus. Each has its own special fish or resource, as with the *Púrpura pansa* snails, abundant for centuries along these rocky bays and known to the Native women who come south to procure them.

Left: Promontory, las Bahías, 1998

Right: Fishermen and tour boat, 2000

Vicente Guerrero, insurgent chief during the last years of the War of Independence (1816–1821) and President of México from April to December 1829, is considered a hero along the coast. Like so many of the people here, he was of the peasant class, of mixed ancestry, and spoke one of the indigenous languages. He was turned over to the authorities at what is known now as La Entrega (the Beach of Delivery) and shot at Cuilapan, Oaxaca, on February 14, 1831. For Mundo, and many other lancheros and residents, Guerrero's story is one of the betrayal of a popular hero. They tell the story when they bring children and visitors to this beach, asking, "*¿Sabes porque se llama La Entrega?*" "Do you know why this is called the Beach of Delivery?"

Maximiliano de Lavariega has written in his family history:

> During the 19th century the port of Santa Cruz was the terminal station, and Santa María was on the commercial route that united parts of the coast with Oaxaca. At the beginning of 1831, a betrayal took shape at the urging of President Anastasio Bustamante and was executed by Francisco Picaluga and Colonel Valentín Canalizo against General Vicente Guerrero, who was captured in Acapulco and disembarked at the Bay of Santa Cruz, on a beach that since that time is known as La Entrega. Oral tradition of Santa María holds that he was immediately taken to that town, where he spent the night tied to the trunk of a ceiba that was taken down a few years back. General Vicente Guerrero was executed a short time after in Cuilapan.[6]

Swimmers sometimes rest in a cave at the beach of El Maguey, not far from La Entrega. When Mundo was much younger, El Maguey was accessible only by paddling through lush vegetation. The fishermen came here to mend their canoes with *chapopote*, or tar, from this area. They would dig in the earth for it, then boil it, and with that they covered the dugout canoes they used for fishing. The canoes were made of one large piece of wood, and it would sometimes split, so they would apply the chapopote for protection. The canoes were about five meters long. Spanish and British derroteros dating to the 1600s show the Isla Brea, the island where tar could be found for mending boats, not far from here, around the mouth of the Río Coyula.[7] The navigators learned this from the ancients, and even the earliest *Relaciones* discuss it.[8]

Here at El Maguey, *murcielagos* (bats) fly overhead in the cave that Mundo believes was a hideout for pirates and probably many others before and after them. He says there were piles of abalone shell here, perhaps left by ancients who came to get mother-of-pearl. Abalone shells were very important in pre-Columbian religious rituals, and at one time pearl-diving was an occupation. The only way to get to the cave is to dive underwater and then swim up into it. The pirates hid at other nearby bays as well. Francis Drake docked his boat in the Bahía de Santa Cruz in 1579, Thomas Cavendish in 1587. What they were after, of course, was the booty from the Spanish ships and other vessels that docked here.[9]

Local stories are plentiful about Cavendish's raid on Guatulco. It is also well-documented that Cavendish found the famed cross on the beach and tried to take it from here to destroy it. But the cross is said to have endured. As local history has it—the story that Mundo and others tell—a priest later divided the huge cross into at least four small crosses. One is said to stand at the newly built fishermen's chapel on the bay; another at Santa María Huatulco, the town that was established inland after the pirate raids. A third

Sunset on the angry sea (la rebalsa), 1998

is in the cathedral in Oaxaca City, with a painting of Cavendish's failed defilement. A fourth, they say, is in the Vatican. Sometimes they tell about a fifth, in the state of Puebla.

The Lavariega family history records the story this way:

> In 1587 . . . the English pirate Thomas Cavendish became the protagonist of the episode with the legendary Cross of Huatulco, upon his arrival. According to the tradition told by the settlers, the Cross was planted more than 2,000 years ago by a man with a tunic and long beard who spoke Mixtec and mingled with the ancients for several days, spending most of his time in prayer. In his attempt to assault Huatulco, Thomas Cavendish did not find the uprising he expected and was accustomed to, so he ordered that the port be leveled and burned. The only thing left standing was the great Black Cross. Cavendish ordered that it be razed with hatchets, which themselves broke into pieces. Intent on destroying the Cross, he attacked it by tying strong cables to it from his anchored vessel, to no avail. Thus, he ordered that it be burned by first applying tar and resin to it and then igniting it. This caused no harm to the cross. And this is how the legend of the Black Cross of Huatulco was born.
>
> As time went by, the fame of the Cross grew to such proportions that people came from different parts of the world to venerate it, including very large pilgrimages from Perú. With as many as 2,000 faithful before the cross, taking pieces and splinters from it, the Cross was getting thinner. There were those who wondered how this now diminutive Cross withstood the fury of the winds that sweep the beach, causing much admiration. By 1612, the bishop don Juan de Cervantes moved the Cross to Oaxaca City and placed it in the Cathedral. This was after a detailed investigation of more than 2,000 pages, mentioning the pirate attempt to destroy it and many other miracles attributed to it through the testimony of many witnesses.
>
> A short time later, the bishop took a large part of the foot which had been thinned by those taking splinters. The bishop also ordered that a large part of the top be cut and made into a small cross which was sent to Pope Paul V. . . . Finally, one part of this millennial Cross remains in the Cathedral of Oaxaca, another in the chapel in Puebla de Los Angeles, another from the same wood is in Santa María Huatulco.
>
> In 1895 the archbishop . . . placed another great cross in Huatulco in the same place where the first one was, which is the same one that is there to this day. As a consequence of the constant invasions and clashes between the pirates and the Huatulqueños, they decided to transfer it to another more secure site that is two leagues from the port.[10]

Don Ignacio García of Santa María, whose family also has a long history in the region, tells the story as well:

Chapel by the ocean, Coyula, 1997

They wanted to destroy the Holy Cross. They couldn't destroy it. Later they tried to dig it out, but they could never find its base. Then they tried to burn it, nothing. But they did destroy it. They say that an archbishop came and tore it apart. In the church is the small cross adorned with silver. That cross has cured many people. . . .

We all gathered together for the procession [to consecrate the fishermen's chapel]. There was a priest. I was in the procession. Many of us were going when we saw the cloud. It was going to rain, and in a little while the rain started. We were wet when we arrived to leave the cross at the church. At that point the priest came out to receive it. He said that the cross was very miraculous, but he didn't believe it. The cross is very miraculous. They say that the priest took the large one apart, but the largest piece was taken to Rome, and they left a little one here. The best they took to Rome.

The old fishermen's chapel, whose consecration don Ignacio remembers, is not far from the new open-air shrine of the Cruz del Monte. Both the chapel and the shrine receive thousands of pilgrims who come to El Pedimento for the First Friday of Lent, and for the Feast of the Holy Cross, on May 3. They come, too, as in ancient times, to trade

foods and goods. They come from the mountains to sell, buy, pray, and swim in the ocean, in the calmest of all bays. They come for entertainment, in recent years at the *kermess* (fair) and *jaripeo* (rodeo), Traditionally, the mountain people brought venison to sell, and bought fish and salt. As doña Nestora Cervantes Domínguez narrates:

In the past, when there were no tourists, they would say, "Let's go to the fiesta of Santa Cruz." They went just for the fiesta. All of the people passed through town. They would all pass through town; they would never stay. Then the fishermen would stay, and slowly they settled, and the town grew and grew. Now it's very large. People went on burros, and they had small thatched stalls because by day they sold things. They sold fish. Some sold nothing but fish. Later, as more arrived, they had little restaurant stalls. Then it was very nice for the First Friday of Lent, because everyone went. Nowadays it doesn't even seem as though there is a fiesta. Then they would come from all places. They'd come from Piñas, from Pluma, from Candelaria, from Pochutla, from all over. But they only [traveled] on burro, only with their animals. They came to sell whatever they had, and to buy.

On the First Friday of Lent, pilgrims come to this bay, Santa Cruz. Then they travel to the village of Santiago de Astata for the Second Friday. On the Third Friday, they travel to other trading villages, including San Juan Ozolotepec. For the Fourth Friday, the big feast is ten leagues (forty-eight kilometers) away, in the inland municipal seat of Santa María Huatulco, where the priests have given up enforcing a somber Lenten ritual. Instead, the people have festivities that last about a week, with dances, rodeos, fireworks, and one of the largest market days of the year. Even many of the people who have migrated to work in the United States come home for this event. This is duplicated in San Pedro Huamelula to the south, where the Chontales celebrate the Fourth Friday of Lent, and in San Francisco Ozolotepec, where there is a sizeable market day. The Fifth Friday takes place toward the state's capital, Oaxaca City, in the town of Etla, an early trading partner with towns nearer to the coast, and in San Pedro Mixtepec. The Sixth Friday is celebrated in various locales farther inland, in places where the old traders would travel. At the ends of this region, the trading network expands and includes Mitla, the village next to Oaxaca City, which people hope to visit, like Mecca, at least once in a lifetime, to pay homage to the dead.

Here at the Bay of Santa Cruz, one of the main activities is for entire families to stay overnight on the beach and swim in the clear blue ocean. They bring the bare necessities and drink water from the local springs.

There are large banks of white coral at the Bay of the Holy Cross, but the people have noticed so much devastation of late, and local ecologists concur that the coral is vulnerable. There is erosion. The tractors that flattened some of most sacred sites to make way for the naval base on one side of the bay, and for luxury houses and tourist hotels on the other, loosened the sand and topsoil, leading to mudslides. Now the naval barracks, built almost overnight and at the edge of the biological park, are virtually empty, their fate unknown.

Around the bay beyond La Entrega is the *bufadero*, a large rock that erupts with plumes of water when waves crash into a cavity at its base. When the ocean is rough, the bufadero is particularly active. The *Púrpura* snail, temptingly abundant all along the sides and cliffs of the bufadero, is safe from most predators. When he was young, Mundo came here with his parents. Mundo says that first they came as a family to get octopus. When the ocean was still, they would use *balsas* (small, light boats) to get close to the rich, dangerous bufadero. Then some deep-sea divers from Acapulco taught him and his brother their methods, and they learned, but only because they were trying to make a few pesos by rowing for the divers. When the ocean was still, Mundo and his brother used the oars to guide the boat while the divers caught lobsters. In the evenings, about five o'clock, they would row with tremendous strength, so as not to be caught in the rocks.

El bufadero, 1998

Organo (Organ Pipe) is a quiet, pristine beach where turtles lay their eggs in July, August, and September. Few turtles come here anymore; they seek more isolated places to nest. Clams are still abundant, although smaller now than in the past. Mundo says that when he fished, there was a rule that no one disturbed a nesting place, as the new fishermen from outside have done. Divers used to measure the lobsters, he says. If they were

Boy running by the kiosk in Santa Cruz, 1999

too small, they would be thrown back. Mundo says that this is no longer respected. "We would always reserve the small ones," he says. "This is why there was always plenty. There were *lapa* (limpet), conch, oyster, and so many different mollusks."

Organ Pipe is followed by Violín (Violin Beach), named because the water screeches like a poorly played violin when it pours out of the rocky cove. "Many people have died here," Mundo says, "and there are many stories of these people." Mundo and others have names for the rocks, which were formed by volcanic activity. There is a bed, *la cama de piedra*, and there is a well-chiseled face that looks as though it was carved during the Cubist period. The face watches this area, where the water is very deep.

Just to the west is the bay at Cacaluta (Crow's Hill), where large waves come crashing onto the vast unprotected beach. Divers on a small motorboat nearby are using a generator and a long hose they take down with them. They say the depth here is forty to sixty meters. The divers stay underwater for as long as one to two hours, taking in air from the hose. They bring up octopus during the spring season, when the water temperature is changing and the whales pass, swimming north.

Mundo says that before the ecologists arrived, fishermen here used to catch gulf turtles for their meat and hides. Now the turtles are protected, and catching them is prohibited. Cacaluta Island, right off the bay, is covered with guano. It is also a great place for *Púrpura* snails, lobsters, fish, and needlefish. Here, he says, the crashing waves signal the *rebalsa*, the engorgement. The ocean is angry at this time, he and many other fishermen say, because it has not rained. From March until the heavy rains of May through July, the sea waits for the rain to come. Then it swells until around October or November, when the tides begin to go down once again, and the ocean "empties." The lack of rain and the low tides keep the guano-covered cliffs and rock islands white and dry. Todos Santos and Día de los Muertos (All Saints Day and the Day of the Dead) coincide with the end of the rains. The dry season is best for collecting mollusks from the sides of the rocks. This is when the dyers from Pinotepa come. They come from up north, Mundo says, and pass through Puerto Escondido, then Pochutla, then here. They work their way from the Bay of San Agustín down to a beach close to Tangolunda.

Mundo says the ocean is a woman:

I will say, and the truth is, that I have had a great deal of respect for the ocean, and I have also had very good luck because I never failed there. I never had a motor stop on me, but once I had something happen when I tossed the palangre [trawl line]. It's a type of fishing line with several hooks attached. The fishhooks have clamps that come from below and are used to catch sharks. When we go to raise the palangre, we take a long boat and go out beyond Copalita, about sixty meters, or deeper still, about eighty meters. One time we shut off the motor and lifted the line over the cimbra [the swell of the sea]. Once we did that, we tried to start the motor. We tried again, but we no longer had any petroleum— we had run out getting our catch. One of the men suggested we take a box and place it on the prow. We did. We let the wind bring us all the way back into Copalita beach. There another launch brought us back to Santa Cruz. We were there all day. We were tired and hungry, but the west wind brought us in.

The terral is the wind that comes at two o'clock in the afternoon. It comes "*de abajo*" ("from below"). It comes from inland, Mundo says, and it blows "you out, all the way out"—"*afuera*"—toward the Isthmus. Perhaps the same current brought the European ships into this bay. Perhaps they used the terral, or perhaps they were brought in by accident, like the white-bearded old man who landed on the shore. In the 16th century, Fernando de Alva Itlilxochitl recorded the stories he heard about the migration of the Toltecs after they were driven out of their lands by foreign invaders. They landed here at the port of Huatulco, present-day Santa Cruz, and traveled inland. Stories of Quetzalcoatl's presence and the Toltec influence were told farther south among the Maya, as well. Quetzalcoatl, it was said, introduced a different religion to his people. Perhaps the Toltecs knew that they must become allied with the peoples to the south. When they arrived in what is now Santa Cruz, they saw scattered but prominent settlements, of which only vestiges remain today. There are dwellings on almost every precipice of the ancient rock curtains. The old ones say they were occupied by "the gentiles," but the cliffs keep their knowledge.

The rivers and bays are the places that tell the most stories now. Río Huatulco, flowing down from the mountains through the current municipal seat at Santa María de Huatulco, meanders to the ocean through Bajos de Coyula, where Tío José, a wise old man, cares for his land. The Xuchitl and Cuajinicuil fill the dry creeks that sometimes, during the rainy season, flood the plains of Bajos del Arenal. Lucino, who is from Arenal, knows that this is inevitable. For hundreds and hundreds of years, salt from Arenal was traded at the very site where the cross now stands. And during the late winter and early spring, the people who came by way of the old road from Huaxayac, now Oaxaca City, to buy and sell goods at the Bahía de Santa Cruz, stopped at the encanto of El Pedimento to implore the spirits' goodwill.

El Pedimento

In the past the cross was smaller, just a little wooden cross. Then La Cruz del Monte appeared, and it is still there. It's a much more elaborate cross. The one from the past is no longer there. It's the same thing with the cross in [the chapel at] Santa Cruz. The cross that appeared is behind, and the new one is in front of it. There you ask for what you desire, and La Cruz del Monte grants your request. Many people come from Santo Domingo Morelos, and the Third Friday is celebrated there.

—Señora García from Benito Juárez

Every year in early spring, at low tide along the Mar del Sur, on the coast of Oaxaca, pilgrims visit El Pedimento, one of the many encantos known to the people of the region. Here large whitewashed stones form the foundation of La Cruz del Monte, the Cross on the Hill. Native speakers of Chontal, Zapotec, Mixtec, Chatino, and Huave arrive on foot, in taxis, and on the backs of trucks, bringing their offerings.

El Pedimento is at one of the most ecologically vulnerable sites in the region. This holy mountain, encircled by bays and marshes, has been partially flattened, like so many other places nearby, to make room for the development of the tourist economy along coastal lands. But the spring ritual continues to bring together a multitude of people whose faith guides them to this place.

With great purpose the pilgrims build miniature houses using sticks, cardboard, the leaves of the red yacal tree for thatched roofs—models of their homes blown away in 1997 by hurricanes Paulina and Ricardo. Small clay figures of people and animals rest alongside votive candles. Sandbags hold down offerings of flowers and food. Silver reliquaries representing legs, arms, and other body parts lie here beside small nests of twigs containing little stone eggs. Grass roofs shelter miniatures of many things, including farmers' implements and fishermen's nets. Old photos rest alongside handwritten notes, some weakly

scrawled with the prayer, "Grant me the ability to read and write," others penned in the elegant script of an aged scribe.

On the Cruz del Monte lies a promise made by an elderly grandmother. Her long, almost entirely gray braid drapes the top of the wooden cross, wraps around the crossbeam, and hangs down to the base. It is sadness, mixed with hope and joy. A woman's once-long hair adorns the shrine as testimony to a prayer fulfilled.

This is a land that has known all time, where past, present, and future are one. Millennial roads cross here, taking travelers north by way of the pediment on foot through the mountains inland, or south to the ocean, then east or west along the coast, in canoes carved from the grand and graceful guanacastle tree. This is the port of the cross, intersected by all dimensions, all directions.

Many different people lay claim to this place as home. They are born here, and here they live on, even after the entreaty from beyond can no longer be ignored. Most of the elders speak two languages. Some speak three—Zapotec, Chontal, and Spanish—and they are neighbors to people speaking Mixtec, Chatino, and Huave. Some of the children and grandchildren speak their languages of origin; many understand the language of the elders, but speak only Spanish.

There have always been fishermen here. They have fed their families with gifts given by the sea—fish, turtles, and shellfish. Hunters continue to bring home prized iguanas for special tamales, and venison for mole. Farmers grow papayas, mangoes, coconuts, coffee, amaranth, sesame, and sugar cane, and tend their sheep, goats, cows, and other animals. There have always been *maíz*, *frijól*, *calabacitas*, and *nopal* (corn, beans, squash, and cactus). And those who till this soil constantly unearth and re-inter fertility figurines placed here long ago to ensure fecundity.

For, although this is a land of plenty, nothing is taken for granted. *Sismos* (earthquakes), droughts, floods, and landslides have destroyed villages. Wars, famines, epidemics, and looting have, at times, made the fertile land barren. Now with the arrival of tourism, big hotels and trails for quadrupeds—motorized tourist buggies—have left much of the jungle broken and bare. More and more people are employed in service to tourists as taxi-drivers, guards, waiters and waitresses, maids, and housekeepers.

These are the people who make the pilgrimage to El Pedimento, to ask for the spirits' benevolence on themselves and their children. And the deities, the lords and ladies, look upon the land with kindness.

Edmundo Cruz Martínez's family, praying at the cross, 1999

Bajos de Coyula | Lowlands of Coyula

This place was a very large hill they called Coyula, because there was a lot of coyul palm, the small, moist coconut loved by children. They did away with the hills, little by little. There were guacamayas [macaws], loros [parrots], perícos [parakeets], chachalacas [guan]. When a chachalaca would start making noise, it sounded as though there was a war, with all the noise the birds made. Chachalacas are the ones that are eaten.

It was a place that was only crossed by that small pathway, which was the national road. Whenever anyone passed, it was necessary to cut away all the overgrowth. Who knows how long it existed? When we fished we caught aguja, zabalote, rayo, jaiba, roncador. For turtles we went to the sandbank of Chacalapa, and they brought the eggs for First Friday and Fourth Friday. For the Púrpura caracol, they'd come from the south, from Salina Cruz, then they'd come down from the north.

—Don José Ortíz

The torrential rains have washed the roads away, a big difference from just four months earlier. The land is dry and parched, and there is some irrigation in the fields, but the farmers are worried. One farmer in the distance is sowing seeds, and a flock of cattle birds follows, eating them. From another part of the village, the hum of voices can be heard. Men, women, and children are walking along the dirt road, chanting, holding the standard of the Virgin of Guadalupe, whose statue they also carry. They pray for rain. Unknown to them, Lucino Arista from the adjacent village has just predicted that the earth will soon have rain. A ring around the sun foretells it. The dry spell will end the following day, bringing hurricanes to this land named for the coyul palm. The palms, which grew here more abundantly in the past, bear small fruits known popularly as *coquitos*, or little

coconuts. Rich with oil, they are ground and used for *cocada* candies and the local *totopos de coco*. The coquitos have a brilliant patina. Local artisans take the hard shells and carve small figures of turtles, frogs, eagles, armadillos, albatrosses, and other animals from the coast.

It is difficult to find don José Ortíz. His wife says that he is tending his fields and animals. He is at least ninety-five years old, and he has gone to care for his papayas, corn, and *ajonjolí* (sesame). Most of his crops were destroyed by the hurricane, and there is much work to do. His land is in the middle of the Río Coyula delta, between the Río Huatulco and the sea. You wade beyond the barbed wire to where the women are washing while the children bathe and play. There, across the river and above the muddy bank, are devastated fields belonging to several people. Among the coyul palms and fallen trees, near a small, weather-beaten thatched shelter, the old man sits grooming his long white mustache in a jagged piece of mirror. He carries a *morralito* (woven hemp bag) on his back and walks with a cane that is as twisted as his feet. He says he doesn't see too well because of his cataracts, but his keen vision makes you doubt any impediment.

Tío José, as he is called out of respect, is one of the most admired elders of the region. He says this hurricane is nothing compared to the struggles the community has known throughout its history. The first fight he remembers, though only barely, is the one involving Pancho Vásquez, who was the *jefe* of Coyula. There was a mayor who stole some

Top: *Pilgrims making their prayers, 1999*

Above: *Prayer for a new house, with a truck and a fenced garden, 1999*

money from the municipality, and the struggle involved litigation between San Mateo Piñas and Huatulco. At that time the land in dispute was one of the mountains that border both municipalities, a mountain now known as San Benito. Ambrosio Ramírez, from Arenal and Huatulco, got up in arms against the mayor and told him to return the money he'd taken. Ambrosio also threatened those who were trying to lay claim to Coyula lands. The opposing side went after him and killed him.

These events marked the beginning of a long struggle between Coyula and the town of

Huatulco. There was a traitor named Ramos, appointed by a General Márquez, who stationed people in strategic places, like Chacalapa and Miahuatlan, strongholds left over from the war between the Mexican national leaders Emiliano Zapata and Venustiano Carranza in 1910. Tío José says these struggles lasted for a long time, and the original reasons for them carried over into other fights, bringing banditry into the area. Men were sent after Vásquez, mostly from hideaways in the mountains. Tío José says that, as a result, people from the lowlands are still afraid of visiting highland areas. Vásquez was later warned to leave, and he fled toward Arroyo Seco. Some of the words from a ballad Tío José remembers give the year 1941.

Ten years later, there was another war. The elders in the area, Tío José among them, all recall the war between this land and Pochutla, the adjacent district. Settlers from Pochutla moved in and intermarried, but some wanted to take the land. Others joined them in the belief that governance of the lands should be under the neighboring district, and they fought alongside their old compatriots against the Ortíz family. Tío José says, "There was a war. They went through the hills of the Matlaxihuatl. They'd come out through the river. A man would go through the thicket where there was prickly *zarza* brush. He would go through the hills, and he would change. They were bewitched—they would become dwarfed men." They called it *la guerra*, the war. It took place in 1950, but people harbored memories and grudges long after. Those who were "for Huatulco" lived closest to Arenal, or the next bay over; those "for Pochutla" lived on the side closer to that district. As Tío José recalls, the people of Pochutla rented the property of Coyula for grazing their cattle, and they did not want to pay the rent, and slowly they tried to claim the entire area.

The sandbank where Tío José now sits, or close to it, used to be called Boca Vieja (Old Mouth), or Punta Cuatunalco. When there was no road but the dirt path, there were *leones* (mountain lions), *tigrillos* (small ocelots), and deer. The path went from Piedra Blanca, past La Garita (the Sentry House), and ended up on the Bay of Santa Cruz. In those days, as legend has it, there was a small lagoon with alligators, but there was also *paludismo* (malaria). Santa Cruz was a fishermen's village. Tío José was a fisherman then, as were his father and brothers. They learned to fish, he says, from an old man from Xadani who fished in the Copalita River. The old man taught them how to make canoes, as well. His name was Bonifacio Torres. He made the canoes out of the guanacastle tree. They cost about fifty pesos, Tío José says, in those days that was plenty.

They used the sulapán for fishing. They made a type of harpoon out of ocotillo. There were three people who went out in the canoe. The fellow at the front was the *tirador*, the thrower or marksman. Another was the *boga*, or oarsman. When the thrower shot the harpoon and did not reach his mark, the boga hit it with a stick. As he speaks, Tío José says:

If I was strong enough, I would build a canoe right now. We would catch as many as fifteen to twenty dozen fish. We don't have nearly as many fish as we used to. We dried the fish and salted them. In those days we had to salt the fish and lay them out in the marketplace, or go up to the highlands in Pluma Hidalgo, because people would come from Miahuatlan and the other mountain areas. In the past, it was dead here, very quiet. There used to be a large market in Huatulco on Sundays. But all the people would go to these markets to buy fish.

He fished for quite a long while, until the wars, when Tío José had to protect the lands of Coyula. This is when Tío José retired, in 1950, after forty years of fishing. He says he gave it up because those from Arenal, Santa Cruz, and Coyula were insistent about their

land claims. By that time, he had his lands, and while he says that fishing paid twice as much as farming, farming became the essential part of his livelihood.

The crops grow well, and the land is very fertile. Here in Coyula, he says that there have been several times when the course of the Río Coyula–Río Huatulco has been altered naturally. At the moment, as he rests under his torn thatching, he points to the most recent devastation. He says that around 1967 a very large guamuchil tree fell over the river, forcing it to flood some of his crops and causing a great deal of harm to much of his land.

He says has always lived here, in Coyula. He is the son of Quirino Ortíz and Ursula Franco, and his grandparents were Tomás Ortíz and Feliciana Robles from Miahuatlan. People would come down from the mountains to work, as they still do, especially on the coffee plantations. It was customary for people from the mountains to come down for the harvest, for what is known as *la pizca* (the pinching). He says, "*La riqueza la teníamos en la mano.*" "We had all the wealth in our hands." Not only the land, but the hands of labor created wealth. Pinching back the harvest created new growth later. They used *reata serrano*—mountain rope, made of the fibers of maguey leaves—to sew netting for carrying the harvest and for many other things.

Tío José says his grandparents had a great deal of cattle. His grandfather had property and money, but he buried his fortune and never gave it to his children. Tío José says that with the earnings from his crops, he has managed to buy land here and there. He has distributed it to his children so that they will have something. He earned one peso at a time—growing bananas, watermelon, corn, and other fruit—and saved it to buy land. He says the land was not expensive then, but it took a lot of work to earn one peso. There was the one small dirt path that came down from Acapulco and went all the way to Salina Cruz. In the days when the coffee plantations were thriving, the owners would come down to Coyula and other areas with their *bestias* (animals) to buy corn and other crops for the people who lived on the plantations. Later, they drove down in trucks to purchase freshly harvested fruits and vegetables. You had to be careful about what you planted, so that it would not rot and go to waste.

Tío José speaks with Nereo Ziga, the descendant of a prominent family of the 1800s who owned much of the property of Coyula. Nereo recalls the name of the leader of the Pochutla side by reciting a ballad:

> *Pedro Díaz had first said that,*
> *With Huatulco he would finish,*
> *He would walk away with Coyula,*
> *And in addition with Arenal.*

The Zigas have defended this land for centuries. José Jesus Ziga, Nereo's *tatarabuelo* or *chozno* (forebear), owned the Hacienda de Apango and is mentioned several times in documents dated 1816 to 1831 relating to land transactions and litigation over land tenure.[11] Tío José says that the prominent families of Coyula were mostly from Pochutla. There were Pablo Cárdenas, Angel Manzano, and Peralta and Lucía Ziga, who leased most of the properties of Coyula. Lucía's father was Justo Ziga, who passed all the property rights on to his daughter, he says. She then transferred her rights to Susana González, who was from up in the mountains of Candelaria. Then Huatulco asked Susana González to transfer the property rights to the municipality. And she did, on the condition that if the municipality at some point decided to sell the lands to individuals, the properties would revert to

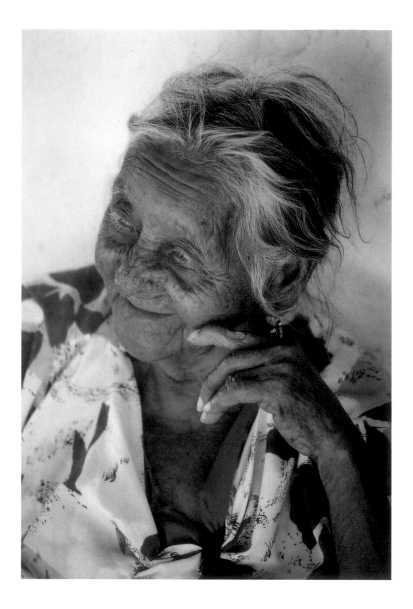

her. They were to remain communal lands. Both the Ziga and the Manzano names are part of Nereo's family.

Nereo's grandmother, Artemia Olmedo Lavariega, is well into her nineties, and don José Ortiz was godparent to one of her children. Doña Artemia, full of wit, still has the voice of a young child, and she sings songs from long ago. She says her husband courted her in Huatulco with serenades, always music and song. Nereo takes after his grandmother, and they sit swapping verse after verse and song after song. Like her husband, Nereo is known as a ladies' man—so says this grandmother about her husband, son, and grandson.

Tía Artemia left her home in Huatulco to live with her husband in Coyula when she was fifteen years old and he was twenty. She says they were *amancebados*, living together in a common-law marriage until their first daughter wanted to marry in the church. Then, she says, "My husband never asked to marry me until it hurt him. When they asked when he would marry me, he would answer. 'She said yes, but she never gave me a date.'" They had

Left: Abuelita Artemia Olmedo Lavariega, 1997

Right:La sobrina (the niece), 1997

ten children, but only two of the four sons survived. Now she has 120 descendants, including several great-great-grandchildren. Her eldest child is Nereo's father, Leonorio Ziga.

She recalls the war of Coyula, and the poverty everyone suffered through that period of about five months. She, along with most of the women, went back to live in the town of Huatulco, while the men stayed in Coyula to fight. She says that Huatulco was relatively depopulated then, and so was Bajos del Arenal. People left for the mountains of San Mateo Piñas and Xanica, seeking help and shelter. Andres Manzano Ramírez, her husband's nephew, fought along with her husband, José Ziga Manzano. Tía Artemia was pregnant with Ismael, one of her sons. She says she would spend her days crying, not knowing what would happen. Since they had no food, they made a type of "coffee" drink by toasting tortillas and grinding them with *jamaica* (hibiscus flowers). Sometimes, too, they would take *plátano macho* (plantains) and use them to make a type of tortilla.

Nereo's grandmother has not gotten over the death of her husband, then in his nineties, whose life was overtaken with sadness after the expropriation of these lands. What Nereo's grandfather was never to know—or perhaps he does—is that the time limit for development expired, revoking the expropriation in this community. For the time being, the Zigas, the Ortíz family, Abdías Vásquez, and others have been victorious in reclaiming Bajos's land.

Tío José has many more stories to tell. The hillsides hide old settlements where the elders speak of hidden treasures, like the coins his grandfather buried. Most people respect these places. But recently one group used a bulldozer to dig up ancient artifacts, anxious to be the first to find them, little different from the pirates of old.[12] When the parishioners wanted to reconstruct the chapel on the bay, Tío José was one of the elders they consulted

Lucino Arista, 1997

Lucino's flock, 1997

Left: Coyote Point, at the edge of the sea, 2000

to determine the very site where the famous cross of legend was placed.

Tío José is everywhere, in his milpa, in his house in Bajos de Coyula, at the Bay of the Holy Cross, and in the main town of Santa María, at the house where he stays when he wants to pay homage at the grave of his ancestors for the Day of the Dead. As Abdías Vásquez says, "*Tío José es el padre de la dinastía de todos los de Coyula.*" "Tío José is the father of the dynasty of everyone from Coyula." Tío José cleans the tombstones with his hands, straightens the cross, and sets out flowers and candles he has brought in his morralito. Then he removes his hat, bows his head, and prays that those from Bajos de Coyula buried here have found comfort on the other side.

Bajos del Arenal | Sandy Lowlands

The main road leading from the bays proceeds to the largest metropolitan area in the country, Mexico City, as well as to the capital of Oaxaca. This is the road most Mexican tourists take, whether home for them is to the north, east, or south. Off the main highway, across from the road to the municipal headquarters and the main town, an unpaved road leads to Bajos del Arenal. At the base of the big rock is the bus and taxi stop. People sit in the shade waiting for taxis taking them to La Cruz or home to the *agencia* (precinct). This unpaved road is a slippery sand path winding down to the left on the edge of the hill, right toward a gully, left again, right, left, and then right through lands planted with papayas, bananas, and low-lying crops of sesame and new corn.

A group of men stands around the agencia headquarters. Some have tied their horses to nearby posts. An emergency meeting has been called, gathering everyone together in the dry, hot sun of midday. There has been no rain, and the crops will be lost soon. It's the rainy season and the clouds taunt the land, then leave without offering a trace of moisture. In the midst of the group stands Lucino Arista, who has predicted rain. With a stick he draws in the sandy ground. He's explaining to the group how the ring that surrounds the sun means that there will be rain very soon. The elders are relieved and get ready to leave.

Lucino Arista is a *comunero* who works this land as his father and grandfather did. Documents of old litigation from 1844 and 1936 attest to the land's continuous occupation, and to the fact that other Aristas have had to defend their property rights, just as Lucino and his fellow townsmen have done.[13] Lucino cannot read, and he says that the authorities wanted to make him sign a document, like the others, with a thumbprint. They wanted to give him a few hundred pesos for his land. "My parents were born here," he argues. "I was born here. . . . There must be respect for that. They come and tell us that they are going to give us land. But how can they do that if the land already belongs to us?" His home is toward the end of the agencia, and when his family sees him coming home from the fields with his sheep, his grandchildren run up to him and mingle with the lambs. His daughters live on the same property with their husbands and all the little ones. And there are many, mostly little girls.

Lucino says he is partial to this place where he has always lived. "The *maquil,* the *nanche,* and alligator's tail; you dig the root and boil it. It's good for hemorrhages. I'm calculating: one drinks this for more than ten days. And the leaves of the maguey plant? The leaves of the maguey plant are ground and boiled. They're calming. There are many remedies from these plants, but one has to know them." He knows the local names for the plants, some in Nahuatl, some in Chontal, and some in Spanish. Most of the Chontal lands are on the other side of the Río Copalita; before marrying his wife, Lucino courted a

Chontal woman and learned the language.

He walks to the bay of San Agustín, one of the most beautiful bays of the area, and he shows you where the surveyor's lines have been laid out for the new hotel. He says what he knows, and what his grandmother asserted to him many years ago when he was a child: all this land is a floodplain. Lucino points to the expansive beach that butts up against the river next to his land. He says that all of this land gets flooded—notwithstanding the plans to put a hotel on it—and that some of the floodplains become salt marshes. Once it rains heavily, the water will inundate this area. It will go from here all the way to the river, close to Lucino's home. This is not surprising. Many of the lands around the region have been well known as sources of salt for inland peoples since pre-Hispanic times.[14]

Up ahead is the sandbank, the Barra del Arenal. Beyond that, where the bay opens up, cruise ships and tourist boats have broken the coral. At the edge of the beach are thatched shelters, makeshift restaurants where the people of San Agustín cater to those who come here by boat. Within a three-year period, the bay has become a small boomtown, dependent on tourism for survival. Fresh fish, skewered on thin branches, are grilled over a wood fire. Cuauhtemoc, his parents, his brothers, and his wife and children were raised here

First Communion dress, 2001

and in Santa María Huatulco. They proudly care for the old dugout canoes they used for fishing not too long ago. One of the old canoes is at the very top of the house on the hill, a trophy of their family's history. They still fish, without canoes, catching what's needed for the day. Their brown skin gets browner, in contrast to their hair, which is reddish blond, sun-bleached from the full days spent on the water. Lucino's youngest daughter, Mercedes, worked for Cuauhtemoc's family briefly, but she prefers staying close to home with her sisters and her new baby.

Lucino is keenly aware of all Bajos del Are-nal's resources. "Look at these little shells," he says. "All the world is in each one. They are things of great value. There are sponges, starfish—things of value to those of us who are from here. That black sand there that is brought in with the tide dirties and stains like ash. It is filth brought in from elsewhere."

Lucino's words echo times past, when shells were traded with inlanders who used them as inlay, for trade, in their architecture, and in many other ways. They were used as vessels and *hachas* (axes), made into spoons and imple-ments for fishing, used for ornamentation, for beading, and for a host of other things. The shells have turned up among other things of great value in archeological sites on the lands of the Pueblo peoples of the southwestern United States, and south through corridors to Teotihuacan. Most recently, research has recov-ered pre-Hispanic sites in Ejutla, in central Oaxaca, where specialized households were involved in the production of ornaments and other goods made of marine shells from the Pacific coast.[15]

Following ancient custom, Mixtec people from the north still come to this place, women who speak differently from those who live here. Many more came in the past. Every year, in January and February, at low tide, they gather the sea snails that cling to the rocky cliffs at San Agustín. The women milk these mollusks to extract a clear liquid that oxidizes the minute it is exposed to air. When it touches thread or yarn, the substance changes from clear, to white, to yellow, to chartreuse, and to vibrant purple. Mixtec women from the north and Chontales from farther south have valued this dye for hun-dreds, and probably thousands, of years. These women have long been known for their beautiful woven skirts. Artist and author Miguel Covarrubias described this in the early 1900s, when he wrote about the use and high value of textiles among women from the region.[16] Cuauhtemoc says that many people serve these sea snails in shellfish cocktails, even though the mollusk is a protected species. Lucino listens intensely and adds his opinions to the dialogue.

Nothing escapes Lucino's eye. He knows the night sky as well as daylight. His house had no electricity until recently; it still has no gas. For running water, his family uses a well next to a huge guanacastle tree. His wife and daughters laugh and say that when they get tired of their old metates, or grinding stones, they go up the mountain and get new ones—new stones that could easily be more than a thousand years old.

His daughters and sons-in-law live here. When each of his daughters marries, Lucino adds another room to his house for her family. As he lays out the space and digs the foundation, he finds seals, whistles, pottery shards, animal figurines, and other things. There must have been an old kiln here, he believes; there definitely was a settlement, long ago. Until very recently, much of this land had been protected from looters, and most of the area had escaped the attention of archeologists. The exception is a brief survey that was conducted in the early 1980s, before the area was developed for tourism. The region has held its ancient sites and monuments safely close to its bosom, with very, very few identified thus far, and then only vaguely. But Lucino and other people who live here know the old places, and respect them as sacred domains.

The day after Lucino saw the ring around the sun, it rained. In fact, it rained and rained, and a few months later, the hurricanes came and flooded the land. The water reached Lucino's house, a few kilometers from the shore. The papayas were lost, and the other crops, and everyone had to make do with the canned sardines and water brought in to help them. Lucino said that the earth was upset and had to resettle, and that there would be an earthquake soon. Two months later, cracks developed in the walls and foundations of many of the new houses in the development. Lucino's home—made of simple thatching and heavy forked branches that support lighter branch beams, or *vigas*—was almost washed away as well, but he reconstructed it quickly. He hung the hammocks and placed the *catres* (cots) on the wet earth.

Lucino attends to all the signs around him. He says he might grow old and see his granddaughters marry, but then again, he might have to defend this land as his ancestors did, even to the death. Lucino and his daughters, especially Eva, dream of building a small school for the local children, and they are receiving donations. Another good thing happened recently: there was a statute of limitations on development, and the builders' time ran out, at least for now. People say the hotels will not be built after all.

Since Lucino's family added electricity, Eva has bought a freezer where she stores fresh fish to sell to the community. The children seem to have set their internal clocks to a popular Mexican soap opera. They run to the television to watch the latest villain and heroine in the drama. The adults, too, can't help but be mesmerized by El Chavo del Ocho (The Kid from the Eighth), and they sit, lie in hammocks, or stand, laughing, continuing their daily chores.

Cacaluta (Cacalotepec) | The Hill of the Crows

Following the old road from El Pedimento to the northwest, a dry riverbed leads to a marsh, and then to the place where a vast lagoon meets the ocean. To the left, a heart-shaped beach embraces a rocky cliff. To the right, a long beach lies at the base of another cliff. This place has been occupied continuously for thousands of years. Local people

The lagoon at Cacaluta, 1999

sometimes swim or take their boats to Isla Cacaluta, across from the beach, to catch the day's meal. The Nahuas named this area Cacalotepec (the Hill of the Crows).

In Chontal stories, the crow is associated with the origin of maize. Legend says that when the ancients followed an ant they had seen carrying a kernel of maize, they found that it had taken it from a cave piled high with ears of corn. People watched the cave to see who owned the corn. When someone finally arrived, it was the crow. People watched to see where the crow got the corn, because he kept bringing more. Every twenty days, every month, the crow brought a new ear of corn. But who knows where he brought it from? No one ever found out. The crow, then, as the story goes, is liked by the people because it was he who discovered maize.[17]

There is not one crow to be seen here, but there is a pottery handle or two, the legs of a vessel in the shape of a bird or turtle, shards left over from looting and scavenging.

People say that this beach is the place where turtles came to lay their eggs. Large vats remain from not too long ago when turtle oil was processed and other parts of the turtle were sold. They say that truckloads of oil would be taken from this area. It is quiet now, except for the maligned quadruped vehicles that roar through, bringing tourists on an adventure. The birds fly away and back. Some of the locals continue to come here to bathe in the ocean, then wash the salt off in the lagoon. A few decided this was an ideal place for a fish hatchery. They brought their belongings and their hammocks, but the project survived less than a year. They are having better luck growing papaya trees. Leucadio's father-in-law lived here as a child and now lives in Coyula with other Chontal families. His nephew was one of the people given permission to plant papayas in this area. With so many struggling to make ends meet, this fertile land has given these hard-working farmers a chance to make a living.

Albina, who is from Pueblo Viejo, and her husband, Amadeo, raised their young family on one of the hills. They pride themselves on having been caretakers of the area for many years. When they were children, they came to this place on holiday with their families. Now Albina and her sisters bring their daughters here to bathe and play in the large sweetwater lagoon.

Cacaluta, lagoon and sea, 1999

Albina and her children sit with their cousins catching what they call *camarones del otro mundo*—shrimp from the other world. Perhaps you are lucky enough to catch one, even a small one. You sit on the moist sand close to the edge of the sweetwater lagoon. If you are a novice, you watch for bubbles rising in the muddy sand, then dig deep, quickly, before the shrimp gets away. If you are more confident, you calmly observe the colonies of small holes. You lightly toss some grains of sand into a few, toying with the shrimp. When you see a tiny claw come up, you quickly dig the shrimp out and save it with the others for dinner. This is what Albina prepares sometimes.

This part of Cacaluta has been designated a biological park, and there is only one couple, whom people refer to as "*los Españoles*," living on the ancient hillside overlooking the bay. Albina and Amadeo abandoned their home here, and she moved back to Pueblo Viejo, to live on the land where her parents and sisters live with their families.

Amadeo used to go back and forth to Texas to work and send money home. Now he stays longer in Texas than he lives here. He is there with his oldest son, who is in his twenties. Albina also thinks of moving to the United States, with Amadeo and their oldest son. "Is it too hard to cross?" she asks, like so many others. Her middle son, now almost twenty, is restless. He wants to be with his father. It has become a rite of passage for young men to go to El Norte. They know the risks involved in trying to get across, the chances of deportation once there, the loneliness. Still, El Norte allows them to make more money in a few months than they might make in years here, and it always calls. Areli, Amadeo and Albina's only daughter, turned fifteen, and her father sent money to celebrate her Quinceañera, this most important birthday to a young girl.

Cacaluta is quiet, except for the quadrupeds. Sometimes there are campers at the

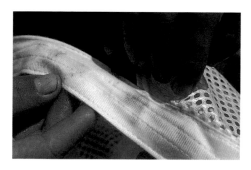

Purpúra pansa snail and its dye, 1997

beach. The lancheros bring people to swim here every so often during tourist season. They drop them off, then come back for them hours later. And the national park has sent teams of scientists and others to study the flora and fauna.

Bahía Chahue | The Place that Floods

The plaza and beach of Bahía Chahue used to be a marshland. Don Ignacio talks about the *lagartos* (alligators) that abounded here. Both the marshes and the alligators are gone. "The alligators are now in the municipal building," don Ignacio says, with dry humor. This place of old *esteros*—"the place that gets flooded"—has been covered over with soil and sand in preparation for development. With a few exceptions, the building lots have been vacant for years, the investment in electric cables, gas lines, and water pipes a bust, so far. The undertow off the beach recently drowned a young mother and son, tourists who had come on vacation, not knowing the dangers that the local people know. The waves seem as harmless as the landscape, silent about times before the present.[18] "What can anyone expect from marshes that have been filled with the sand and soil left over from other development projects?" people ask.

Not that long ago, malaria struck the people who lived here. The *Relaciones* and other sources record that plagues took many lives between 1566 and the 1590s, and again in the 1700s.[19] Don Nacho says that some families from the port moved north to San Miguel del Puerto. That is why that town is called Saint Michael of the Port, instead of its earlier name, San Miguel de Huatulco. The mosquitoes know that the marshes are still underneath. The *monstruo de la tierra* (monster of the earth) is not evident unless you know what to look for. "It is there," don Nacho says, "but you may not recognize it as you did before."

Arrocito | Little Rice

Don Abacuc Luis Avendaño and his sister are from farther north along the coast, where women wear the traditional skirt, the *enagua* or *pozahuanco*. They come here every year to extract *Púrpura pansa* sea snails from along the cliff rocks. At low tide the water is low enough to try this risky task. People here talk about the people who come from the Mixteca. The Huatulqueños call them *las inditas* (the little Indian women), or *las de Pinotepa*, (the women from Pinotepa). The women spend several weeks along the rockiest bays here—as long as they can—dyeing their *madejas* (skeins of cotton). It takes more than 200 sea snails to dye one skein, and several skeins to weave a pozahuanco, the long cloth they wind around their waist. The rocky coast at Arrocito[20] and Playa Consuelo helps preserve the tiny snail until the women return the following season for the harvest. Don Abacuc and his sister have been working with Javier, a biologist, Marta, and others to conserve knowledge of the dyeing process, and of the *Púrpura pansa* and its fragile ecological niche.

The people of the area—Mundo Cruz Martínez, Lucino Arista, and the fishermen and boatmen who see the women every day when the tide is low—speak respectfully of the Mixtec dyers. Nearby hotels sell postcards and paintings depicting these women as they work. They used to wear their cochincal- and Púrpura-dyed cloth skirt and no blouse. Marta, who has been working with the Mixtec dyers, remembers how a nineteen-year-old cultural worker called the women's attention to the fact that they were bare-breasted and suggested that they wear something to cover themselves. Like Eve, they were driven out

Arrocito, 2000

of Eden. That was about twenty years ago, and since then the women have worn a type of halter or apron top.

The dyers come from Pinotepa de Don Luis and Puerto Escondido, then farther south and east to Pochutla, San Agustín, Cacaluta, Santa Cruz—to as many bays as they can. They bring small parcels of food and bundles of undyed cotton thread, and they sleep on the beach. The fishermen and others have come to expect them, and, more important, to try to make them to feel at home. Among the drawings on an old Native map, you can identify two women in wrap skirts walking together along a path, people who have been coming to this coast for hundreds of years.[21]

Alvino Cruz, 1999

Punta Arena | Sandy Point

Between two bays that have already been sold to build hotels and expensive residences, there is land to be planted, a field owned by don Albino Ortíz, or as don Félix calls him, *mí compadre*. In the scorching sun, Albino draws water from a well he has dug, as people have done forever in this land.[22] During the rainy season, farmers don't need wells. When it is dry, they find aquifers almost anywhere they dig.[23] With a pump and small generator, Albino waters the tomatoes on the side of his property closest to the ocean. He doesn't have too much time because he does all the planting himself, and he has to prepare his land for the ajonjolí that grows abundantly in this region. In addition to sesame, Albino grows watermelons, cucumbers, and lemons.

Don Albino doesn't remember his language of origin. He is Indian, he says, born very poor. He taught himself to read with the Bible, and he's worked and saved his money. He bought this land from Señor Narciso Valladares and has all the papers to prove it. But the developers are slowly moving in on him from both sides, and the exclusive Conejos retreat would like to buy his land from him. He's one of the last holdouts along the ocean, if not the last one; he's not certain he'll survive. Others who have lost think he'll get tired of the struggle eventually and give in, but he's tenacious.

He speaks, standing in the middle of the field, where there is no shade from the scorching sun. He decides that something to drink is in order. He climbs the coconut tree, and there, with the machete he uses to cut weeds, he slices the top off a coconut. Coconut is not only thirst-quenching, he notes, but it also kills parasites, just as the guayacan is good for diabetes. Willy, the gringo weaver from Oaxaca City, has been coming by for years to collect natural dyes from the plants and other things on Albino's property, and the two men visit for long stretches of time, drinking coconut milk.

During the early stages of development, Albino gave the government two hectares of his property so that the new road could be completed. He was willing to support a public effort. "Now," he says, "they want more. They want to keep going." Don Albino and his wife used to have a small restaurant. They found it burned down one day.

Their children are adolescents, and don Albino wants them to get a good education. All his efforts are for them. He says that as long as he continues to work his land, the developers and politicians have no excuse to seize it. He has good attorneys, but he is realistic. He is an avid reader, and he does as much as he can to keep abreast of old and new laws. He may be better informed than many local lawyers.

Tangolunda | Beautiful Woman

A beautiful woman dressed in white walks along the shore, elegantly balancing a basket on her head. It is sunset as she gracefully crosses the beach. This, the finest stretch of sand, is now occupied by expensive hotels. Onlookers stop, mesmerized by the woman's presence, which feels almost out of place. Or perhaps it is they who are out of place. She has been coming here since she was a little girl helping her mother. This is how she makes a living, selling tamarind fruit and beads made of shells and seeds.

Tangolunda is the name of this bay. Few people know its meaning anymore. Artemio Cervantes says that it is the original local word for "beautiful woman." At least this is what he learned as a child. The old derroteros include drawings of the island off the bay, and they call it Tangolo, Tangolo.[24] The Chontales say that its name is Tecualo, the Place of the Rocks. The ancient Chontal dyers came here, too, to collect the snails that gave their cotton thread and clothing the vivid purple color so highly valued throughout the world.[25]

Abel Martínez, his brothers and sisters, and his future in-laws, the Cervantes family, grew up on this land. Abel's father and grandfather owned cattle and grew sesame, papaya, corn, and other crops. Artemio's very large family had land in the mountains, including a coffee plantation. His wife, Francisca, Abel's sister, was his neighbor on Tangolunda, and the daughter of the largest landowner. It is prime land, now claimed by various resort hotels. There are encantos here as well, though one has disappeared. Artemio says there was a cave along the ocean. He played there as a boy. Now this encanto of Tangolunda Bay has been dynamited to allow the construction of a prominent hotel.

It is early in the day, and Francisca is cutting a portion of the pig that Artemio and their son have just slaughtered. They are hearing news about another son, Ulíses, who is in New Jersey. He works two jobs there, in landscaping and construction, and calls his parents every Sunday. They are grateful for the news. Artemio ties a rope in the middle of the kitchen where he hangs pieces of pork that he will distribute to other members of the family and to friends. Artemio's family made their living as fishermen. Now he has a taxi concession on the sidewalk in front of one of the largest hotels, and a large parcel of land in the hills. This land has become a homestead, where he, his wife, and his sons live. It is called Rancho Tangolunda, or La Javalina (the Wild Pig).

Francisco, a third son, married Jacinta, who is from Barra de la Cruz, one of the Chontal communities nearby. They have four young daughters. Francisco is a wise young man who knows many of the stories his father and relatives recount. His passion for the land is evident as he describes its uses and customs. As young as he is, not quite thirty, he knows what it was like to be a fisherman, to cast the *atarraya*, the round nets used to draw in fish. He now works as a guide, taking tourists kayaking and horseback riding through wooded areas where he explains the uses of plants and describes the animals. Although he sees himself as a protector of this land, he also feels the pull north. There is a man who regularly calls to invite Francisco to work with him in Colorado. Perhaps if he went for a short time, he could save money and come back with equipment he needs for his business. But Jacinta worries about this, and Francisco's business is already flourishing, thanks to his love for this land and his knowledge of the region. With cell phones, they can easily arrange to conduct tours. He brings people here in the evening, after a busy day, and gives them a meal prepared by Jacinta and his family. He owns several horses, a truck, and kayaks that serve him well on his tours.

Yet the Cervantes family continues to yearn for their home at Tangolunda. They feel some resentment, naturally, because of the unfair way in which land was expropriated by the government and resold for development. Their family has done better than most, but it has been hard to watch Tangolunda become a playground for tourists, off-limits to most local people except those who work in the hotels and restaurants. It is hard, too, to know that Tangolunda is constantly changing hands, bought and sold by the wealthy, because the hotels have not been as successful as investors hoped. And now the subsistence farmers and fishermen, like the hotels, are dependent on tourism and must also wait for the tourist season to earn a living.

Abel, Artemio's brother-in-law, who is married to Floralice, don Félix's daughter, lives by the ocean close to Tangolunda Bay. This place is called La Bocana (the Mouth). With their four young daughters and one son, they have managed to create a community like

Santa Cruz, view from the sea, 2000

the one in which they grew up. The families, who were neighbors on two of the bays, intermarried, as many have.

The Ríos, Cervantes, and Martínez families all have children and siblings in New Jersey, where they live next to each other, as they did in Huatulco. They preserve the memories of Tangolunda, their childhood, and their family history. Those who can, maintain homes nearby, close enough to see the comings and goings of Tangolunda Bay, where beautiful local women and little girls walk along the sand, selling bracelets and seashells, and braiding tourists' hair.

Barra de la Cruz | The Sandbar of the Cross

A young woman sweeps the earth around the hammock where her son lies sleeping. The baby's grandmother, Luisa, runs out to greet the passersby. Luisa is from San Miguel del Puerto, in the mountains, where coffee is grown, and she knows everyone there. She came to this village with her husband, who was originally from San Isidro Chacalapa. The Barra, as it is known locally, was settled by people from San Isidro, and by Chontales from other pueblos. She knows many of the people from the nearby villages. They are all related, she says. She sees everyone who comes and goes. She knows that Jacinta's parents are home, but that Jacinta herself hasn't arrived yet this weekend. As she speaks, the rooster follows the hens and the turkeys watch, their necks moving forward in unison.

She gives you directions to follow to the village, farther down. She will be here with drinks when you return. The rest of her family should be home by then, and her husband will be back from feeding the animals. It takes him three hours to walk to Zimatan in the morning and three hours to walk back.

Outside the village there is a lumberyard, now closed. Three *socios*, businessmen not from the village, said they would fix the roads and pave them if the villagers allowed them to open a lumberyard. There has been quite a bit of deforestation here recently. The tourist development requires a constant supply of the best woods. The socios are today's colonists, seizing the opportunity to do business with the developers. But since the three partners started this venture, new laws have been passed prohibiting cutting many of the trees. The laws are almost too late. Some of the special and most sacred trees of the area have been lost—some were lost long before the most recent incursion. The *aserrín* (sawdust) lies over the dry earth creating more dust. There will be no rain until the dry season ends several months from now. As the road winds closer to the village, there is a large fish hatchery to the right. Storks and cranes stand guard over the *mojarra* and other fish growing in this lagoon. The villagers take turns looking after the hatchery. Down the road a few adults and children run toward the soccer field. The earth is less parched closer to the center of the village, and there are more homes and more verdant overgrowth, including cultivated papaya, coconut, and banana trees. It is Christmas afternoon, and everyone is dressed in Sunday finery, especially the children and the women. From the small hills around the town almost everyone can see the comings and goings of those taking part in the Christmas pageantry.

Isabel, Félix's wife, was born here, as was Jacinta, Francisco's wife. Jacinta's parents live on the cliffside, next to the large plum tree. She and her family, as well as Jacinta and Francisco and their children, come here for the festivities and the dance. Isabel's father, don Isidoro, too, likes to be in Barra for the holidays and in his old age often travels between his home here and Isabel's home on the Río Copalita.

The dance is held at the basketball court, next to the church. On both sides of the court, on a stage where the bands will perform, are speakers about five feet tall. On one side is the *banda*, and on the other the *marimba*. The musicians alternate playing different dances—*cumbias* and *sones*. The men prepare the stage while the women decorate the area with flowers, painted *jícaras* (gourds), and gifts of bright plastic—pink, blue, green, red, and yellow pails, combs, bowls, cups, and other things that will be given away. The gifts are very important, and the food is one of the gifts.

It is an honor to be a *mayordomo* or *mayordoma* of a feast day. The man or woman selected to take charge of organizing the festivity must have gifts for everyone and must serve enough food for the entire village. This is true in all the neighboring Chontal villages. There is great respect for this responsibility, and many people—men, women, and families—take their role very seriously and save for many years to fulfill it. As in the other towns, there are people who leave this village for extended periods in order to save money. They find jobs elsewhere in the region, around the tourist development, or as far away as

Development at Santa Cruz, 1998

Luz, working in the hotel at Tangolunda, 2001

the United States, and send their earnings home for these occasions.

Barra de la Cruz is noted locally for its Christmas festivities. Taxis, buses, and trucks arrive filled with people. Many visitors are staying in the homes of relatives and friends, as the dance will last all night. There is music, the exchange of gifts, dancing, laughter, food, and drink. Women, dressed in embroidered *huipiles* and enaguas, carry large painted jícaras filled with the brightly colored gifts and prizes. You offer a small donation to offset the cost of the festivities. The mayordomos and organizers of the event are under scrutiny by everyone in the village, and from nearby villages, over how well the event is organized and how much is given away. Some years are lavish; others are lean. Everyone compares last year's festivities with this year's. Then, too, events like this are an opportunity for the village to show its strength and pride to guests visiting from other communities.

People throughout the region know the calendar of feasts and celebrations and plan their holidays accordingly. Jacinta and her daughters come to stay with her mother. Flora Ricárdez visits at least once a week when she is off work as a waitress, and she never misses Christmas or the special feast days, such as the Feast of the Holy Cross. Isabel and her daughters love to get involved in all of the activities. Because of her restaurant, Floralice can't make it to all of the feast days, but she sponsors a big event for Our Lady of Guadalupe's feast on December 12. The local paper often carries articles describing these events.

For many people who live in La Cruz or Crucecita, in Rancho Tangolunda or Copalita, Barra is home, grounded in tradition, color, celebration, and pride, and the place to which they always return. Don Isidoro, his son-in-law don Félix, and Francisco—three generations—were captured by the beauty of the women here. Don Isidoro, Floralice's grandfather and Isabel's father, was from a town in the northern part of Oaxaca, but he married a Chontal woman from Barra, and he always made sure to be here for the feasts.

Now, foreigners and others are trying to buy the comuneros' land. Some have built modest houses in the area. In most cases, if comuneros sell their land, it is out of need. Sometimes there is no other way to survive. Most people, however, are adamant about keeping their land intact for their children's future, and about maintaining their customs and rights of use. The village will gather together and make decisions about what is best for all. And next year's Christmas pageant will be even larger and better, and everyone will come.

Before another Christmas, there is sad news. Don Isidoro, the quick-witted teller of long stories, has passed on, leaving all with the memory of his humor. Now they will tell their own stories about his stories, for many Christmases after.

Ríos | Rivers

Río Copalita — The River of Incense — and La Bocana

I speak here about some bells that were made in San Mateo Piñas. In those days, San Mateo belonged to Santa María Ozolotepec. So they asked Santa María Ozolotepec for a bell. The bell was very heavy. So they set it down in order to rest, while they were carrying it over a mountain that is called Espinazo del Diablo, or the Devil's Backbone. The bell rolled down into a deep hole. They went to look for it, but they never found it. So we say that the bell ended up in San Mateo del Mar [in the Isthmus with the Huave people]. And there is an Englishman, a historian who toured the area. He went to San Mateo del Mar and he saw some men making nets and asked them what they were doing there. Well, they said, "Here we are taking care of the bell, so that the naguales [spirits] who brought it from the sea won't take it back." So, it coincides with our story.

We believe that sometimes the nagualismo is irrational, but if we think about it and look at parapsychology, [we might] think about how things become transformed. That tradition coincides with the story in San Mateo, and that's the place we call the hondura encantada, or the enchanted hole, because many who looked for the bell never found it. It is in the Río Gijón of San Mateo Piñas. The bell was made around 1766. The Río Gijón feeds into the Río Cristobal, which feeds into the Copalita River, whose mouth is right here. It is possible for the bell to have floated down to the mouth of the Copalita River and down to San Mateo del Mar.

—Don Cástulo García García, San Mateo Piñas

If you stand looking south at the waves rolling onto the shore, straight ahead is the Mar del Sur, the southern sea. To the east, cliffs of volcanic rock unfurl. Roosters and other birds greet the orange, red, purple, and blue hues of the dawn. Fishermen in canoes seize the moment of quiet to seek unsuspecting schools of fish. A father and son bring in the nets they cast before the first light. The canoe glides forward. A man jumps off and drags the canoe safely onto the shore. His son unloads wet bags, nets, and buckets of fish.

They walk slowly, carrying their morning's catch, nudging the curious dogs aside. They talk as they make their way up the stairs of the small restaurant, where a painted sign says *Mariscos* (Seafood).

Inside, Esperanza carries Grecia wrapped in a large white towel. The toddler is wide awake. Her mother is taking her to see the healer. A radio is playing. One of her cousins, a

Left: Evening catch, Copalita, 1999

Above: Bells of San Miguel del Puerto, 1998

young man who has come to help wait tables in the dining room, lies under a white sheet. He's listening for more morning sounds before he rises to sweep the floors. The heavy storm kept most of the family awake last night. Lightning, which plays a part in the ancient religion of the Chontales and others from this region, put on a show. The spectacle was most pronounced here, at La Bocana, the mouth of El Río Copalita, the River of Incense.

Copalita beach at la Bocana,
after hurricane Paulina, 1997

This river winds down from the clouds, receding and expanding, serving the many peoples whose lands are bounded by it—the Zapotec, Chontal, and others. It cascades from the highlands, past the town of San Miguel del Puerto, to the lowlands, past the hamlet of La Ceiba. Near the ocean, it broadens into lagoons that feed sweetwater plants and fish. Here, on either side of the river's mouth, communities offer their allegiance to separate jurisdictions and districts— Santa María Huatulco on the west side, San Miguel del Puerto to the east. All rivers have two sides, but the Río Copalita—the largest in the region, named after the copal tree whose resin is burned as incense for offerings—is one of the prime boundary markers here, and several mojoneras are located along its length.

On one side of the river, an unpaved road leads to homes made in the traditional manner, with round palm thatching. Houses with the same layout, the same dirt foundations have been found across the river, excavated from under mountains of earth, and dated to around 800 C.E. or earlier. A cemetery serves those who live and lived on both sides of the river. This is where the ancestors are honored. On the other side, too, are government property markers and vestiges of a ball court from an early period, as well as dwellings that once belonged to an unknown elite.[1] It is a place long abandoned to its grandiose intent. In the recent boom years, the local tourist industry tried to name the mountain point, from which you can see the sunset and the sunrise over the sea, Punta Celeste, or Celestial Point. But the specialists who are studying the site asked for the traditional name to be kept. It is quiet here now, with only the infrequent footsteps of its most recent caretakers, the occasional archeologist, and probing tourist to be heard. Cement paths, known as *andamios*, have been laid for ecotours and archeological research, but are quickly overgrown. Only those who know what to look for can see as a bird, lizard, or deer makes its way through the brush. Don Félix recounts the number of times in his life he's seen the bright, burning lights through the thicket, where scholars, too, have discovered the ball court.

This land by the river is abundant with life: opulent fruit trees—coconut, papaya, guanacastle—many types of birds—gray, white, and pink storks, egrets, cranes, and herons. The people who live at the mouth of the river walk along the bank remembering the coconut trees they planted when their children were born, and the many more trees they use for healing. They care for each branch the way they care for their grandchildren. These old comuneros have worked this place for generations, but they no longer own it. The

property has been expropriated and privatized. Their families now live in small houses that belong to the government, and they are officially caretakers of the land to which they once held claim.

Don Félix's daughter, Esperanza, gave birth to Grecia here, where she was born. Soon the baby will be three. Until her great-grandfather Isidoro died, she listened to his stories and watched him walk through the thick foliage toward the river and along its shore by the ocean to bathe and to survey the land.

Her grandfather Félix, in his khaki uniform, baseball cap, and rough-worn, sandaled feet, leaves early and comes home quite late, after he inspects every inch of land along the river and on the mountain and by the cliff. The very old remember how, as a young man, don Félix fought along with others in an adjacent community to help keep their lands from being taken by the town of Pochutla.[2] Don Felíx was born in 1924 on Las Palmas, a ranch that is part of Santa María Huatulco. He courted Isabel, or Chavelita, in Barra de la Cruz. For at least fifty of his years he has been the custodian of this place now being conserved for future research and ecotourism.

Floralice and Abel, whose father owned the largest portion of Tangolunda, have the prime view of La Bocana. People come here from far away to be dwarfed by the waves, to see the ocean that recedes with hurricanes. Tourists come in busloads for the mud baths. The mud baths are a favorite place for children to play, as well.

These days, don Félix bows to his children's hopes and aspirations. He watches as they build their dreams. His eldest and her husband slowly expand their beautiful restaurant, using *horcónes*—slim tree trunks or long branches—as pillars, thatching, and serpentine stone from between Santa María and Benito Juárez. Esperanza has started a business to support herself and her daughter, selling coconuts, refreshments, and lingerie. Don Félix's son, Esperanza and Flora's brother, calls every Sunday from New Jersey, sending his wife and son money for their living and to save to build their new house. He sends money home for a Mother's Day gift, as well.

Don Félix, 1997

Río Seco | The Dry River

During the dry season, from about December to June, the riverbed is empty, and the path to the village looks parched. The clothing of the people walking along the riverbank is the only color you see. More than seventy-five years ago, don Irineo and his bride settled here in what the old ones know in Chontal as La Filai. Now he is ninety-eight years old. His vision is not as sharp as it used to be, but he goes out every day with his machete to cut leña (firewood) for the oven and for cooking. His brown skin is lean and taut like jerky. He says the secret of his health is that he only eats seafood, no food from animals that walk the earth or pick up things from the ground. Once every few weeks he goes to the village of his birth to make sure his lands are well-tended. He takes the bus and stays a few days. His wife, doña Luciana, ninety-six, her hair falling over her shoulders and onto the hammock, recalls their courtship and his songs as she holds her sewing needle and looks out the door to the past. She sighs with love. Later, he sits watching his wife blow away the transparent fibers of the dry pumpkin seeds, and he recites love verses and tells stories about the Japanese ships that docked along the shore and the things they brought with them. Their children and grandchildren live next door, across the way, and all around them. His son and grandson are weaving a hammock, and his daughter-in-law is baking

Panorama from Río Seco

Left: Doña Luciana García, la abuelita, 1997

Center: Don Irineo García, el abuelito, 1997

Right: García cousins, 1997

bread in the oven her husband built. A granddaughter is resting on a hemp cot.

They say the dreams that haunt you are ones to which you must attend. Therein lies the secret of the *nagual*, the animal-other or spirit-other that exists in an unseen dimension as a guardian. You must go back to the source of the dream in order to recapture the spirit that has drifted away.

The conversation is about the spirit of the family, of the community, of the earth and how we all relate to one another. One grandson, Leucadio, went away and completed his service in other parts of the country. Now he wants to pursue something he can do here. Other members of the family join the conversation. An elderly aunt and uncle, Esperanza and Victoriano Gómez, come to visit and bring fresh boiled turtle eggs, a delicacy. The pungent, ping-pong-ball-like eggs are the best offering that can be made, and everyone is grateful that the presence of guests has given them a reason to enjoy this special food.

The Gómezes are childless. They are affectionate to all, and their family knows that they treat their animals as they would their children. They have compassion for their dog whose paw is injured, and they put a salve on it. They know all the plants in the area and their properties. The national school gave them a certificate for their knowledge. With or without a certificate, villagers have always come to them to be healed. What are turtle eggs good for? They are high in protein and vitamins, doña Luciana says.

There will be a wedding on Saturday. The women are preparing turkey, chiles, chocolate, ajonjolí, totopos (tortillas baked crisp), and the other dishes of the wedding feast. They make the *relajo*, a round, cage-like structure on top of a long pole in the middle of the dance area, and set out two chairs, for the bride and the groom. There are *coronas* (crowns) for the *padrinos* and *madrinas* from both sides of the family. The bride's family lives all around her, but the groom is an outsider—he has no one here to wear a crown and take a place of honor. Everyone wonders why. One guest will serve as a substitute family for him.

Above: The wedding: dancing under the relajo, 1998

Left: Ariana Ríos, 1998

The bride and groom first marry in a civil ceremony, as ordained by civil law, then return to the village for the feast. The bride dresses in a white dress, though all the women around her wear their best huipiles and enaguas. The young couple is photographed in her home, next to her parents' wedding picture. Then they walk out to greet the guests. Tall stacks of tortillas and large dishes of mole, turkey, chicken, beans, and rice are passed to the guests. The entire village is here, all related. The members of her family and the person chosen to act on behalf of his family are adorned with coronas, and they dance with the newly married.

All the young, unmarried women are called to the relajo at the center of the dance area. Each brings with her a small clay olla. As the young women are called, they form a circle and dance around the bride and groom, and one by one, each of them breaks an olla at the feet of the couple. The vessel will be broken. Then the young women take the cords of the relajo and circle it, unwinding its colored-paper wrapping, releasing confetti and flowers. Towards the end, two doves are released from the relajo and fly out to the applause of all present. The marimba plays the *zandunga*. It is sunrise before most of the villagers make their way home from the dance. The grandparents have long since gone back to rest on their hammocks. There are animals to feed in the morning.

Zimatan (Cimatlan) | The Root of the Mountain

Present-day Zimatan is a hamlet, but at one time it was formidable in size and prominence.[3] Cimatlan means "at the root of the mountain" in Nahuatl. This place seems as
though it was pulled out of the soil at the base of the foothills of Xadani. Old records
describe Zimatan as being between "Guatulco Viejo, the Port of Guatulco, and Guatulco."[4]
It once held promise of wealth and abundance. It was granted to Pedro de Pantoja, one of
the conquistadors, around 1525. Later, it was ordered abandoned. Within the last century,
portions of it belonged to the Ricárdez family, a prominent Chontal family who owned
several large parcels of land from the mountains to the ocean, including the coffee plantation El Faro. One of the Ricárdez children, a daughter, was a *diputada*, a member of the
Mexican Congress.

Fishermen's camp on the ocean at Río Seco, 1997

Simio and his Purpúra-dyed hair, 2001

There is a pun about Zimatan. Taking the "Zi" for an assertive "sí," and "mátan," as in the Spanish "to kill," Nereo says, "Sí mátan, pero no entierran." "They kill, but they don't bury." Jokes contain a grain, or more, of truth. For all its past prominence, this place, as well as the former Suchitepec, now Xadani, is known as a good place to escape the law.

Zimatan feels like a ghost town, or perhaps the spirits of the past pervade the rocks and stones that are more profuse here than in any other part of this land. Everywhere you look—in the riverbed, on the hillsides, as the foundation for most homes, around garden plots, as fences, and separating the houses from the road—there are rocks of every size and shape. It must have taken a long time, and an enormous amount of strength, to move these huge rocks to this hamlet and set them in place. It is even harder to imagine how life is lived among the rocks and stones.

Simio, who works by the sea in Santa Cruz, grew up here, and his mother still lives here. Simio has dyed his hair with *Púrpura*, squeezing the snail's purple secretions on small sections of his hair a little at a time. There are a few men whose hair is dyed this way—they believe that it makes their hair grow healthier and fuller. But the stench leads most people to wonder whether it is worth it.

Simio is proud to be "Indio." He says he doesn't know what kind of Indian he is, but his mother and aunts speak "in dialect." (His aunts live in La Merced de Portrero, a Zapotec village, hidden in a valley higher up in the foothills, where the *topil*, a town constable, blows a shell horn to call the council to meetings.) Simio is a brilliant young man who wonders why things are the way they are. Most young people from the region have grown up with the experience of expropriation. The region has changed a great deal in the last ten or fifteen years. The young people of Zimatan, like those of so many other hamlets, leave to work in the new hotels, or they migrate north, to the United States. Simio is eager to do this for awhile, but he loves his home, and he is dedicated to supporting his mother. She has suffered many hardships, he says, and she wants what's best for him.

Montes | Mountains

Xadani | Foothills

At the base of the mountain is a stream. Although the road runs down to the water, you can only cross it on foot. A woman washes under the shade of large guanacastle trees, next to bananas and guanabanas. She has chosen a place where the water runs clear, and where she can lay shirts, blouses, and undergarments on the rocks to dry. Her small child splashes and plays in a shallow pool by the elephant ears and other plants growing along the water's edge. The source of the stream is a spring. Water as clear as glass cascades over the sides of a square cement tank made by some locals who decided to well the source for profit. People say that since the source was welled they can no longer see the snake that used to guard this place. They say that the water is not as abundant as it was in the past. The woman washing says that there is always water, no matter how dry the season, but that the damming did bring misfortune: one of the men who tried to profit from this enchantment was found dead soon after it was dammed.

Xadani, literally "at the foot of the mountain" in Zapotec, lies within the remote area on the way to San Miguel del Puerto. Among its early names were Axochitepec, Suchitepeque, and Xuchitepec—Flower Hill, because of its flowering trees. Around 1579, Gutierre Díez de Miranda was the *corregidor*, or magistrate, of this place where people spoke Chontal.[1]

At the church, a fork in the road leads to the Zapotec village of La Merced del Portrero and to another road that takes you up to the coffee plantations of Monte Carlo, El Faro, and up farther to La Constancia and the peak of Cerro Lobo, Wolf Mountain. The other fork continues to San Miguel del Puerto. Along the way, you pass smaller rancherías. The coffee plantation of La Gloria, with its waterfalls and clear pools, has become a tourist locale. This is the site of another encanto, a spring where the locals say that gourds of many colors appear. Most of the Native people living in the area have come down from the mountains to work the coffee. Some of them have small parcels of land on which they grow coffee to sell to the coffee growers association. But coffee is at its lowest price, and it gets harder and harder every year to make a living.

Left: Cerro Lobo, 1998

Above: Church at Xadani, 2001

Above: El encanto de Xadani, 2001

Left: Mountains on the way to San Miguel del Puerto, 2000

Here in Xadani, across from the cemetery, a young woman is waiting for the taxi to give her a ride into town. Her little brother has been keeping her company, and she shyly says goodbye as he walks away. She stays in La Cruz from Monday through Saturday, in a room she and some other young women rent, and comes home on Sunday to see her parents. This is the way many of the young people from the hamlets live—some as young as fourteen or fifteen—to make ends meet and help their parents. Some eventually come home, like the young dentist who recently returned here, where there is a great deal of need. Others meet someone and go off to live and raise their families elsewhere.

San Miguel del Puerto, the Wingless Saint

From its source kilometers above, on its long descent to the sea, the Río Copalita winds past this coffee-growing town in the mountains. By the short route through La Hamaca (the Hammock), San Miguel del Puerto is only an hour and a half above the bays and Santa María Huatulco. The long route, by dirt road through Zimatan and Xadani, takes three hours or more, through mountainsides covered with coffee plants, the tiny beans barely visible at this time of year. It is July, and the sweltering heat and humidity are offset by the shade of the guarumbo and guayacan trees overhead and the cooling sound of waterfalls in the distance.

The trees and mountains serve as natural fortresses, protecting the town of San Miguel del Puerto and the many small hamlets nearby. It is easy to miss settlements that lie just over a rise in the land or beyond the fork of the road. Small plots of coffee saplings are invisible unless the eye catches their cultivated symmetry among the shade trees.

On one side of the *vereda*, the footpath barely carved out of the slope, are ferns, brush, coffee plants, trees, and unwelcoming rocks and crevices. In places, the mountain is held up by the macahuite or matapalos, the strangling ficus tree that entwines everything around it, from smaller trees and shrubs to rocks and boulders. Brilliant turquoise blue and green loros, or small parrots, flash by. There used to be poachers here.

They . . . came from Santa Rosa. . . . They would capture the parrots. They'd bring large cages with gum. They'd bring parrots, parakeets in cages. The caged birds would scream, and flocks of parrots and parakeets would come and get stuck on the gum. Their wings would get full, and they wouldn't be able to fly. They finished with the parrots. They would take them to Santa Rosa.

Then there were parrots, parakeets, loros, macaws, beautiful parrots with white breasts. By chance you see one now. I don't know how the federales found out. The federal police in Pochutla didn't let them get through. They opened the cages and let the birds fly away, and they prohibited the men from coming back. You can still see a few birds.

—Don Ignacio García

On the other side of the path, trees cover the mountainside all the way down. The umbrella-like leaves of the lanky guarumbo seem to hover, more than thirty meters overhead, shading the coffee plants. The sun filters in streaks through the forest. Orchids and other bromeliads grow lushly on their host trees everywhere the eye can see. The ceibas have witnessed the long history of this land, but they keep its secrets. Luis, Eme, and others who have lived in the mountains know that those who kill a ceiba die along with it, although Eme says her uncle knocked one down and he's still alive. Luis is from El

Mirador, a coffee plantation at the edge of the encanto, and Eme runs the plantation her grandmother managed alone for most of her adult life, in the jurisdiction of Huatulco.

At El Mirador (the Lookout), the path starts its descent toward the big mountain and the Yuviaga River. People from the area say that Yuviaga means "*cántaro de agua*," or "pitcher of water." Fresh, cool water pours from hidden caverns and springs. Through thousands of years of wet and dry seasons, water that seems to come from within the mountain has sustained everything that grows. This source, known as El Nacimiento, the birthplace or origin of the spring, is honored in February on the feast day of San Felipe, patron saint of the town on the other side of the mountain. Luis's father says that in times past hundreds of candles lined the Nacimiento. These days fewer people leave candles and flowers to honor the saint and show respect to the great snake that sometimes appears to those who stop at the spring.

The climb upward is gradual, but sometimes rough, and the foliage grows thicker the higher you climb. Rustling leaves mean something else is moving as well. At a precipice, the Río Copalita is visible way in the distance, too far to walk before sundown but comforting nonetheless, for you know that it leads south to the sea, not deeper into the mountains. A rock face looms, filled with niches, caves in which to find protection. Blue and ochre pigments, barely visible at first, form a shape like a human figure, and another like a cat, and others like the sun. The caves hold the secret of this enchantment and may also lay claim to those few who seek it, people say, for they don't return. People say that giants painted the narratives on this great wall in ancient times. No one knows who they might have been. There is evidence of smoke along the base of the rock face, and there are caves within caves. This is a holy place, guarded by the snake of the spring and by the stories people tell. Only a few who live here maintain the knowledge of this place, on the boundary between San Miguel del Puerto and San Felipe Lachillo.

On the way down from the encanto you come to a store at the edge of town, and the public telephone. Women and children who have come to town from the nearby hills sit here visiting and talking. The women ask people who pass what they are doing, where they are going. This is how news spreads. They know all the deliveries of goods, all the trucks and vehicles that are familiar, all the ones that are not. Voice travels as quickly as a bird's call. The women are surprised that anyone has found the encanto. It only makes itself evident to some, they say, and they never return. The women have never been there, nor do they want to go. The owner of the store, a former mayor of San Miguel del Puerto, Señor Hernández, says that a geologist came here once with some hobbyists, but he doesn't know what they learned. He is hoping that the place will be preserved before it can be despoiled. There are stories here of *mamuts* (mammoths), and large bones that people have found. They believe that giants inhabited this land once, because of those bones.

A child with a long ponytail walks along a path with a fragile woman, prematurely aged. Water running down from the mountainside has made the dirt road treacherous, and they stumble on rubble and thousands of shards uncovered by the wash. They are walking toward a tiny, thatched shack on the hill. The child, Alicia Mariela, four now, lives with her grandmother. Her mother died from eating poisonous mushrooms. Her father abandoned her. They are from San Felipe Lachillo, the Zapotec village just over the mountain, abutting the cave.

The steep stairs leading up to their one-room home are carved from the earth along the hillside. It is a makeshift house, vulnerable to the elements. There's a *comal* (griddle) where the grandmother heats tortillas. Alicia's uncle, twelve years old, works at San Anto-

Above: El encanto de Yuviaga, 1997

Right: The Zapotec woman at the strangling fig, 1997

nio, one of the *cafetales* (coffee plantations). The owners were kind to help him out, aware that he is supporting his sickly mother and his niece. He climbs the hillside, carrying a load of branches, kindling his mother will use for cooking. She says they will probably move closer to town because Alicia will start school soon.

A few months later, Alicia comes running down the steps. Her grandmother follows, saying that Alicia told her that the *chigüiro* birds visited in the morning and announced that people were coming from far away. The chigüiro says, "*Allí vienen, allí viene*"—"they're coming, they're coming"—she says. She was wondering who it might be, perhaps one of her sons who moved far away. Cynics may raise their eyebrows. How could birds speak? When asked, an old man from La Ceiba, a hamlet along the Río Copalita, answers, "Of course they speak. The chigüiro is the one who makes the announcement. There are other animals and birds that do this, too."

The hurricanes of October swept away their small house. A large tree fell over its roof, and the steps were washed away without a trace. Several people had their eye on little Alicia, and the wife of the doctor thought it might be possible to adopt her. When she and her grandmother were nowhere to be found, the owner of the store in town said that they were living at El Mirador. Luis's family has hired Alicia's uncle and is providing a home for Alicia and her grandmother. Alicia plays with Luis's daughter, and others of her uncles have come to work at the cafetal for the season.

Coffee was first brought here around 1880. During the latter part of the 19th century and the beginning of the 20th century, many Europeans came to the region to acquire land for coffee growing. Among the earliest coffee plantations was San Pablo, run by a company from London.[2] The company leased part of the communal lands, which raised issues of titles and jurisdiction bearing upon Santa María de Huatulco, San Miguel del Puerto, and San Mateo Piñas. By the early 1920s, Europeans—Germans for the most part—were buying land in the highlands, ideal for planting coffee. In the 1930s, when President Lázaro Cárdenas nationalized the petroleum industry, he also enforced an article of the 1917 Constitution that restored communal lands taken by large haciendas. Many of the German holdings and those of other foreigners were expropriated. By then, however, several European landowners had married local residents. The conditions of the remaining fincas vary. Some have been abandoned, a few are being revitalized by tourism, and others continue to produce coffee, and to employ local workers, despite the depressed prices for coffee around the world.

Luis's parents are descendants of the families who came to the region in the first part of the 20th century, and he is related to people on other peaks. His mother remembers how, when she was a child, families would travel down the mountain for a holiday by the ocean. The children were carried in baskets slung like saddlebags over a horse. She says it was a rough trip and quite treacherous. Luis has inherited his parents' passion for this land. His cousin owns the plantation of Monte Carlo and lives just down the way. Now the growers are all trying to make ends meet, struggling to keep one of the main businesses here from disappearing. Many Native people from the region are dependent on the success of coffee sales for their livelihood, as laborers and as small growers themselves. Yet it becomes more difficult every year to hire people from the mountains to work. They prefer to try their luck elsewhere.

On May 8th, there is a fiesta, the celebration of Saint Michael the Archangel, the patron of this village. On the Catholic calendar, the feast falls on September 29th, but here, the wet and dry seasons govern all events, even those Catholicism introduced. So on Septem-

Young bread-seller at San Antonio cafetal, 1998

Above left: La niña, Monte Carlo cafetal, 1998

Above right: Alicia's twelve-year-old uncle, carrying kindling, 1997

ber 29th, a simple mass is said in honor of the saint, while the May fiesta lasts several days. The women and men of the village use the kitchen behind the church to prepare the feast. Roast chicken, mole, and tortillas in large quantities are distributed to the villagers. There are basketball tournaments on the court below the church, and all along the one real street there is a marketplace of stalls. Everything anyone might need or desire locally is here, from herbs and foodstuffs to brassieres, trousers, toys, cassettes, and kitchen implements. People come from Xadani, and Simio is here with friends from Zimatan and Santa Cruz to play basketball. It is his first time here, and he will stay overnight. He is happy to see a young woman he knows, with her father and mother selling clothing, and his attention has been returned. In the local bars, men are drinking and talking, more concerned with the political relationship between San Miguel and Santa María Huatulco.

There has been a competition for land here since 1539, when the ancient title divided this region between Santa María Huatulco and San Miguel de Huatulco, assigning the area beyond the Río Copalita to San Miguel. Everyone who knows the history admits that the people of San Miguel, now San Miguel del Puerto, are from the same families mentioned in the original title on the port of Guatulco. And this, they say, is why for awhile the people of San Miguel had a hard time keeping their patron saint from returning to the coast.

Don Cuauhtemoc Méndez was born in the highlands, but he has lived in Huatulco for many years. He works as a scribe and advocate for many people who cannot read, but who want to secure their land for their families. He is also one of the local historians, and he tells the story of the saint:

There is a fragment taken from the scribe Melchor de los Reyes, who, in his routine notes, referred to the disappearance of this icon. It took place about 1879, when one morning, upon opening the church, the caretaker noticed that the saint was not on the altar. He made a report to the authorities, and they immediately ordered a search throughout the town and surrounding areas. Since the saint never appeared, they decided that it had been stolen. It was a grave sin that someone would steal something from a church.

The bells of San Miguel del Puerto, 1998

Three months passed—some say it was three days; we are more inclined to believe it is three months—when a family that lived in Santa María Huatulco visited their relatives in San Miguel. In the course of the conversation during their visit, someone raised the case of the saint. One of the visitors from Santa María asked why the town of San Miguel had returned its saint to the Bay of Santa Cruz. The saint had been there for awhile. The people from San Miguel thought he was joking. When they realized that he was serious, they notified the authorities.

So, the people of San Miguel commissioned the topiles and fiscal officials of the church to assess the situation, dispatching them to the Bay of Santa Cruz, where they indeed found the icon. They returned with it to San Miguel. At first, the townspeople thought it must have been a practical joke. But after the second, third, and fourth time? They believed it might be a miracle. Despite their vigilance, the saint escaped.

Then came the time of the fiesta in May, and the priest from Santa María was brought to officiate. After learning about the escapades, he ordered the carpenter to cut off the saint's wings and to place them in a niche in the sanctuary, apart from the icon. And it was done.

An unexpected incident occurred after the priest had officiated for three days of the fiesta. The priest left San Miguel del Puerto very early in the morning accompanied by a steward who was to take him to Huatulco. The priest was riding on a mule, and his steward was leading another animal carrying the priest's belongings and gifts. It so happened that it had rained heavily the night before. When the steward and the priest arrived at the edge of the river, the servant heard the thunderous force of the water coming from upstream. He suggested to the priest that it might not be advisable to cross at that time, but the priest answered, "Man of little faith!" Whereupon the priest rode into the wide river, and by midstream the strong current took him away.

The steward, who had stayed on the bank, returned to San Miguel to notify the authorities. They ordered the entire village to go down to the river to look for the priest, but they never found him, nor the

Wolf Mountain   "Lobas"   Oaxaca-Mexico

One of Las Lobas, with her niece, 1998

mule. And since then, that place on the river is called "the curate's pass." At the edge, where the servant stood, there is a small cave that to this day is known as "the devil's cave," because one year later, to the date, a priest was seen there on his knees praying the Miserere for the sin he committed under the devil's influence.

There are, of course, many versions of this story, but this is the most credible.

And it is the most credible. The other versions are told in the dark, on the way across the river, going up and down the hill to and from San Miguel, and at the chapel of the Bay of Santa Cruz, by the sacristan who knows the stories. Some say the priest was stabbed in the back by Saint Michael's sword, and that he was found, face down there, in the river. Luis's mother sponsored the restoration of the saint. She said that not only is it very old, but it is true that the wings were cut off some time in the past.

Cerro Lobo | Wolf Mountain

From the closest neighbor's below it takes one hour by car and two hours or more on foot to get to this pinnacle overlooking the region, which was once a Zapotec holding. The highest peak in the area, Cerro Lobo stands in the midst of clouds, often surrounded by fog. Two sisters, called Las Lobas (the She-Wolves) by the people around here, inherited the land on the mountain from their father. They live here, isolated from the other plantation owners, most of whom are descended from Germans who came to México around the time of World War I.

Although they use antiquated methods, the sisters are known for growing and roasting superlative coffee. With their mules alongside them, they walk down the mountain to the closest water source and bring back large vessels of water for processing the coffee beans. One of their siblings is a doctor who lives in the city, and another's child is here with them now. A three year old, she watches everything her aunts do. She plays with the little dog that often sits at the peak, looking out toward the ocean.

Amid the foundations of an old settlement are large upright stones inscribed with circular designs that have yet to be deciphered. People say that there was an entire valley of Wolves in ancient times. Las Lobas are the only living residents on this pinnacle, but the space is occupied by legends.

Cuajinicuil | The Place of the Cuil Tree

It is 1997, and hurricane Paulina has just passed, leaving terrible devastation. Two young boys, cousins of twelve and thirteen, walk uphill on their way home from school. It's a three-hour walk. They leave home at five in the morning to get to school by eight. Sometimes they catch a bus on the way, but the roads are bad now. Landslides caused by the storm have washed away many of the roads and left others impassable.

On the day of the hurricane, many of the local people were told to go to the schools for shelter. The boys spent the night there. Their parents had no idea what had happened to them, nor did they know how their families were doing. Many houses were torn apart, their tin roofs blown away, but some that were made with palm thatching survived intact. This is Cuajinicuil Alto, on the hill, one of the contested areas between Huatulco and San Mateo Piñas. In San José Cuajinicuil, down below, next to the Río Huatulco, the school was swept away by the force of the river.

On this Día de los Muertos, in this place named for a tall Mexican tree, the Méndez family has much for which to be grateful. Some of the boys' aunts and uncles lost their homes, but thankfully they have their lives and are all right. Today when the boys arrive home from their night in the school, their parents come to greet them. One mother, two aunts, and a grandmother are in the adobe kitchen stirring mole and warming tortillas on the comal. The small white wooden table is set for at least eight people, and the roosters are walking in and out, trying to avoid being stepped on. A cat sits on a ledge, waiting for the end of the meal. On the plastic tablecloth, a blue gingham pattern with small clusters of red flowers, is the rich, dark red mole and chicken served on *peltre* (pewter) and in deep-blue-rimmed, enameled dishes. The women take turns warming the tortillas as others eat. Once this is done, it is time to turn attention toward completing the *altares*. This is the men's domain.

La familia Méndez on the steps of the school at Cuajinicuil, 1997

The uncles prepare the altar table and bamboo arches adorned with threaded marigolds, magenta-colored cockscomb, crab apples, and greenery. Votive candles, incense, *pan de muerto*, chocolate, mole tamales, and the favorite things of the family's dead rest before their photos. As the children run by grabbing treats, grownups share the offerings with family and guests, and the spirits consume the essence of what has been presented to them. This year everyone gathers together for a family photograph, some patiently, others less so as they wait by the steps of the school for what seems hours. After one of the worst hurricanes in years, they are all present and accounted for.

Xuchitl | Flower Mountain

This place bears the Nahuatl name for a flower, or rather for the guamuchil, a fruit- and flower-bearing tree. Now bougainvillea and yellow and orange flowers grow abundantly here, in contrast to the earthen roads. Xuchitl is an orderly town, with a beautiful little plaza and church decorated with streamers of paper, on the way up the mountain toward San Miguel del Puerto, before crossing the Río Copalita.

On this particularly hot day, Señor Rogelio Gabriel sits on a bench with his cane beside him, wearing no shirt, but a lively smile. He has cataracts, and he struggles to see the children who surround him. A dog sleeps at his feet, and there is a pet rabbit hopping about. His daughter-in-law is preparing a meal, and she lets him know what everyone is up to. The boys are playing ball out front. His son is busy inside the house. A woman from Astata goes by selling bread, and his daughter-in-law mentions that she comes by often. Tío Rogelio travels in his mind, recalling the places he knows:

I first visited Huamelula and Astata when I was twelve years old. My father would take me, and we would go almost every New Year. I knew Astata fairly well. The last time I went was about three years ago. We went to see people we know, people we visited with. There is this man—what is his name?—I recognized him, and he recognized me, and he welcomed me into his home. They're very easy to speak with. I know a number of people, but if I saw them today, I wouldn't recognize them.

We would fish in Tangolunda in order to eat. I know all of the places—Bajos del Arenal, Coyula.

The Gabrieles founded Xuchitl, more than a century ago. "Well, this is the way people settle here, when they don't have a place to live or to work," don Rogelio says. "First one

Above left: La abuelita Méndez placing offerings on the altar for la Día de los Muertos, 1997

Above right: The Méndez men constructing the altar for la Día de los Muertos, 1997

comes, then a few more, then more. Pretty soon there are plenty. In the past everyone spoke only in dialect. Now they don't."

The first mention of a Gabriel (Gavriel) appears in documents dating from the 1700s. It is made by someone who says he is a friend of a Gavriel, a man who says he is from China and leases land from Astata for cattle grazing. Catarino Gabriel Lavariega, don Rogelio's father, and his grandfather, Nicolás Gabriel García, were born in this area, as was don Rogelio.

My grandparents came with the branch that came from Piñas. They're the Gabriel family from Piñas. Those who are here are the ancient ones. I stayed here. I had ten siblings. We're all Gabrieles. There are some here next to us, and on this side [he motions to the right] there are several as well.

This place has been here for a very long time. People inhabited it beginning a long time ago. There are hills here where they built their homes, places where they lived from ancient times.

He says he loved working in the fields, there was always something to find. Sometimes it was hard to prepare the fields, he found so many mounds made by earlier people. "When I worked up on the hill, I found pots, and there was a place where I found metates they used for grinding." He got water from a source at the Cerro del Sombrero. It was called Sombrero Hill, he says, because it is shaped like a hat, very steep at the top. He says you climb it by going around and around. It's labeled Cerro del Cimarrón on the map, but they call it Cerro del Sombrero around here. From its peak, he says, you can see the beach and all of Huatulco. An abandoned hamlet, El Hule, is named after the rubber trees, because, as don Rogelio says, *"Así le pone la gente."* "That's the way people give names." It's the way Piedras Negras' name was given, his son says. "All you see there are these black rocks."

Don Rogelio talks about how certain hamlets are made up of families that keep growing until some move away. Other places are abandoned when the land can no longer produce. Here in Xuchitl, life is peaceful, don Rogelio says. There are no *pleitos* (fights). The tortillas are ready, and so is the soup. Then it is time to rest.

Benito Juárez

There's a young man who always goes to the encanto. I haven't been there, but they say that there is much fruit. You can eat it, but you can't take it away with you—nothing, you can only eat it there. And if you take any with you, you turn into water. . . .

— Don Filomeno Martínez García

The encanto is a hill close to Huatulco, known as Cerro Huatulco, but in the past it was known as Cerro Isla. Half belongs to Huatulco and the other half belongs here. The hill is deserted. The river on the other side of Apango is the Magdalena River, but on this side it is a small creek we call Arroyo de Hierba Santa [Creek of the Holy Plant]. So they call it Cerro Isla [Island Hill] because there is a great quantity of water. It is within the river and the creek: it becomes an island.

According to the people of long ago, there was a large plateau and a lagoon. They say that people found a garden there with many fruit trees. It was a place no one went to. The people who went hunting would get lost, and this is how they would arrive at that place. When they got out and wanted to return, they could never find it.

— Santos García

One of the boundaries between Santa María Huatulco and San Mateo Piñas is the Cerro Huatulco, the mountain behind the town of Santa María, beyond the shallows of the Río Huatulco. A dirt road hugs the base of the mountain on one side and the river on the other. There is a stretch where it looks as though loose rock will fall if you whisper too loudly, and if the rock falls, the road will be closed. In places the mountainside reveals the beautiful, rust-colored serpentine rock that has been quarried for so much new construction. This is one of the latest areas of contention. Part of the mountain falls within the limits of Santa María Huatulco; the other part belongs to Benito Juárez, in the jurisdiction of San Mateo Piñas. The people of San Mateo say that Huatulco is selling everything and now wants to move farther up the mountain. The mountain is also an encanto.

Santos is a noble young man, well-groomed and very gracious. He worked as a waiter at the coffee kiosk in Santa Cruz. But he needed to be home—especially now, as his father's leg is injured—and he has been working here, cultivating and harvesting the coffee his family grows. Besides, most weekends, on his days off, he left the café to visit his family and play in a soccer league that includes many young men from the local villages and hamlets. He has a near-religious devotion to the game.

Santos was born in Benito Juárez, as were his father and grandmother, and he is interested in the village's history. He sits and talks with the abuelitos. Once, most of the people knew Zapotec, but now only the very old speak it, and those who come from San Mateo Piñas, farther up in the mountains. Santos listens to his father talk about the boundaries of Benito Juárez:

The Llano Suave area is the boundary with Huatulco. From there is the plantation Miramar, and the boundary goes to the finca of San Pablo, and from there to Piñas. The land there borders Piñas and Magdalena.

Xuchitl, 2000

It is three hours by foot from the plantation of San Pablo to the finca of El Nueve. From El Naranjo there is a direct route. Mixteca is a ranchería of people from Benito Juárez. It borders with the Río Sal [Salt River], which belongs to Benito Juárez. The Río Sal was named that because of the trees that grow there. They call them salt flowers or salt branches. These are branches encircled with white flowers. When they are blooming, they smell like saltwater or sea water, something like that. They used to use these trees to make doors because the wood is very hard, and for broomsticks. And they used palo mulato for paper, and also coíva.

The milk of the palo de hule was used in the past to make balls, and for glue. They made balls to play mano fría [cold hand]. Now they call it [pelota]. So that ball is the same as the one that was used in [the ancient Zapotec city of] Monte Alban in a ball game played with the hips. They cut down many trees in the past. Now they're scarce, but there are still some. I used to use it when I made kites. I'd cut into the bark of the tree and use a little pot to catch the milk that would drain. I glued kites with it. I still have some small balls and they stretch [motioning with his hands].

Through this side—Pato Jícara [Duck Gourd], as they call it—they say there is un encanto. They say that people become enchanted in December, around the 24th, before the morning of the 25th. The problem between Benito Juárez and Santa María is that they never bothered to mark the boundaries. Now they want to do it, but they can't find the papers. The border is close to the bajadero de piedras [the quarry]. Well, it's closer to the lightpost where they put a sign that says Danger, High Voltage. From there it's about fifty meters.

Don Filomeno Martínez García, 1999

Santos's grandmother Chole, doña Soledad García, has just returned from the most recent First Friday of Lent celebrated at El Pedimento. She says that people still come to pay their respects to the Cruz del Monte and to make petitions. She hears that her son and grandson have been talking about the encantos, and she offers what she knows:

The man, Ulidio García, who went to the encanto is dead now. They say he was hunting, and he found nothing but light there, nothing but good things. All you see are lights. They say you go camping, and you're there a while, and suddenly you're in a different place, and you don't know how you entered. You see mango, orange, and banana trees. You can eat the entire time you are there, but if you want to pick the fruit to take it with you, you can't.

The finado [late] Juan García went camping, and he entered the encanto. There was a man there who said, "Don't take the fruit because the earth will swallow you." So he wasn't tempted to pick the fruit. He was there about an hour, I think, then he left. Later, his son went, and he told his son, "Don't pick the fruit. There is plenty, but don't pick the fruit." And his son stayed an hour before he left. If you stay longer, you can't get out. People go in, but they come out within an hour. Many people saw the encanto in the past.

There's another encanto in Hondura. There, at night on Christmas Eve, a baby cries. But no one wanders out then. In Hondura they say that you can hear water pouring, but no water comes out. There is a large rock, about four meters high, where you hear the water gushing out. They say that right below, at the base of the rock, is where the baby's cry is heard.

And they say that in Arroyo Sal, a river around here, you see what looks like gold, but you're not supposed to follow it, because it's an enchantment. If you follow it, it will take you in. You will keep on going and never return. There were also gourds, when the river was full. They would see jicaras from the morro tree, gourds like the ones that they used to fill with grease—which are nowadays plastic—the kind that were used for drinking coffee.

Of course this is frightening, but once I went to catch shrimp. There used to be sweetwater shrimp in the sand by the rock. I heard a baby cry, and I told myself, "You're crazy."

The people of the mountains knew about these encantos. There used to be people who lived in Santa Lucía. Now they've come to the village, and many have died. My grandmother lived there, and my great-grandmother, whose name was Crispina, told me that in the past it was a town, but at the time of the Carrancistas [one of many armed groups during the Mexican Revolution, around 1915], it was a center of battle, so they left the place. The hamlet is abandoned. There is coffee growing there now, and we graze our sheep there.

This leads into a narrative about her life. Santos's grandmother doesn't know when she was born.

My husband died more than twenty years ago. I was left with six children when they killed him. Those were bad, bad people who entered at night and at gunpoint. We heard the gunshots through the door. Nowadays it is peaceful. People can walk at night and nothing happens.

Doña Soledad García, Benito Juárez, 2000

My father was born here. I was orphaned. My mother had already died when my father took ill. We went to Pochutla, then to Zapotengo, by the ocean. We were there with my father in April when he got ill in the rastro [planting field]. My sister and I went to take him his taco. When we arrived, we screamed, "Father, father! Where's my father!" He was struck, and he couldn't speak. I asked my sister, "What should we do?" We called for our godfather. My sister was crying. It was about noon, everyone had gathered to eat, and I told my godfather that my father looked as though he was dead. "My father can't talk." That damned fever! My godfather carried him gently and tried to help him, but we were left, the two of us.

Her parents weren't there to select their son-in-law, and she was forced to marry a man she didn't love. She would return home and be told to go back. Santos interrupts and says, "But later you loved grandfather." And she agrees that although at the beginning she cried because she had no choice but to be with him, later she learned to love him. Still, she reminisces about how a mother and father used to pick a good husband for their daughter.

When a suitor went to ask for a young woman's hand in marriage, the family would take a branch, a thick one, as straight as they could find, and they'd spin the stick to see how it fell. This is what they did with my mother. They would make a plate of the hottest salsa and a pot of very hot coffee. They'd give the young man a large cup of hot coffee to wash down the hottest chile to see how much he could handle. They'd make him perspire.

Doña Maura, another of the abuelitas of Benito Juárez, is well over 100 years old, and the stories she tells are written in every line of her face. She cannot hear very well, but she picks up a thread and continues where she left off the last time, although that conversation may not have been with you. Most of her stories have to do with the Revolution and the incursions of the Carrancistas, events that took place between 1910 and 1920, factionalizing the people in the villages and hamlets. Everyone ninety and older can recall the way the partisans swept the region, wreaking havoc on what was sacred—the churches and the women. Doña Maura was hidden from them. Later, she too was forced to marry. Her husband was a widower.

Since neither my father nor my mother knew how to read, I didn't know how old I was. Because I couldn't read, I didn't make note of it. I was born in Cuajinicuil Alto. I had ten children, eleven including one that died. My father was from Huatulco, from Santa María. You see, Cuajinicuil belonged to Santa María. [My parents] came up here during the Mexican Revolution. The military hanged a lot of people, and they robbed people of everything they had. Everything we made to eat had to be hidden, because they stole everything. You couldn't have a meal prepared or they would steal it.

Upper right: El fogón (the oven) at Xuchitl, 2000

Lower right: Escoba (broom), Benito Juárez, 2000

Her son interjects, "She says she buried her money, so they wouldn't steal it, then she forgot where she left it. I think the man from the corner found it [and didn't return it]. Many people hid their money."

Her daughter adds, "She used to tell amazing stories about how it was during the time of the Carrancistas. They would hear the sound of the trumpet all the way up here. It was a warning that the Carrancistas were coming to eat everything. If they found anyone, they would hang them from the highest branch if they didn't turn over their valuables. It was around 1912 or 1915."

Doña Maura continues, "I was forced to marry. In those times they would ask for your hand in marriage, your father, your mother. But when I was twenty, they married me off to a widower. I thought, 'This isn't possible! To a rancher!' I wanted to run. He wanted to take me to the ranch."

An announcement of a meeting comes over the loudspeaker from the town square. The men are discussing ongoing claims regarding Benito Juárez. The most recent one, they say, was registered on March 13, 1972, and today is the anniversary of its resolution. The treasurer and the one responsible for all documents, don Filiberto Peralta Gabriel, says that it was an agrarian conflict between San Mateo Piñas and Huatulco:

The primordial title encompasses San Pedro Cuajinicuil, known in ancient times as Almácen, . . . Miramar, Piedra de Cal, Piedras Negras, El Portazuelo, Loma de Nanche, El Maquil, Río Grande, Llano Juárez, and Cerro Isla, which falls in the trine point between Benito Juárez, Santa María Huatulco, and the private property known as Apanguito.

The treasurer's voice over the loudspeaker trails off, and he addresses those in front of him. The town square is the meeting place, in the center of the hamlet, with a beautiful view of fertile land where coffee, cacao, bananas, oranges, rubber trees, and many other plants thrive. This is one of the areas most heavily contested between Santa María Huatulco and San Mateo Piñas. Documents #2, #7, and #17 in the town archives testify to claims dating from 1766, 1762, and 1895, and the argument about the ownership of this land hasn't stopped to this day. In earlier times, some of the discord had to do with the production of cochineal.[3] As don Ignacio from Huatulco explains:

The cochineal was made from a small red insect they got from the cactus. It is still produced, but since they don't use it now, production has dwindled. That's how they dyed cloth. They used so much of it in the past, they planted a great deal of cactus. There is still plenty of cactus. Some people in Benito Juárez have plots. People would come purposefully from a place known as Don Luis, not far from Acapulco. They would bring a great many skeins of white thread. People here would then give them the cochineal, but I never asked where they were going to sell the skeins, or what factory they were taking them to.

Don Filiberto's voice can still be heard in the background, talking about the anniversary of the accord between the competing interests:

According to Huatulco, the conflict arose from commissions that existed in the past. But in reality, it came to be a conflict between Piñas and Huatulco, and from the conflict, the community of Benito Juárez was formed. This conflict is more than 100 years old.

Within Piñas and Huatulco, it came close to war. They fought hard, because Piñas came with many people. The people from Piñas left, and soon after those from Huatulco arrived on horseback, all armed. Well, this type of machismo existed in the past. The threat of agrarian reform followed. From the 6th of July 1972 the conflict de-escalated. Piñas and Huatulco signed a document in the Agrarian Department. This is where they pledged to respect the possessions that belonged to Benito Juárez. Both towns made that commitment, as it states here:

"The settlement represents 466 campesinos who fulfilled the legal prerequisites to be considered comuneros. The said community lacks titles to support its ownership of the land whose recognition and titles it solicits, as mentioned in a manner expressed in its written request, the towns of Santa María Huatulco and San Mateo Piñas, according to presidential resolution of August 30, 1973. Published in the Official Diary of the Federation on the 26th of November of that same year."

Little Abril, who is six, is looking for don Filomeno down by the river. Her mother says that she goes to him for everything. She wades across the water to find him, but he's not there, so her mother calls her back. Then he suddenly appears, a lean man of average height, elegantly dressed in the traditional white cotón pants and shirt that few from here wear now, although they are comfortable in the hot weather. His hat is large, with a straight wide brim, made of tightly woven straw, and it, too, distinguishes him. He is in his eighties. He carries a large stick he's using as a staff in one hand and an orange in the other. He wears a smile and a pensive look at the same time. They are still recuperating from the hurricanes, and don Filomeno says he is thinking of all they have to do.

He has coffee plants, animals, and an orchard across the river to attend to, and he is building this new house where his daughter, a nurse, will live. Don Filomeno lives farther up the hillside, with his wife, children, and grandchildren. He says that Abril wants to learn everything. She asks him how to say this and that in *dialecto*. She asks him every question she needs to have answered. Don Filomeno says, "Here I am looking the way I do, and she wants to take me to school with her. Many of the young people are not interested in learning the language."

He says his great-great-grandfather or *tatarabuelo* founded this place back in the 1840s. He and his family asked for permission to settle this land. Don Filomeno says:

I was born July 5, 1920. I'm from Benito Juárez and Pueblo Nuevo. This town was called Pueblo Nuevo in the past. My great-grandparents went to San Mateo Piñas to seek a ruling, because the service they gave [in exchange for a homestead] had to be in Piedra de Cal, and they had to come all the way from Piñas, and it was just too far. Their little mule couldn't make it up the hill, so they walked eight hours. They took a stack of tortillas to eat on the way, and went to see if the authorities would consider giving them another place, and they did. That was in 1844. That was my great-great-grandfather, whose name was Eugenio García García, and his son-in-law, whose name was Gerardo García. The other was José Cándido García.

My forefathers founded this town. They slept here on the way to another place. They had a peaceful slumber. If they had no dreams, it was a good sign. This is how they formed their opinion. It depended on the dreams they had.

They went to another place. They were looking for a beautiful large valley, like this plain in Llano Juárez. Sometimes people worked here plucking corn from the stalks, picking fruit. My forefathers asked, "Well, why not here, if it is very pretty. . . ." They went to the Arroyo Sal and elsewhere. It took a year and a half [before they came to a decision]. It was better here. It is cool here.

One family came first, then others arrived. According to the beliefs of the past, decisions depended on whether there were dreams and what type of dream.

The people were Indians. Some wore enaguas, long skirts, and the other part was the cotón. Cotón was what it was called, tusi is what was used to make it. But now things are changing. With this new generation and the youth, I have no one with whom to speak. I ask myself, "With whom will I sit and speak about our memories? Whom will I ask, 'Do you remember?'"

The language was beautiful, pure [Zapotec] language. For whatever purpose—bestowing and accepting the mayordomía [a civic responsibility]—it was all done in the language. In the past, although the old people died, the young people who remained still practiced the old ways.

The stories of the past are for educating, to correct children, to teach them a great deal of respect. There is no better child than one who gets a good upbringing. The children these days say, "Grandmother." But in the past they said, "Becha." "Becha" is a form of great respect. It means "Good morning," or "God bless you." They would say, "Papa, becha. Good morning. Nana, becha. Good morning."

"Son of good faith, don't come in." "Pardon me, Mother." Nowadays, they don't greet you with good morning. "Tata, good morning." That is over.

Don Filomeno says that the old people called La Cruz del Monte, La Cruz Huam Ito, the Cross on the Hill by the Sea Where You Make Promises. He says that those who visit the cross note the date, in writing or in their minds. He says that the old name for Huatulco is Quetz Tuhuao, the Town of Huatulco, combining Zapotec and Nahuatl words.

My father died in 1921 when he was twenty-eight, and I was left at six months. I never knew my father, but my mother spoke the language [Zapotec]. She spoke half Castilian and half in language. When she scolded me it was half in Castilian and half in Zapotec. But the people just let [the language] go. Some left, and others didn't want to teach it to their children, which is what happened with me. I didn't teach my children.

I have five children. We're all descendants from San Mateo Piñas, not Huatulco. This place is not Santa María Huatulco. It belongs to San Mateo Piñas. There has always been a struggle, from ancient times to this day. Now everyone has titles, the government gave them titles: "You must go to Piñas." "You must go to Huatulco." First they were fighting, now they say each stays within its limits.

In the past Benito Juárez, was called Pueblo Nuevo [New Town]. That's the way it still is in the Agrarian Department in Mexico City. It was called Pueblo Nuevo around 1800. In 1917 my father changed the name to Benito Juárez. Huatulco has nothing to do with this place. Huatulco now is a stretch of commerce and tourism. The sea was part of Huatulco, but now it belongs to tourism.

Poblados | Villages

Cosecha de jamaica   Oaxaca, Mexico

Santa María Huatulco (Coatulco)

Between 1909 and 1920 there still remained . . . people residing in that place known as Pueblo Viejo [Old Town], according to Maximiliano Amador, parish priest of Pochutla. . . .

They lived there for several years with a certain amount of tranquility, but the privateers continued to visit them from time to time. To avoid this they decided to move, this time following the directions of the old ones. In the silence of the night, they all moved toward the west, praying with interest, imploring the mercy of God, from whom they awaited a signal of that place where they would settle permanently without further annoyances from the Moors or pirates. That pilgrimage lasted all night until they found, at the hour the roosters sing, an opulent river, which they crossed.

They camped in the place that today is called La Erradura. However, at night one of the ancients heard the voice of the Virgin of the Immaculate Conception say, "Son, this is not the right place. You are all mistaken. You must return, and before the river crossing there is a plain. This is where I wish to have my church established and reconstructed." They built the foundation of the new town of Santa María Huatulco that is conserved until our days.

— From the notes of Silverio Lavariega, written by Maximiliano Lavariega[1]

The name of the town of Huatulco, as it states in the document of 1539, is "Our Lady of the Very, Pure, Clean, and Immaculate Conception." It sits nestled on a high valley, far enough away from the original site on the Bay of Santa Cruz. It took the community more than two hundred years to find its final destination after the pirate raids, though the way the stories are narrated, it seems as though it took just a few years.

Coming from the back road through Piedra de Moros, you pass Pueblo Viejo, then Limoncito, Las Pozas, Todos Santos, Arroyo Limón, and Hacienda Vieja. Higinia Alcántara Mijangos walks the dirt path with some children. She's on her way home to Santa María from the small rancherías after she's finished giving some of her pupils their lessons. On the way, she greets Genaro Ortíz, ninety-two years of age, and his granddaughter, Araceli Ortíz López. They are related to don José Ortíz, but they come from La Soledad, Miahuatlan, a town along the old trade route. Tío Genaro says, "*Allá, el terreno ya*

Left: Tío José Ortíz adorning graves at the pantéon (cemetery) in Santa María Huatulco, Día de los Muertos, 1998

Above: Jamaica (hibiscus) harvest, 1997–1998

no nos da para comer. Lo abandonamos. Allá la tierra no nos mantiene." "Over there the land does not give us enough to feed ourselves. We abandoned it. Over there the land does not sustain us." So they moved outside Santa María, where he is now using half a gourd to dig a posthole for a fence that will stop animals from trampling the young corn. Here the land is very fertile.

Higinia is well-versed in the oral history of Santa María. "Every place has its history," she says. This land of abundant resources has always been a refuge. She says that Huatulco comes from the Nahuatl and that it means "huatulco, el lugar de mucha agua y de las ceibas," "the place of much water and many ceiba trees."[2]

This is why the coat of arms of the town bears the Blessed Virgin, and at her feet there is a ceiba tree. Well, not exactly at her feet, but to the side there is a ceiba. It is the tree that we have as the tree of Huatulco, the ceiba. The first settlers of the village dressed in cotton cloth, white pants and cotton shirts, traditional for an Indian. Our people also spoke dialect, a different dialect, Zapotec and Mixtec. Now we don't speak in dialect that much, we speak in the manner of Castile—that is, Spanish, no more dialect, though there are still people who continue to speak it. We are natives of the town.

St. Thomas appeared after the Holy Cross. It was a grandfather who brought it. It was after the cross that the footprint of St. Thomas appeared. My grandmother, Victoria Lara Franco, would say that a grandfather arrived from the ocean and planted the Holy Cross. There at the edge of the beach he planted the cross, and there is the Holy Cross, the place where the wood is revered.

When the fishermen found the piece of wood . . . see, fishermen always have a piece of wood that they use to clean the fish, to take out their intestines. Thus, they were cleaning the fish when suddenly there appeared the painting of the Blessed Virgin.

The fisherman had cut the piece of wood, and when he realized that something was appearing in it, he washed it with water from the ocean to see what it was. He took it out of the water and rinsed it and let it drain upright. And the following day he saw the Blessed Virgin. Well, they began to call her "Our Mother," the Blessed Virgin.

Up on a hill, under the protection of a palm-thatched veranda over a smoothly swept dirt floor, a hammock hangs from two posts. Marco Antonio, just about a month old, is nestled in blankets in the middle of the hammock between pillows hand-embroidered with willows and stalks, his eyes, nose, and mouth barely visible. His mother is working, and his aunt goes to sway him back and forth. His grandmother Virginia comes to check on him. (The priest who often comes to visit wanted to name him Nepomuceno, according to the calendar, but his mother was adamantly against it.) His grandmother has listened to her daughter begin the story of the appearance of the image on a piece of wood, but then she says, "No, my daughter, it wasn't on a piece of wood, it's a cloth." She continues:

Now then, without dates, because I don't know the year. I do know the story, because my mother had a history book that said that Huatulco was founded when the Blessed Virgin appeared there at the Holy Cross . . . . I know about those Moors, and all of the indigenous people, because the Moors had a large table of the Blessed Virgin as though it was no big deal. They used it to cut fish, and there was a large lienzo [linen or cloth] of the Blessed Virgin that these fishermen would place on the table.

The Moors were people from far back. They did not get along with the Indians who received the cloth of the Blessed Virgin. The Indians venerated the image that had appeared there, and later they took the lienzo, washed it, mended it, and started the veneration of the Blessed Virgin.

Señora Virginia Mijangos, 2001

But the port there wasn't open. Now then, they [the Indians] thought that, with this lienzo of the Virgin they venerated . . . through her they would found their village. So they started congregating there.

The port was a great estuary, a very large estuary. They filled it in with silt and leaves so that they would have their town there. Then it came to pass that there was an epidemic, because of all the things they left in the estuary. They started to die. . . . That's when they died off.

Other Indians left. Instead, they said, "Well, we are not going to build our village here. Let's take the Blessed Mother in this direction [she motions]. Let's take her from here and see what she says. We will come here and sleep. Let's see what she says." And they did sleep there. They dreamed that the Virgin told them that they should leave, and they went from that place. She said to go up ahead, well, that they should come in this direction.

So they gathered their belongings and they came in this direction to a place that they call La Garita at Llano Grande, beyond Piedra de Moros, on the way to Santa Cruz. That's where La Garita is. It's a very large plain. They slept there to see what the Virgin said. Then they dreamed that the Virgin told them to move to that rock, the one they call Piedra de Moros. "Good, we will stay here. Let's see what the Virgin tells us." They dreamed that the Virgin said, "A little farther ahead."

Then they came to Pueblo Viejo. They arrived here, and they said, "Surely the Virgin will like it here." They dreamed that the Virgin said, "Farther ahead." They asked, "Why should we move if this place is so beautiful?" Later they dreamed that the Virgin told them to go a little farther.

So they went to Cuapinolito, next to the tree they call cuapinole. They came to the plain of Cuapinolito. Later they went to a place called, well, historically it is called Casquito de Burro, because there was a beautiful rock and it had the shape of a donkey's head. And she said, "No, a little more."

Many of them dreamed that they had to go farther up. Later they came, they say, beyond the river. They crossed with a great deal of difficulty since the river was so deep. They went to the plains of Erradura. It was a beautiful valley. It used to be very pretty in the past. It is no longer that beautiful.

Once they arrived in Erradura they slept there. Then they dreamed that the Virgin told them, "Just a little farther back." So they said, "Let's go to Hondura." They crossed over and they stayed. This is where they built their church. They venerated the Virgin beautifully. It was a small chapel. I was born in 1937. I must have been ten years old when I saw the chapel, but it wasn't from that time. No, those were historic times, far beyond. . . .

As they say, "She knows why she chose the place." It has its history. That place has some mystery. A woman, Tía Luisa, says that it is because there is a mine there. Cerro Huatulco has many diamonds, and it is the wealth of the Blessed Virgin.

The place was isolated until the Indians came. They then began to build the temple, because they had nothing. So they built their chapel, and then they began to venerate her. But what they did not like was that at the foot of the Virgin there was a damaged piece on the painting. The ayate [cloth] where she is painted is torn.

It was a very strong cloth. They restored the cloth, the ayate, where it was torn, at her feet. It had another tear on the other side, where the fishermen tore it. This had remained. So the people later said, "Let's take it to Oaxaca to have it restored." (It is clean because a restorer came and placed a piece of linen over it to clean it, to take off the dust. The tear is not restored.)

This story I am telling says they took the Blessed Virgin. They took her happily. They arrived in Oaxaca. They went to speak [to the restorers]. "Yes, sirs," the restorers said. "Don't worry, we will restore the Blessed Virgin. It will no longer have a tear." They were happy. But it came to pass that the restorers hid the Blessed Virgin because they could not restore her. So they hid the Virgin and gave the Indians another. They gave them a copy. The people of Oaxaca said, "The Indians won't know."

Then the Indians said, "Let us go. It is not in our best interest that the Virgin is in Oaxaca. She is very miraculous." When they went to retrieve the cloth image of the Virgin they had left with the restorers in Oaxaca, they said: "They restored her beautifully. She is very beautiful. She is a beautiful Virgin." It's in our history, but my mother lost that book. They said, "Look how beautiful she is."

El vecino   Oaxaca-Mexico

They went to their inn. At that moment they were about to leave Oaxaca on foot. They were leaving happily, but the sky began to thicken with rain clouds. They were going to leave, but they couldn't. They asked, "Why dear Mother? Why don't you want us to leave?" Water and more water fell. The water was rising, and they were sinking. They thought it was because they had retouched the Virgin.

At this point doña Mijangos says that the Indians knew that something was wrong with the Virgin that had been returned to them. They went back to Oaxaca, where the restorers told them:

"Here's your Virgin. We could not restore her." They said they would lay the fabric and it would not work, "No, sirs, your Virgin cannot be retouched." The Indians became saddened. Why would anyone want to take their Virgin? But they knew. Well, the heart knows a great deal. Happily the Indians took their Virgin. Immediately the sky became clear. They got their Virgin, and they returned. They brought her back all the way from Oaxaca.

So I tell the priest, "For as much as one would like to restore the Blessed Virgin, it can't be done."

She remembers other mysteries. "When I was a little girl I saw six bells. Now there are only three. The ones from Pueblo Viejo became enchanted. There are occasions when the bells can be heard. The legitimate ones from Huatulco were made of gold, but the Indians buried them. The Hill of Huatulco is an enchantment, so are the footprint of St. Thomas, the Rock of the Moors, the Bells, the Hung Woman, where a woman hung herself because she stole the necklace of the Virgin."

Farther down, entering Santa María Huatulco by the path the ancients took to found the village, is the home of don Ignacio García. He lives with his daughter, and with his son and daughter-in-law, who have eight children. Their houses are lined up next to each other, at the edge of the unpaved road. Tío Nacho sits under the shade of an *enramada*, a shady, palm-thatched veranda where one of the family serves drinks to the passersby. He

Above: La Viejita, 1999

Top: Don Ignacio García and his family, 1999

Día de los Muertos at the pantéon in Santa María Huatulco, 1998

listens to what everyone has to say, but he watches the traffic going into town. He is one of the Huatulco elders, over ninety-two years old without one gray hair visible on his head.

He rarely takes off his hat, just tips it back every so often. He is known as one of the town sages, and as a man who "reads" people. He knows about the mojoneras, the boundaries, because he walked every one of them in his younger days.

San Miguel del Puerto is a brother with Santa María Huatulco. It was [as if it was] another family. It was one town, but they divided it among themselves. That family left Santa Cruz. It was one town, one people. But they say that there was an estuary and that later, that family, that village, had to cover the estuary with wood. They cut good, fertile wood. But they say that an epidemic came, an illness. This is how they separated. Half of Huatulco came here, and the other half went toward the mountains.

And this is how it came to be called San Miguel del Puerto, because the saint has the name San Miguel and as a surname it has "of the Port." The name of the Virgin of Santa María de Huatulco comes from there. Santa Cruz is the original. Huatulco borders San Miguel and San Mateo Piñas. The boundary ends behind the mountain. . . .

The Copalita is divided between Santa María and San Miguel. It empties at La Bocana, at the beach. The primary rivers are the Copalita, Huatulco, Magdalena, Cuajinicuil Alto, Xuchitl.[3] The others are creeks, three creeks. Limoncito is one. There is a place known as Hacienda Vieja (Old Hacienda). My mother would tell me that all those places had a great deal of cattle. That's why that place is called Hacienda Vieja. There is a ranchería, a school, everything. . . .

The boundary between Huatulco and Pochutla is on a large rock at the beach, on the ocean. The beach is known as Salchi, and in Pochutla it is known as Cuatunalco. There's a large rock there where the boundary line starts. We all helped place the boundary markers. In those times, Governor Alderete had the task of marking the boundaries. Alderete, who was the authority, was twenty or twenty-two years old. The boundary line was already there, but it had to be reinforced. There is a Cerro Cigarro (Cigarette Hill), and this is where the top boundary lies, and you follow higher, higher, to a place known as Santo Tomás, on the old road, which used to be the main road. At that place, there are three crosses. One [boundary] goes through on the edge of the hillside. Then it follows a small hill that is known as Cerro de las Rabias (Hill of the Furies). Then you go to Cerro Espina (Thorn Hill). Cerro Chino (Chinese Hill) is centered in Huatulco. The boundary line passes through Xuchitl, through a place

called Cerro las Nubes (Cloud Hill). That's where there are coffee plantations. Originally San Andrés was part of Huatulco, and it still is.

From there you go to a place known as El Carril, where there is a marker with San Miguel. There is a marker that passes through the back of the hill and has its name. From there you climb a hill that is called Santa Lucía. The hills are small. I went with the authorities from Piñas and from Huatulco and Benito Juárez to the boundary marker of Santa Lucía in order to reconsider the limits. We made our peace. Piñas was the most powerful, the strongest. But we all went to defend our limits. Now we all defend ourselves with the authorities. We have no reason to fight.

Above: Night of la Día de los Muertos at the pantéon, 1998

It is Día de los Muertos, and Tío Nacho is talking about how it used to be, before the believers of other religions came and told people to destroy the idols and not to put up altars. For two days at the cemetery in Santa María, the townspeople and many others, some walking from great distances, have come to pay tribute to their dead relatives. They keep coming all through the day and night, to clean and whitewash the tombstones, to lay the flowers, candles, and offerings. Don Ignacio sees everyone walk by, and he compares the festivities of the day with those when he was young.

In the past Día de los Muertos was very enjoyable. Nowadays there aren't as many altars as before. Everyone had an altar with flowers and bread. . . . My grandfather loved the cigarette, we'd put some on the altar for him.

Everyone participated in the homage. There is a flower that is known as the "flower of the dead." People made altars. They placed fruit, tejocote (hawthorn fruit), bananas, garlands of small apples, large apples, oranges, and limes on the altars. On the days following there were many young men and women who would dismantle the altars. They got permission to take things. They'd take all of the fruit as gifts and distribute them. This is how they helped each other and others. This was a custom from times past. There were a great many fireworks. A dozen firecrackers were very inexpensive. Now they're too costly.

In the past you heard only violins and jaranas, which are like small guitars. They would sing indias and malagueñas. Indias are verses, long verses. They would sing these beautiful verses. People would dance accompanied by the violins in the cemetery and in the homes. They would play a box [cajón] that was square-shaped, made of wood, with holes. At night they were still installing the altars. For the following day, they would offer tamales, bread, and chocolate. That was the custom in the past. Now they're letting it go. . . .

There is incense called copal and another known as astorque.

Top: *Sweeping the tombs in preparation for la Día de los Muertos, 1997*

Center left: *Visiting the grave of a child, 1997*

Lower left and right: *Leaving offerings for the dead, 1998*

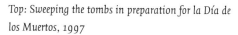

The astorque is a small, hard ball. It is produced in the trees. There is a worm that pokes the wood and out oozes the astorque. It is the same with the copal. There is some in the mountains. It was used for that particular time. They would put it in small fumadores [incense burners], in small pots. There they placed coals, copal, or astorque, and it would start smoking.

They placed it on the altar. They would prepare it in the morning, sometimes at twelve, and then again at night. There would be a distribution. The distribution would take place in pairs. In the morning they would leave cariñitos [tokens of affection], bread, chocolate, tamales. They would take it to the compadre. They would serve a cup of wine, liquor. And there they are, conversing like compadres. That was the custom. They shared and distributed the food. Nowadays you don't see any of this. Only in the home is it practiced.

Whitewashing the tombs for la Día de los Muertos, 1997

Don Ignacio's son and daughter-in-law have become Jehovah's Witnesses, but he and his daughter Soledad, who inherited her father's wit and thirst for knowledge, are a bit cynical about some of the religious practices others accept without scrutiny.

Now there is a Pentecostal temple and as I see it, it is almost the same Bible. There's another temple they call "Inca" that is on the other side of the cemetery. People say that, among themselves, the Jehovah's Witnesses murmur that their religion is better, that they have better studies than the others do. Who knows which is the better doctrine?

The Jehovah's Witnesses say that they will be reborn. Well, that's one hope the Bible gives. The Pentecostals say, no, that it's the spirit that has to be reborn. Recently with the elections for [municipal] president, they had more than one deceased person voting. So the dead have been revived again. They say that don Cirilio Cántaro just came to vote—all the dead came to vote. The dead mother of the person who is going to be president just entered into candidacy as well.

We'll wait and see who will be [municipal] president. . . . We're supporting the person who is from here.

Young Beto has helped out at the municipal building for many years. He is a clerk, actually more a political apprentice, and he is quiet. He is an Avendaño, a familiar name here and in Astata. His maternal grandmother has a *panadería* on the main paved road leading

into the municipio, with a large oven in the back, where she makes and sells bread. His mother, Ana Luz, has an altar in their main room, and the table is set for those who come visit. She serves her tamales—made with almonds, cacao, chile, sesame, and other special herbs and ingredients, wrapped in banana leaves—and freshly ground cacao from the mercado (market), boiled in water with sugar to make chocolate: all products the land around has to offer. The lights are dim, the television is on, and her three daughters are there with the littlest brother, who is wearing his cowboy boots to bed. They greet those who come by and offer a plate of food.

Beto was present when the municipal documents were found, strewn in the warehouse. A conservator from the archive at the Institute of Anthropology and History came to assess them and to let the town know how they should be stored. Ever since, Beto is the one who has known their condition and whereabouts.

The mayor in 1997, and others in office then, agree that it was a most difficult period. Guerrillas rampaged through the area in defiance of decisions that were not in accordance with what they believed was for the good of the people. No one admits to knowing who they were, but many do. Then hurricanes Paulina and Ricardo ravaged the area. Soon after, there was an earthquake. All the while, issues of land ownership and boundaries never subsided. At times, they became even more intense, as tourist development took up more land, and the people who were given other property or moved to homes with running water, gas, and electricity got wiser.

Paulina and Ricardo may have devastated homes and natural boundaries and changed the course of rivers and the contours of the shoreline, but the storms were also the impetus for rebuilding homes. Tractors, cement, bricks, steel struts, different kinds of wood,

Jamaica harvest, 1997–98

and other materials were poured into the region to solidify a new infrastructure, including heavy roads, fortifications, and pavement. Help for those in need came from all over México and from other countries. Corrugated metal sheets were distributed for building and roofing materials, perhaps not such a help in this hot tropical region where intense sun radiates through metal and heats homes even more. Some traditional houses of adobe and palm thatching withstood the elements better than other structures.

The building boom added to the growth of Santa María. Its population, more than 25,000, includes people living in the surrounding hamlets and agencias under its jurisdiction, as well as residents of Santa Cruz. Santa María itself is a beautiful small town far from the tourist traffic, fortressed by the surrounding hills and mountains. The roads leading into town follow plains and valleys through a series of hills. During different seasons fields are planted with corn and many other crops. Toward the end of the year, brilliant magenta patches of *jamaica* (hibiscus) are visible on the hillsides. After the branches

Church of Santa María Huatulco, decorated for the Feast of Immaculate Conception, 2000

of the jamaica bushes are harvested, families pull them through y-shaped sticks to separate the flowers from the stems. The flowers are dried on tarps on roofs and patios, and later used for teas and other thirst-quenching drinks. *Agua de jamaica*, made with water, is also a diuretic and can alleviate muscle pain.

The Church of Santa María is across from the municipal building. The church, which was restored and reinforced after the earthquake, sits on a low hill surrounded by the townhouses and shops of the original settlers of Santa María. The building stands out, white with red bell towers, against the backdrop of the deep green Cerro Huatulco and the low-lying clouds. It is no longer the small chapel built by the caciques, but a moderate-sized church, and people overflow its doors during Sunday mass and on important feast days. The high ceilings are decorated with simple floral motifs and vines, and the niches and side altars hold the saints most venerated locally, including a part of the Holy Cross and the lienzo of the Immaculate Conception. Next to the church on the same plaza is the old mercado, a large veranda-like structure of concrete and wood beams with steps leading up to it, where many of the local fiestas and contests take place and where films have been shown in the open air at night. For the Fourth Friday of Lent there are the traditional *toritos*, when a man wielding a bull made of fireworks chases courageous children, mostly boys. Large *castillos* (firework castles) illuminate the town square for admiring eyes, every year's pyrotechnic display even better than the last.

At the town square, too, they have contests for the best Día de los Muertos altars made by local associations, schools, and other organizations. During the festivities, while many are at the *panteon* (cemetery) a few blocks away, others are here. It is all part of the same corridor of traffic. There is a poetry contest. Local poets, children as well as adults, write verses that parody death, satirically describing local characters and events. These verses are called *calaveras*, or skulls, and they signify the fundamental nature of a person, place, or event. No one escapes this burlesque poetry, any more than we escape death.

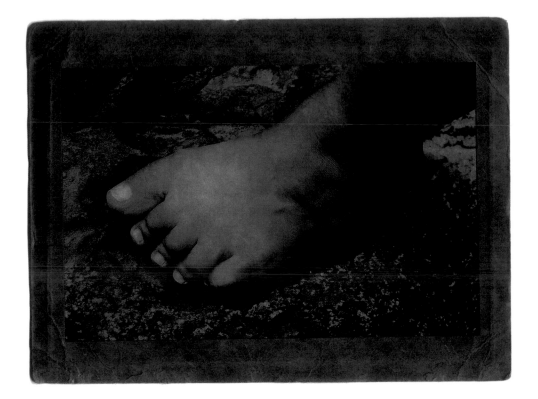

Erradura and the Footprint of Santo Tomás

Erradura and Santo Tomás sit side by side, small hamlets made up of a few homes scattered about. The road between them leads toward some of the coffee plantations in the highlands of Pluma Hidalgo, one of the highest mountain areas, which gives the local Pluma coffee its name. It is also the old road to Oaxaca, for large stretches easier to walk than to drive due to innumerable holes and small gullies created by rain gushing from the hillsides. Don Ignacio notes, "Besides this one there is another road, a highway coming from Oaxaca to Hualtulco. I think it [the new paved road] is good because it will give life to Huatulco [Santa María]. Huatulco is dead. The municipal seat is dead now that the complex is in Crucecita. There is no work here, nothing. Everyone from here goes to work in Crucecita, to Tangolunda, and to the hotels. Here the municipal headquarters is not a place that attracts tourists."

After the hurricanes, the waters of the Río Huatulco swept away the bridge, folding steel like paper and tossing concrete into the river, along with the boulders that lined its bank. Had the bridge been washed out just a short time earlier, before the highway connecting this region to Oaxaca City was built, the impact would have been more devastating. For now, the people who use this old road cross the river at a shallow place about a quarter of a kilometer away.

The journey is slow. Don Ignacio, or Tío Nacho, is greeting and being greeted by ninety-two years' worth of acquaintances. His daughter Soledad, too, offers comments in passing on every place and every person. Her father knows people at every turn and tells about each one's history and genealogy. He speaks about the deep hole in the river where he and his friends played as children. He says there is a rock you can enter at the bottom, where it is possible to breathe and hide. It scares the unknowing that you can stay so long underwater without coming up for air.

Ceiba tree, 2000

Erradura gets its name from the old activity on the road. Don Ignacio says, "It is called Erradura [horseshoe] because this is where the first wagon cars rolled. There was a warehouse where coffee was stored. The coffee was first carried on mules and donkeys. The first carts could only hold eight sacks of coffee and the two people driving. The driver's cabin was made of wood. It was very simple."

Few cars come through here now, but some people do come by, since this is a juncture and a highly contested space. "They say that there was an attack by the Chontal on the other side of the mountain," Don Ignacio says. "The people of past civilizations lived there, but there were wars. My mother died at 120 years of age. She lived a long life. Another woman whose name was Piedad died at 130 year of age. Her name Piedad Lizama. She lived on the street of the musicians. They are the only people I have known to live that long. But they remembered a lot."

Don Ignacio is hesitant about this foreboding place beyond Erradura. Everyone talks about the enchantment of Santo Tomás, where the saint's footprint is marked for all time. Tío Nacho and his daughter say that it has been there forever, fossilized—proof that it is old—in rock a few feet from a very large matapalos ficus, literally meaning "wood killing tree" because it covers and devours everything around it. "A matapalos is a fig," he says. "It is said that a tree is *malpariando* when it is blossoming outside its cycle. When its fruit is fully ripe, deer and cattle eat it. Those that are in the creek give very large figs because of the humid soil."

Soledad and Tío Nacho say that Saint Thomas was plowing his land in his bare feet, and this is why his footprint is there next to the prints of two hoofed animals, one a large one and the other a small one. "Here is the footprint of Santo Tomás, the footprint of an animal, an ox, and some coins. The footprint is very large, but look at how it imprinted. At the moment when he placed his foot, he wanted to leave the imprint of his bare foot. He was accompanied by someone else because there is another footprint and a small handprint. They say that he was sowing in the fields."

The hillside where the footprint lies is surrounded by graves. Don Ignacio says they are the graves of those who had a "*mala muerte,*" a bad death, brought about by homicide or tragedy. Although they are buried outside the cemetery, these unfortunates are remembered during the last day of the Día de los Muertos vigil. The roots of the enormous matapalos tree twist around the rocks and graves. Tío Nacho says:

Others chose this place as a cemetery. The footprints were here first, before the cemetery was built. But only bad people are buried here and little angels [children]. It evolved a long time back, from the confrontations between the communities, as with Coyula for example. They brought them [the dead] here because this was the accessible road. It was the old road. But supposedly it was also the place of the witches, those dedicated to casting spells, bad omens. Communities performed their rituals here. This is a very powerful place. There might have been a few homes, but they had other customs. This place was dedicated to the people who studied magic. In the old books, they would say to recite three rosaries. They would attempt to cast a bad spell on a person, in accordance with Satan. Very few of us ever walked at night around here. In the past people would cause harm with a bad air or wind. We would say, "We're not going to get together with them, because here is the enemy."

Washing at the spring at El Nueve, 2000

A taxi driver acquaintance on his time off is accompanying the group, and he comments that since this road marks the boundaries between the contested lands of Pochutla and Huatulco, the graves are the result of the struggles over those territories.

There are several other encantos in the surrounding areas that Soledad and her father discuss, like the one in the Cerro Espina, where there was much fruit, and the one in Paso Ancho, close to the mine. "Here in Huatulco the stories say that there was an iron mine. They dug shafts, but they couldn't work them, because the mountain was enchanted and it would scare them off. Well, perhaps it was Satan. But they couldn't take anything out. Now they go in with those machines, but they still can't take anything out. Who knows if it is true or not? At least this is what the people who have worked there say."

Santo Tomás left his imprint, but according to Higinia's grandmother and others, the imprint was left there after the white-bearded man arrived on the shore at Huatulco. The history the people recount is embedded in the great rocks of this land, or, like the large matapalos, has roots entwined deep under the surface, below the most obvious.

Judith "Eme" Juárez Sánchez, 2000

On the Way to San Mateo Piñas

Judith, or Eme as she is known, runs the Café Huatulco with her husband and two children. Her grandmother established the coffee plantation El Nueve on part of the land Eme's grandfather had owned. The finca is well over 1,300 meters above sea level, high even for this coffee-growing region. As she checks on the new growth of the coffee plants, Eme points out the mojonera, the boundary between Huatulco and San Mateo Piñas. She

Cleaning coffee at El Naranjo, 2000

sees don Cástulo's wife, carrying her baby wrapped in a rebozo, walking down the dirt path with her young son next to her. She's on her way home on land belonging to San Mateo Piñas.

Eme's grandfather, Manuel Sánchez, was killed more than fifty years ago during the "war" involving the people of Bajos de Coyula, and pitting those of Pochutla against those of Huatulco. Manuel met Eme's grandmother, Ernestina, at the San Pablo plantation store, where he had gone to buy cigarettes, and they married there in 1938. Manuel purchased San Pablo with his brother-in-law and another man. Eme's mother, also called Judith, was born in 1939.

After don Manuel was killed, Ernestina was left to deal with the plantation alone. Through the kindness of an old friend of her husband's, she was able to buy a part of it from her late husband's partners, and she later gave her cafetal the name El Nueve. Here she mortgaged the land and built her house, the *beneficio* where the coffee is processed, and a chapel dedicated to the Virgin of Guadalupe, to whom she was devoted and whose feast she celebrated on the 12th of December. She built homes for six families who lived on the land, and hired temporary workers when it was time for planting and harvesting. As Eme points out, the work generally requires at least fifteen people throughout the year, and during the time of harvest, sixty to seventy people are hired. For cleaning the coffee, they hire thirty or thirty-five people. Eighty percent of the workers come from the sierra of Miahuatlan and are Zapotec speakers; the other twenty percent come from the coast. The *acasillados*, those who have a home on the land, generally live here for fifteen or twenty years. Judith's main caretaker, her compadre Canseco, who is from Santo Domingo Ozolotepec, and his wife Margarita, have lived here for fourteen years. Margarita is from San Gabriel, close to San José Ozolotepec. Traditionally, the people offered work are from neighboring communities that get along, as opposed to those from towns that have been at odds with each other for centuries. This is why the responsibility for selecting workers is left to those who live on plantation land.

Up until the day she died in 1987, Ernestina managed everything alone. Her grandmother's work, sacrifice, and vision "is what unites us," Eme says. Now the house is in dire need of restoration, eroded by time and cracked by earthquakes, but it is still the refuge where Eme's grandmother's spirit prevails among the old photographs, the kitchen, and the upstairs rooms with their views. To one side you can look out across the mountains to Xanica, the closest village though still far in the distance. On the other, the view is of the coffee-drying court, the houses where the caretaker, his family, and a few other workers live, and the small chapel where Ernestina's grave lies.

Don Cástulo García García has come from his finca at El Naranjo to call on Eme after she spoke with his wife. He takes time to reflect on a number of subjects, including his own identity, saying, "I am an Indian. You may think I'm not because I'm fair-skinned, but I am an Indian. The priest of the village was responsible for the color I have, but I am Zapotec, I was raised Zapotec, and I speak the dialect." Don Cástulo is in his sixties, and his son, who is four, sits on his lap as he gesticulates expressively. Don Cástulo has written and published his own history of his village, *Breve Historia de San Mateo Piñas, Oaxaca*.[4] "In our region there is no library for any kind of documentation," he says. "On the other hand, I make an inroad, believing that the dialect or language need not become extinguished, but on the contrary, it should be fomented. The parents of families that know

Don Castúlo García García, 2001

Making tortillas at El Nueve, 2000

how to speak it need to teach it to their children because, in actuality, the superior schools where a career is launched for bilingual professors require speaking in dialect."

He is about to publish his second book. He is a man of much experience and wisdom who is content to spend hours ruminating about every aspect of life. If a comment is made about his intellectual curiosity on every question, he answers like a true sage:

When they speak to me about my wisdom, I'm embarrassed by my ignorance. In reality, there is so much to see, there is not enough time.

[In the past] they had a manner of dressing that was very special, which, at first glance, one knew, "Look, this is a yote." It was of an elevated culture. Like the one who placed the cross here, as a sign that the people were at an elevated spiritual level. This was here in Santa María. So this "race" was very cultivated and was known as "yote." But now that word or title is taken as a derogatory term. What I would give to belong to or be a "yote."

The ancients venerated natural things. The Spaniards arrived and took all of that away from us. For example, the goddess Tonantzin: all religions of the world have always had a representation of Mother Earth. The Aztecs [Mexicas] had the goddess Tonantzin, and year after year on the 12th of December they had pilgrimages in different parts of the nation. . . .[5]

Here in Tonameca there was a very large rock where corn was venerated. Close to Oaxaca there was an ear of corn that was the symbol of the earth and that the old priests used before planting. They would go with an ear of corn before planting. It was the symbol of fertility and the nourishment of the human. For us here, the tortilla is used in the wedding. A tortilla is divided by the maid of honor who gives half to the bride and half to the groom as a symbol of unity. So the ear of corn is venerated as a symbol for all of the cultures established in México.

Here in the coast, there is very little knowledge about what was venerated. In San Mateo Piñas we had the Piedra del Temblor [the Rock of the Tremor]. Paulina [the hurricane] came and took it. It was a rock of the Pedimento: any man or woman would go with a great deal of devotion and take rocks or

Rooster, Santa María Huatulco, 1998

coins, and within a few months to a few years he or she would find his or her match. The rock is gone, but there is another one called Llano Mujer [Plain of a Woman]. This is a rock where people who did not have the strength or luck to keep animals go to give their reverence. For example, they would buy a mule and it would die, their chickens did not lay eggs, etcetera. They went there to offer their reverence, and this caused them to have an abundant supply of animals.

I was at this place. This place is exactly where the sun rises, and it coincides with this rock. Then to the side there is another rock that has the face of a woman very well-sculpted. People of late have not given it its importance. They slash and burn. They plant, and they don't understand its value. There's another that is known as Mano de Mujer [Woman's Hand]. Speaking philosophically, if one is to think of these rocks as the trilogy of the Man, Woman, and Child, I would say that the rock of the sun [Llano Mujer] is the maximum astro that gives life. Then there is the sculpted woman, and the Mano de Mujer. People know these places as Llano Mujer, Mano Mujer, etcetera. They used to go quite a bit, but they're letting that practice go.

Don Cástulo is well-versed in politics, philosophy, and just about any other intellectual musings and where they might lead. He offers a great deal of thought and insight into issues of local and regional land titles, sovereignty, and identity. He says:

I witnessed the disagreement and accord [between Piñas and Huatulco]. I was a representative as Municipal President of San Mateo Piñas three times, and I had the good fortune of taking part in the facilitation of the agreement. The primary problem that influenced this conflict was the struggle for Benito Juárez. Huatulco wanted Benito Juárez, but it fell within the boundaries of the San Mateo Piñas. The original people of Benito Juárez were part of a ranchería belonging to San Mateo Piñas. This is the location where they would complete part of their service. (A Spaniard established himself in a plain known as Llano Juárez, because his name was Juárez. And to simplify matters and not be in favor of the devil or God, the congregation became a precinct that later answered administratively to Pochutla, so as not to answer either to Piñas or to Huatulco.)

Thus, when it was time to resolve the issues with Huatulco, we convened before the Agrarian Reform Board. Our decision was that we would divide the land of Benito Juárez with an imaginary line. It would be divided in two by this imaginary line. Both Piñas and Huatulco would respect the accord before and after the resolution. . . .

But the problem is that the communal representatives are not aware of the accord as it was. If we were to look at the Río Bravo [Río Grande] as the boundary between the United States and México, it is never a straight line. So each rancher began to mark all of his property lines.

Don Beto Peralta [of Benito Juárez] was the representative of bienes comunales [communal property] when I was municipal president, and we were here in a roundtable when the Agrarian Reform took place. It lasted two or three days. There were discussions, proposals, and resolutions. . . . Once there is a study done, boundary markers must be placed in the presence of the proper authorities and representatives of each bounding area, so that it is marked with the proper measurements. But the problem exists when the boundary is just on a document because they're too lazy to go up the mountain. . . .

The struggles between San Mateo Piñas and Huatulco are based upon the time when Hernán Cortés arrived at the beaches of Huatulco. The original people of the town of Huatulco gave him a fine reception, and they laid out where their possessions were and incorporated San Mateo Piñas. Then Piñas reviewed its property titles and reinforced its possessions. This is where the struggles began until they came to a mutual accord. There were some rancheros in Cerro Leon who began to cultivate the grana, which is a small insect used to make pigments and paints. Then those from Huatulco began to charge taxes to the people of Cerro Leon. So the latter asked, "Why should they do this, if this is not the property of Huatulco? Look how far away Huatulco is."

This was around 1540, more or less, because Piñas is a pre-Hispanic town, just like Huatulco. Around 1744, Piñas solicited the viceroy for its own titles and legal documents. In 1758 it was granted its document as first authority. As a result of this, Piñas no longer wanted to pay its tribute and Huatulco protested and began to take measures against Piñas. So here Huatulco wanted San Mateo Piñas to pay the tribute for the lands being used on Cerro Leon for growing the grana. Huatulco believed Cerro Leon was theirs. . . .[6]

They were never able to compromise. There were many reunions, many meetings in the hamlets. Authorities came, but it was difficult to reach any type of friendly accord. They would invade us, and in order to cross to Huatulco it was a difficult problem. There was a period in which there was so much crime, and they killed so easily. . . .

Don Cástulo is equally interested in the town's earliest history.

San Mateo de las Piñas was known previously in the National Archive as Respaldo de las Piñas [Backbone of the Pineapples]. There is a mountain range that leads to all of the towns of Los Loxicha. It is a natural configuration uniting all the Loxicha communities with San Mateo Piñas. Loxicha in Zapotec means—lo equals place, xicha equals pineapple—"the place of the pineapples." Long ago there was an abundant harvest of pineapples in San Mateo. But once coffee came along it displaced the pineapples. Cerro Leon is a little cold. It is possible that these are a different type of pineapple, like the pine cones from the ocote. But it is the word for pineapple.

There's a legend that a man fell asleep under the tree known as coralillo, and it so happens that he dreamed that he should establish the town there and sculpt the image of San Mateo [Saint Matthew] in this tree. That is the legend. I don't believe it. First, the pineapples were here long before the Spaniards. Second, Piñas was a pre-Hispanic village. When the Spaniards came they began to evangelize the villages and assign each one a patron saint. So they gave us Saint Matthew of the Pineapples. Since they brought the saints with them and we were an ancient village, I discard the legend of the dream as the reason why the town was established. The Spaniards did it to distinguish the village names, assigning a saint's name to the ancient name.

The Chontales occupied all of this land, from Huamelula all the way to Ozolotepec [the municipal seat of San Mateo Piñas]. Piñas is within the Ozolotepecs. [There are several] in addition to this place. Earlier, Chatino was spoken here. But the influence we have here is from the Chontales, whom they say came from Honduras, somewhere there, to colonize all of these lands. When the Zapotecs came—warriors who came in great numbers—they dominated and combated with the Chontales, and they slaughtered so many Chontales that in the hillsides there were piles of cadavers and bones. And the Chontales sought refuge around San Carlos Yautepec. . . .[7]

I think that we, after those wars, lived in caves, and so did many others, and we ate fruit, and this is how the hamlets and villages came to be. So I think that this is why we have certain physical features—a phenotype—all of us from San Mateo Piñas, that match those of the Isthmus and those of Huamelula, Santiago Astata, all over. Perhaps not myself, they tell me that I'm fair-skinned. They say, "You certainly don't have anything of the Zapotec or Chontal, or anything like that." They're not referring to my stature, but to my skin coloring. But I tell them that the legend of San Mateo Piñas is that a Spanish priest arrived in the village of San Mateo Piñas to evangelize the people. Since he couldn't leave because of the mountains and the rivers, he stayed there, and he mixed with the Native women of the place and this is why we're a bit fair-skinned, "güeritos."

From one town to another the language varies a great deal. For example, San Mateo Piñas and Xanica are bordering villages, and they cannot understand each other. It's Zapotec, and these are highlands. The Zapotec from the Isthmus or the coast is also different. But San Marcial and San Mateo Piñas do understand each other a little. Piñas and Benito Juárez are the very same people. There was one professor of Chontal from Huamelula who said that our Zapotec in San Mateo has some semblance of Chontal.

House at Piedra de Moros, 2001

Piedra de Moros, 2000

I don't believe the Mixtecs came here, because there is no influence here. The Zapotecs formed an empire. The Mixtecs and Zapotecs did not let each other get through their territories. . . . I think it is very difficult for the Mixtecs to have been strong here at all. What I do think is that when they came for their exchanges and commerce, they came in a caravan of twenty or thirty people, so that in case of any aggression, they would be able to defend themselves.[8]

So the groups of Mixtecs who were great merchants would come here to get fish and shells. Since they did not have lime or cement, they made a mixture using shells for building their homes. They had to take shells from the ocean. They did it in caravans, to take everything. They carried it all.

Piedra de Moros | Rock of the Moors

We would stand on top of Piedra de Moros and throw a stone, and it would sound, "tan, tan, tan."
— Don Ignacio García

The distance from the Port of Santa Cruz to the town of Santa María Huatulco is twenty-nine kilometers. Halfway there is Piedra de Moros. According to tradition, the Moors or pirates found that Pueblo Viejo was uninhabited. They looked for the Huatulqueños in order to exterminate them, but when they arrived at that place, there was no clue allowing them to know the direction the people had taken. Thus they left and never returned to bother them. This place [Piedra de Moros] has a peculiarity in that if you let a rock drop from its precipice, a metallic sound emanates from its base. Piedra de Moros has been known since the beginning of this [the 19th] century.
— From notes written by Maximiliano de Lavariega and the Lavariega family

People said that there was a giant, dark gray rock that grew as though it was alive. Others from all around heard about it, and those living in the surrounding lands were sometimes frightened by this enchantment, particularly at night. The climb up to its precipice is gradual and unalarming, weaving in and out between trees and across meadows where nothing grows but short grass, until suddenly you are on top, more than thirty stories high. Some say the name Piedra de Moros dates to the time when the pirate ships invaded the coast. From this rock you can see the ocean toward Tangolunda, the island of La Blanquita, and the Bay of Santa Cruz.

On the way you pass a small hamlet known as Arroyo González, a few homes divided by the dirt road. Small plots of banana trees grow close to the creek, and on the other side there are equally small plantings of corn and papaya. Down past the school is Piedra de Moros, the hamlet that sits at the foot of the great rock. Doña María García has a small store at the place where the shortcut to Santa María Huatulco meets the newer, wider dirt road to Pueblo Viejo. Doña María is from San Mateo Piñas and came to live here with her husband more than thirty-three years ago. All of her children were born here. Many young men from this hamlet have gone to the United States, and many have returned to their family home. Doña María's sons are still gone. The one who is twenty-six lives in Cancún; the twenty-two-year-old lives in Oklahoma.

She wastes no time on her way to the piedra. She comes here every so often to collect wood for kindling. Next to a well she passes an old metate used as a washing stone. She says some women wash here, in the privacy of this lush vegetation, because they don't have running water in their homes. Doña María's house has running water siphoned from the arroyo, which is usually full. On occasion, if the water is scarce, she, too, washes from this well.

There are many trees with yellow flowers that doña María calls *cajón de caballo* (horses' box)—she says they're good for heart palpitations and for the stomach. And everywhere along the path you have to be careful of a thorny plant, the huizache *(Acacia arnesiana)*. Cerro Chino becomes more prominent the higher you climb, and the ocean, which begins as a glimmer seen faintly in the distance, slowly grows until it shines brilliantly at the horizon, tiny specks of land—the small islands—disturbing the sea's straight edge. Doña María is not that familiar with the piedra's history, she explains, because she's not from here—the Lavariegas are the ones who know. She calls it Piedra Mora (Purple Rock), because of its dark, purple-gray color. The color has also been compared to the complexion of the people once called "Moros" ("Moors")—the black sailors and runaway slaves who jumped ship at the harbor in Santa Cruz during the 16th and 17th centuries. In some documents, the great rock is also called Piedra Prieta (Dark Rock). This landmark is often mentioned because it was one of the places where the settlers believed they might stay before they arrived at the present site of Santa María.[9] Close to the top of the rock is a very large copal tree, an appropriate place for offerings. A cross has been placed here to mark a sacred spot. There are also mesquite and cacahuanance trees with pink flowers. If you have a rash with fever, you can grind the leaves and rub them on your skin, dona María says. The cacahuanance is also called *madrecacao* (mother of cacao) because it is used to shade the cacao plants where they are cultivated. She says that there were many more plants in the past, but that the area was used for grazing cattle, and this is why so much was lost. Animals are prohibited from being set loose in the area now.

Many people make this climb to see what the great rock is, and sometimes they come to celebrate a mass where the cross stands. The patron saint of this place is St. Peter, and in June there is a large fiesta in his honor on the rock. Continuing upwards are giant steps carved on the rock's large, slanting stone face. There is a flower, known as *robador de montañas* (robber of mountains), that looks like a marigold; it is used for general fatigue and an achy body. The precipice is tranquil. There is no sound. Another tree, leafless until the rains come, prompts everyone to warn you not to get too close. It is the tatatil tree, poisonous to touch, although its black berries are edible. There is *palo rayado*, a striated tree,

The Lavariega girls, 2001

and zacatín, with white spots and always-small fruit. Mountain papaya and pineapple grow here and there, as well. Doña María says that there used to be small deer, unique to this region, and tigrillos, but the people who brought cattle here did away with them, and now the wildcats are in the mountains and hills farther away. Iguanas may be spotted every so often. Doña María makes her mole the way the grandparents made it, with small birds and animals, like the iguana. Others use the armadillo, and still others appreciate the chachalaca, large black birds with red bills and throat sacs that look like a living vestige of a prehistoric past.

Here there is no nopal, as there is in San Mateo Piñas, doña María points out. She says that there they gather the cochineal used for dyeing. She says she knows a great deal because her children sat down to study when they returned from school, and while she prepared dinner, she'd listen to them doing their homework. "*Yo moliendo y ellos leyendo,*" she says. "I ground [chiles], and they read aloud, and I learned everything. But I never went to school, so I don't know too much. They didn't put me in school, but my father taught me a little at a time." She says that whatever her mother read, she also learned. What her mother was given to read were brochures about the pride women should have in their housework. The brochures stated that housework was not a punishment, but something in which to have pride.

At this late hour, there are a few *urracas*, crested blue-and-white jays with long tails, still visible in the trees above. People of the region call them *urruacas*, in imitation of their song. They make a racket before daybreak, at about five in the morning. Almost everyone in this hamlet is awake by six. The *molino* (mill) is nearby, beneath a tree where an urraca sits in waiting, perhaps for tomorrow morning. The stone beneath your feet going up and down the formation doña María calls *techale*.

Gabriel and Albano Olea Lavariega and their uncle, Baldomero Torres Ramírez, sit at doña María's store early one morning. They were all born and raised in Piedra de Moros, and they say that when the great rock kept on growing a priest came and blessed it, and this is why there is a cross at the top. They say there is also a cave in this rock that has never been located. The rock is covered with *hierba de sapo*, good for foot sores. They say for at least the last few years, sportsmen from all over the world have begun an annual trek here to compete in a race that includes climbing the legendary encanto.

This land was settled by the Lavariega family, and every person in the entire region associates the Lavariega name with Piedra de Moros. Members of the family have settled in Xuchitl, Santa María, Santa Cruz, and Palo Alto, Tío Gabriel says, and in other local hamlets, but the cradle is here, in Piedra de Moros.

Document # 60, dated 1969, is a notarized copy of the original solicitation of purchase from 1886–87 that Luciano Lavariega, Gorgonio Martínez, and José A. García—*naturales* of Huatulco—made for the purchase of these lands in order to graze cattle. The official in

Pochutla, where the papers were filed, was Justo Ziga, the same man who purchased part of Bajos de Coyula. The land title designates boundaries that at that time bordered San Miguel del Puerto, the Cuajinicuil River, Xuchitl, Palo Alto, and Hondura del Toro, and reach a place called El Mirador de Buenavista (the Lookout of the Good View), Cerro Zopilote (Vulture Hill), and the Pacific Ocean, at the hill between Arenal and Coyula, the Ziga lands. The three partners were recognized as proprietors of the land on the condition that local custom prevailed; that people be allowed to grow their crops as in the past; and that settlers be free to take wood, iguanas, and fish as long as they respected the property and did no harm to the cattle or the good farmland. In 1904 the titles were turned over to Luciano Lavariega, José A. García, and Concepción Manzano, Gorgonio's widow.

Luciano Lavariega's descendants have kept their history, writing it down and passing it on to their children and grandchildren. Silverio Lavariega now has it. He, his wife Marcelina, and their daughters live on the edge of a high plateau, overlooking a creek and several hills and mountains. Since this hamlet is mostly family, he is surrounded by siblings, as well as other relations. Using the red earth of the area, Silverio and his brother make and sell brick for local construction. On the way down to the creek, there is a small area where brick is laid out under the sun of the December dry season.

Marcelina Lavariega is Mixtec. "They're the old ones," Silverio says when talking about his wife's people. Silverio married her when she was fourteen years old and brought her here from Jamiltepec, a Mixtec village north along the coastline. Marcelina speaks Mixtec, but her daughters are barely learning the language. It is the day after the Feast of the Virgin of Guadalupe, and the girls went to a dance that lasted the night. It's not yet time for the afternoon meal, and they're still in bed. Silverio recounts the history as it was told and written by his grandfather and uncle, and as he has drawn it from his own experience.

Silverio has worked in different places along the coast, following a path that other fishermen follow. But he has been all the way up the coast to Sinaloa, Sonora, and Baja California Sur and Norte, as well.

I had to ensure that I knew about this and that, because one can't remain the same, and just be satisfied with the status quo. One has to learn new things. For example, there are too many people who want to go to the United States—"I want to visit California."—There is so much to know. This is just one part. So I asked questions: let me see this, what is that?

We fished a great deal. As young men of fourteen and fifteen years old, we docked at the cooperative of the Isthmus. At night we caught fish. We caught four to five tons of large shrimp. We fished a small quantity of dolphin. . . . And then in Ensenada, Baja California, we belonged to the cooperative for a small bit of time. In Baja California we also caught shrimp. At that time we were on don Aarón's sardine boats. He had twelve [boats]. Then we went to Puerto Madero, and to Guaymas [in Sinaloa] to fish for shrimp. I fished for sardines as well. There were large clams before. Now there is very little clam, caracol, and octopus.

The area surrounding Piedra de Moros is easily visible from where Silverio sits. In the distance, you can see organ pipe cacti on a hill. The hill is called Rincón de Burro because there used to be so many animals there they raised clouds of dust. Other landmarks visible from his home include the Cerro Chino. While the word "*chino*" can be translated "Chinese," it is also used in México to mean "curly." Silverio explains the name Cerro Chino: "It's got a tall grass that has the name chino because it curls, almost as though a woman had been curling her hair. Many people use the grass the way we use palm, for thatching."

Marcelina Lavariega, 2001

Silverio Lavariega, 2001

Cerro Sombrero, described by señor Gabriel in Xuchitl, is known as Cerro Macahuite by the people of Benito Juárez, Silverio says, and also as Cerro Cimarrón (Wild). Then there are Cerro Limoncito (Little Lemon Grove) and Cerro Huatulco. "Cerro Huatulco is where there is a mine. I've been there. They would take large rocks and ship them to the laboratories in Monterey. They extract the metals from the rocks—iron, silver, or gold—silver mostly. They do this in Nayarit, as well as in Sonora. It dates to the time of Porfirio Díaz [around 1910]."

Silverio thinks aloud about his interest in this region. "Often people don't study because of lack of resources. The parents are poor and don't have enough, but one more or less thinks up different ways of doing things. If you start to ask and read there is such a great deal to say about Huatulco that we would never finish today or tomorrow."

Maximiliano de Lavariega, Silverio's uncle, contributed to the ongoing history of the family and to a briefer history of Huatulco and Piedra de Moros. He used documents his family had, as well as interviews with the old people of the area. He also used some of the most notable bibliographic sources from the very few about Huatulco that were available to the local citizens. Some of the notes he compiled were clearly used in a brochure produced in 1987 to support the imminent tourist development, but otherwise his work appears never to have been published.[10] Silverio, however, keeps the material close to him.

Maximiliano wrote: "Bays of Huatulco: soft sands that embrace, transparent waves, birds that fly and sing in the blue interminable sky, the awakening sun, sunset of love and star-filled night; flowers, palms, tropical fruits, a dream, in Huatulco made real."

Maximiliano de Lavariega, and many other lugareños (local people), made it a point to be informed of those who came to town and for what purpose. He drew from early reports and his own knowledge about preliminary archeological surveys conducted primarily around the bays of Huatulco prior to its development.[11] Numerous sites were identified, based on Lavariega's and the community's knowledge. He believed that the region was densely populated during pre-Hispanic times, with the oldest settlements located along the margins of the Río Coyula, where there were permanent water sources, as well as fertile soil that assured good farming. He discussed other sites as having large shell landfills and foundations that incorporated shell in several ways.[12] He also mentioned the fortified points that reveal the commercial routes important in post-Classic times. These extended into small dominions of exchange headed primarily, as he stated, by Mixtecs, Chatinos, and Zapotecs. He quoted from the *Relación* about the Mixtec monarch 8 Deer, under whose authority the highland and coastal Mixtecs were unified, creating an empire that ruled from Tututepec beginning in the 11th century C.E.

Silverio Lavariega proudly refers to his family notes, but shares his own experiences about the Piedra de Moros. There are pottery shards broken from the legs or handles of many unknown vessels, very similar to those of Cacaluta, underfoot here and there, buried in the earth swept smooth by Marcelina, especially around her home. Silverio says:

I feel as though there was another race of people living here, another culture. This place goes back centuries upon centuries, to the time when the end of the world was coming. They say that the people of the past didn't die, they continued to play, and they made things of clay like animals, figures. But we didn't see that. We find these objects tossed about, and we wonder about who might have made them.

The old people spoke about them. They say they were Mixtec, but they are all gone. They were another race of very large people. There are many ruins all around. At night, however, there is always a light, or a fire one sees. It's visible because there are gasses that escape from below.

His wife Marcelina says, "One sees them throughout, all below. Every once in awhile we see them coming off the rock as well. When my mother lived by the rock, she would see light in the early morning, or at about midnight. She would see something lifting. She would see green and reddish-blue light."

Before the Spaniards came, the road that leads from the ocean toward the Pedimento to Piedra de Moros—the same road that cuts behind Doña María's home at the fork, through the hamlet of Todos Santos to Santa María—was the well-traveled pilgrimage route of the ancients.

We've known it since childhood, and the grandparents talk about the way the rock was before. When the pirates arrived and after, there were many people who would come to see the rock. But the rock continued to grow, because it was an enchantment, and people said that they stopped coming, because the rock killed at least five goats and who knows how many cows. Those who did go to the rock placed candles so that it would stop growing. I'm talking about 1587, but that's all there is because the notes are the only thing that recounts it, nothing more. They say the rock has seven points. There's a cave, but who's going to find it? No one. There's an echo. The cave could be above or below.

But when we were children, the age of my daughter [about six], we had many animals, and we would go watch them, and in the rock a woman appeared wearing a black shawl. We saw her. The shawl she wore was like those used for going to mass, the ones worn in mourning. She wore it on her ascent. She climbed the entire rock to the peak, and when she was at the crest she disappeared. She was an enchantment. We never saw her face, only her back. We would go looking for her, but we wouldn't find her.

La Laguna Culeca, 2001

Paso de los Robles

The old *terrenos de los Robles* (lands of the Robles family) embrace the edges of Chontal lands, from the source, or *nacimiento*, of the Zimatan River, all the way to the ocean, to an encanto known as Cerro Culeco, between two lagoons. This is in part private land, belonging to the descendants of the original titleholder, the García Robles, now the Ricárdez. They are a prominent family, with ties to San Isidro Chacalapa, Huamelula, Astata, Zimatan, Barra de la Cruz, and some of the coffee plantations, including El Faro, the first finca owned by local people. Doña María Escamilla's grandmother from Huamelula was Juana Robles, also of that family.

A small portion of the land is known as Rancho Paraíso (Paradise). The property encompasses a large lagoon, the Laguna Culeca (Roosting Hen), surrounded by dense vegetation, including palms used for making thatched roofs. The lagoon's muddy banks —milky terracotta—give the impression that something alive has been thriving here for thousands of years. It is an encanto that people from around the immediate area believe to be hiding gold.

Don Beto Ricardez narrates some of his family history, as well as a part of the relationship of the land to the people of the region. He says his mother died around 1997, when she was ninety-four. In the early 1800s, her great-grandparents went to Oaxaca City to ask for the title to the land on which he stands.

The family is from Huamelula. My mother was born in San Isidro Chacalapa. My mother's grandmother was Carmen Robles, who had a daughter whose name was Martina. On the day my mother was born, her mother died. Her grandmother raised her. Since the grandmother had some money, she was the one who helped build the church [in San Isidro Chacalapa]. She ordered the virgin from Switzerland. They brought her the virgin, but who knows where it is now.

There were several individuals who had settled this land and had titles from the colonial period. . . . The names [on the titles] are still known because my mother remembered everything. The parents passed on everything by word of mouth to their children, since they didn't know how to read, and they recorded everything in their mind. They never forgot anything. And I, who know how to write, never wrote it down, and I don't remember the names. But being that names are passed down from parents to children, I know who they were. Some were Robles, and their names have been passed down through many members of the family through all these years.

The fact is that this land was privatized because they were people who had an education, more or less, and they brought a topographer and an engineer who drew out the plans for the Robles lands. The property was drawn up and recognized in accordance with the authorities of Huamelula, Tehuantepec, and Oaxaca. . . . When Huamelula needed a presidential decree for their lands, they based their petition on the plans of this area that the Robles had. They respected the survey because these plans were the oldest that existed of all of the properties. . . .

There was a man from Guerrero who came around these parts because of the alligators, because there were so many. He came to catch alligators. This was forty-five years ago, more or less. Then he came to ask for a cash loan, and it was agreed that he would repay us with corn. He was given the money, to be repaid with his work. But then there were two bad years of harvest. So he could not repay the money within those two years, and he said to us: "Look, sirs, I can't pay you everything I owe, so I will return these lands that I worked in order to pay you the money. I am going back to my land, and I don't want to leave things unresolved."

My brothers came and saw this garden, this paradise, and they fell in love with it. They went to my mother's granduncle, who was alive. My great-granduncle's name was Martín Robles, and my brothers said to him, "Look uncle, we loaned this man some money and now he is giving us this land in return. What can we do? You are the representative of all of the owners. You are the only landowner of the old Robles."

And my uncle said, "Look, sons, my brothers told me that this specific region was for the only daughter, the only sister of all of them, and she was your mother's grandmother. So this land is rightly your mother's property. You see, we never gave it to her, because she has El Faro [the cafetal], and well, we just never spoke to her about it. Your mother was never allowed to come here, although it was hers. So why don't you take it, because it is yours." They should have returned the land to my mother.

So my brothers looked into how the title was documented, and it was in the name of the Robles brothers, but almost all of the brothers had passed away, except for my uncle. Thus, we began the process necessary in Oaxaca and in México City. . . . We were able to get all the rightful documentation. So it was that it was left to my brothers. There were many of us. When it came time to divide what our father had left, I picked this place. It turns out that this was the best land, but in those days no one wanted it.

When I first came here I fell in love with this place. I arrived here when I was a young man. I fell in love with all of the stories, from people who would go from here or there to work. I told my brothers, "Say, that place you got? Let me have a little piece." When I got here I went crazy with joy to see all of this. I had a scholarship to go to Brazil to study economics. But I chose to stay here. I didn't go.

Don Beto tells some of the stories about the land:

This was all virgin jungle that was conserved by the Robles family. Since ancient times it had always been held as sacred, because the Laguna Culeu is where people made their idols, their figures, and

everything they needed for their offerings. There is a cave, a grotto, where they would come to pray. This is what my uncle told me. . . .

He came to see me every day to look around. One day he took me to the cave, and he said, "Look son, here is the place where the old people said people came to make their offerings, and here the leader of these people lived. They called them "the gentiles." The head of these gentiles, when he was a young man, at an age when he could lead his people, would be brought to this cave. He would stay one entire lunar phase. The one who later became the head of the gentiles would stay here until he was old enough to fend for himself.

Then he would be followed by the nomad tribes. My uncle did not tell me the names, but they must have been Aztecs or Nahuas who would come from the north and continue on to Guatemala. Not too far from here was a hill where the gentiles lived and where they would hide. They had lookouts, and when the nomads came, they would hide all the food. They were a peaceful people, the original people of this land. And these people were Chontal.—They would say that they spoke their own language. Subsequently they were called Chontales [a Nahuatl name], or rather they are called Chontales.—They lived off the land and from fishing. This is why they performed all rites in these places, in this lagoon, in Mascalco: they fed themselves from there.

But if what my uncle knew was right, they didn't put up a fight against those who arrived. Instead, they took everything they had to eat, and they hid it very well. Better still, they took the food far away. Later when the others arrived and found the vestiges of their dwellings, they broke the metates and all of the utensils in vengeance for the owners' not waiting on them and not paying tribute.

This is where the lagoon extends, the Laguna Culeca. It is dry now, in this season. The water evaporates and holds salt, and it takes on that red color. At some point, I gathered salt here, but now it is too much of an investment, and salt is very inexpensive. . . . This is where the lagoon continues, but that part has already evaporated, and it is heavy with salt. When the salt is piled high, the top part turns a beautiful pink, but once it continues to drain, it gets whiter—meaning that there is a chemical change. Salt has its chemical composition, that is why it has these colors.

On the other side of the hill is Mascalco. This lagoon is called La Culeca, because there are times

when it does not produce, and [like a hen] is roosting—as she is right now when she is red, when the pH, the salinity, is high. And then it comes back—her chicks hatch—because at that moment shrimp and fish grow, and they are fed during the whole season.

For centuries, lagoons in this area provided inland peoples their ration of salt. Acquiring salt was an important reason to undertake the pilgrimage to the coast, and salt was traded at the large markets that took place on the Primer Viernes (First Friday of Lent) in Santa Cruz, Segundo Viernes in Astata, Cuarto Viernes in Santa María Huatulco and Huamelula, and so on. Producing salt was one of the principal economic activities of the coastal Chontal, and the seven marshes that were the primary sources of salt—Coyula, Arenal, Santa Cruz, Mascalco, Rosario, La Culeca, and La Colorado—were titled in early documents. Now the salt-producing lagoons are concessions, leased to commercial operators.

Pedro Carrasco, doing research in the early 1950s, was told that the mountains were encantos. They were women, and often they would be called "hens."

In the mountains resides another spirit of the earth. It is a woman named "Chontal nahio," meaning "girl" or "hen." Some people may see her and hear her shout. Men in love often see her, and she entices them, calling them and making gestures to them. They follow her, and when they realize who she is they have already walked deep into the mountains and are lost without having been able to overtake her. Then people say that the woman of the mountain deceived them. She is always described as a woman. She is heard shouting or laughing; usually she shouts three times in the evening. It is said she was the moon's companion who stayed on earth when the moon went up to the sky.[13]

Before they permitted the Mixtec dyers to come here, don Beto says, Chontales collected *Púrpura* snails from the rocks along the shore. "The men did the dyeing, and the women wove. They carded the cotton they got from the pochote. They also used the cotton that comes from the ceiba. They made hammocks from the palm. There are a few who still make them, very few, but they're beautiful." The ocean yielded clams, oysters, and lobster. "They also ate alligator. That's what they lived from. This is why in San Pedro Huamelula they have such love for the alligator. It was one of their modus vivendi." Now, however, the understandings that governed the exploitation of these resources have been forgotten.

People come here to take the turtles' nests apart. They take the eggs, and it is so sad that sometimes, if they don't find eggs, [the poachers] get so angry that they take them from her womb. It is so sad and even embarrassing that anyone would do something like this. Thousands of turtles come out at night. In uses and customs only the Chontales are permitted to eat them, just the Chontales, but others have taken to selling eggs as a business, and they take them out. Within the community they sell for 150 pesos per 100.

When the workmen from the plantation came here to use the pasture for their horses while they planted coconut palms, each one was given permission to kill two deer a week. They would eat one here, with their women, and they would take the other to the sierra for their families. They also had permission to catch alligators, but not those that were less than three meters long. When this started, those from Guerrero began to kill the smaller ones. . . . I've been here for thirty-five years, and there were still alligators in Mascalco, but now there are very few. They are almost extinct. It's probable that it was because of a strong dry spell, that they did not have enough food. Mascalco was where there were many. Ayuta, which is the next town, means turtle. Its original name in Chontal is Li Pojo, something used to tie the hair [lipo] and lije, or rock—perhaps the River of Rock.

Don Beto has had a long career as an educator and administrator, first in Santiago and then in Oaxaca City, but he kept his ranch here. "I came back every year and for vacation," he says. "As the director of schools and the coordinator of production, I was in charge of production, and here on my ranch I didn't produce a thing. Well, I guess it is because there they paid me to attend to those things and here, there was no time. On vacation I dedicated myself to my daughters, to taking them out, and then to coming here." One of don Beto's daughters is still studying at the university. His elder daughter is a prominent leader, an elected official whose term has just ended. For years, she has worked to represent the needs of the Chontal and other people of the region.

He continues talking about this place that he loves:

What I want to stress here is that the people who lived in these places had a culture of admiration, of making their offerings deliberately in the caves. To them, the caves—specifically like the one within the rocks [on the ocean]—were where they would catch fish. They drew their nourishment from the sea. Thus, my uncle said that the person who was going to be the leader would go to this cave, and to another on the two or three special days when nature allows access. This is where the person soon to lead the people would go to live. He would go with wet nurses and eat nothing more than milk from their breasts and food he caught within the cave. They were healthy women who had just given birth. This was how he was able to receive emanations, by not consuming any other foods. He was about eighteen to twenty years old, a strong young man, son of the highest official. My uncle told me this. They called him the "new guide of the gentiles."

The encanto at Cerro de la Culeca, 2001

Later, I was told that when there are at least three days of strong northerly winds, which hit in the middle of the ocean, the waves recede. This is when the other, larger cave is accessible. My great-granduncle passed away, and there is no one to give me more details. All he said was that there were periods in which nature allowed access to that cave. I asked him to take me, but we only got this far. My uncle was a very reserved man, very discreet.

This is why the people of Huamelula make offerings in all of the caves, such as the one [El Boquerón] whose entrance was filled in by the priest. I don't believe they found anything more than the place where the original people performed their rites. After all, the people would say, "Well, if I performed my offerings [in the church], and this year went poorly for me, it's because I didn't perform offerings to the deities of my people. If this means I'm favoring the devil, who cares! If I don't do it, who knows what may happen?" This is how the priests made them feel, converting their gods to devils. And now they say, "Well, if they don't adore God, they adore the devil."

The deities were very important. Thunder and lightning were important because they would bring the most benefit, the majority of times. People were afraid of the earthquakes, just as with those things that they could not see. This is what they feared the most. This is why there are so many beliefs regarding the bewitching hour. It is the hour of the night when the strange or unknown presents itself. It terrorizes. It doesn't have a fixed time; it varies. This is when La Llorona (the Wailing Woman), the spirits, and the witches come out, those changelings who become transformed. Many have these beliefs, and I respect them. But I think the fear is so strong that that there are some who may call themselves brujos [sorcerers] so that others will respect or fear them, and they can impose themselves on others.

My uncle said that they normally practiced their rituals in caves, but there are some who practice in their fields. They try to hide what they're doing so that other people don't find out. They make three offerings. One offering is made to the earth and the rain, another to the gods, and another to the devil.

The rain, the sun, the moon are all considered. The moon is important because of the ocean tide. It influences the sea. People know perfectly the hours for the low tide. They leave their communities to arrive on time to take advantage of the low tide.

What I have noticed about those little ceramic heads of women [found in this area] is related to what I have just said about the novice leader—that he would come here and be nourished with mother's milk. There are many figurines of fired clay that emphasize the breasts. There are even some that are only the breasts, and they were made purposely this way. This is what they made here at La Culeca, on the dry land. There is a red earth that is good for kneading. There were also some ovens there at the edge where they fired them. I've found such figures, but since they no longer make them, they are disappearing.

How I love being here. The lagoon drains within these trees. One can't see it, but the water reaches very far. During the rainy season, the minute it fills with water it stretches much farther. My grandfather on my father's side came to acquire land in El Faro with his brothers. They didn't have much money, so they started working, little by little. My father would leave on foot to purchase cattle, and to buy other things. He would go all the way to Ejutla, which if one can imagine is a minimum of eight to ten days' walk. The largest market day in all of Oaxaca is on Friday in Ocotlan. My father would return home, bringing goods such as fabrics to sell by the yard in the towns of Chacalapa, Tapanala, and Astata. . . . From this land to the plantation was about three to four days' walk. When I studied in Miahuatlan, we rode in baskets. It would take us three to four days as well, with the animals. When they drove cattle, it took even longer to get to Miahuatlan and to Ejutla.

Just at the time that the sun is about to set, don Beto sees a bird. Its name is the *pajarito caballero*, the gentleman bird. It has a mask. He says it is a nocturnal bird, and he tells its story.

This bird was a spectacularly beautiful bird. It had the plumage of the peacock. This is what the Zapotec story says. One day the peacock arrived to speak with the gentleman bird and said to him: "You know, I feel this great admiration for you because you are the most beautiful bird there is. There is no other like you. Look at me. My clothing is dark, perhaps even ugly. I cannot bear to go out like this. There is going to be an invitation. Many animals of my region will be going, and I would like you to lend me your plumage for this fiesta. Upon my return, I will give it back to you."

The gentleman bird told him: "Fine. I see no problem if you return it to me promptly."

"Of course," said the peacock. "When the fiesta ends I will return your plumage."

The peacock was just about to leave, when the gentleman bird asked: "What's your name?"

"My name is the caballero," the peacock said. And the peacock left. That one who was going to return the gentleman bird's plumage never returned.

The gentleman bird now only comes out at night because he is ashamed to be seen. He is not the same beautiful bird he was before. He calls out every night: "Caballero! Caballero!" And wherever you are walking, he flies by and stands along your path. He cuts into the road and then you hear the call, "Caballero," because he's looking for the peacock to return his feathers, so that he can come out during the day.

View from Rancho Paraíso, 2001

San Isidro Chacalapa | The Place of the Sweetwater Shrimp

San Isidro Chacalapa is reached by a straight path through hills and dry rocks. Farmers slash and burn the few patches of land available for farming. The *coa*, an ancient pickax, is still the most widely used tool for tilling the soil, and also the easiest to carry. A man walks along the path and through a gate he's made from tree branches. It is hard to imagine why *chacales* (freshwater shrimp), the food the river offers, and San Isidro, the saint attributed with the characteristics of the ancient Tlaloc, the god of rain, would be associated with this place. Here the parched land of stone seems to have been forsaken by the deities.

An old and beautiful Chontal woman walks slowly down the road, carrying a basket of laundry on her head. Her posture is straight, and the basket so still it appears to be floating. She smiles and greets everyone along her way. When you finally reach the river, it is splendidly lush. Fish are visible in the clear water, and egrets stand attentively about, ready in an instant to placate their hunger. Other women are already here, seeking out the little shade while they share the day's news and do the wash.

A large tamarind tree and a guanacastle stand out in front of one of the homes. Children carrying banners, flowers, and food walk with their teacher toward a field where they will play. On a slope above the sparsely populated town is the main church. Really, there are two churches. One is a shell, with the sky and the clouds as its ceiling, and trees growing through what was once the altar and by the wall. This is the old church built by the Robles, don Beto's great-grandmother. Still visible through decades' worth of soil, leaves, and small plants are bits of beautiful, cobalt blue pigment and traces of decorative swirls and vines, testaments to a time of grandeur. Few constructions of this style exist in this

area. Most shrines are four-posted, thatched chapels. The three traditional bells set apart under their own shelter show a founding date in 1881, under the jurisdiction of the Isthmus of Tehuantepec. It is Mother's Day, and on this day a young woman has chosen to be with her grandmother, who lives next to the church of San Isidro. They both go and pay their respects to the Virgin and to the Christ of Esquipulas, the miraculous Black Christ. A Chontal man once went to see this figure among the Mayans in Guatemala. Upon being healed, he promised to bring the Christ back to the community for veneration. And here he is, in Chacalapa, and in another Chontal village, Los Cocos.

Outside San Isidro Chacalapa, 2000

Santiago Astata | The Place of the Storks

Astata is a little less than seventy-five kilometers from Santa Cruz de Huatulco, on the Río Astata between Santa María Huamelula and the hills that hide San Pedro Huamelula. The old people call it Guelaapig, from the Chontal words *apig*, meaning rock, and *guila*, beast. The current name, Astata, is from the Nahuatl word for stork, *astatl*. Juan Bello, a Spaniard from Salamanca, was granted the encomienda of Astata for having been one of the first conquistadors to fight against the Chontal. Shortly afterward, in 1527, the Inquisition

29. El Encanto   Oaxaca Mexico

Enchanted aguaje (grotto), on the road to
Astata, 1999

denounced Bello for blasphemy. His land passed to his daughter, who was married to Gil González de Avila until 1566, when he was executed for taking part in a plot against the second marquis of the Valley, Martín Cortés, the legitimate heir to Hernán Cortés.[14]

In the depth of the rocks on a hillside along the road leading to Santiago Astata, there is a sacred site, an *aguaje*, or grotto, where water springs forth, cascading down into a pool. Sometimes this place is full of people washing or filling jugs with water. At other times it is so quiet, under the awning of the trees, that it doesn't seem to belong here, so close to the road and the thatched stalls selling food and drink. This story has been told many times, over the chatter of the women washing. Once, a woman who was washing here tried to touch some multicolored jícaras, or gourds, that appeared to be floating in the center of the pool. As she reached for them, she was carried away into the depths of the water. When she returned the women she washed with were gone. What she thought had been an instant took years and years.

El Señor de la Piedad, the Christ of Mercy, appeared long ago in this same place. It is one of the most important landmarks of Santiago Astata, a shrine dedicated to him. The main pilgrimage to Astata takes place on the Second Friday of Lent, when people come from all over the region to pay homage at this encanto as they did in ancient times.

Doña Celia Piñon, who lives in Astata, says:

Regarding the Lord of Mercy, and the aguaje or the church, well, they say that he is the saint who appeared in the grotto that you see in Los Mangos. The only difference is that that saint was lying on a flat, smooth rock next to [the grotto], as opposed to here, where the rock is standing. Well, what they tell us is that the saint was here and that the people from times past lifted the saint and left him in a small church. They made him a small palm house like that one [pointing to a thatched home]. They then made a table of rock. But when morning came, he was no longer there. The people came to see, but the saint was no longer there. When they got to the grotto, he was here, the Little Lord of Mercy. Finally, they had a celebration, the women prayed, they cried, and they say that he stayed.

Now, we believe it because people say that when they built the highway . . . the engineer placed the mark for where they should dynamite the hill right in the midst of the grotto, where the spring is. This had to have been less than ten years ago, because this road, the way it is now, was not here before. There was nothing here, but the construction crew kept coming, slowly working their way in this direction. Then they say that the engineer said, "Tomorrow, bring the equipment to blast the rock so that the tunnel passes right through there." The plans had been drawn. There wasn't going to be a curve here.

They say that in his sleep a man came to the engineer, awakening him from his dream, and told him, "Don't touch my rock where I lay or you will regret what will become of you. There's a solution to straightening out your road so that you won't bother [the grotto]. Otherwise, you will regret what will become of you." With the memory of that dream, the engineer could no longer sleep, and soon after he began to speak to all of the people from here.

"Look I had a dream, but in the plans I have here, I have the design layout that shows where I'm going to make the tunnel through the hill in order to come out to the other side. But in the dream I was told that if I was stubborn about it I would live to regret my decision."

The people told him, "Don't do it, engineer. Don't do it or you will have an accident. Leave the grotto alone because it is a spring. If you'd like to get water for your car, and you fill an amphora with water, you who have these studies, look at how clean the water is. By comparison, the running water we have here, in one or two days it has impurities. The water of the spring has none."

There are people here every day. The water is crystal clear, beautiful. This water is clean. I who have no formal education ask, "Why?" This tap water has little bugs and that spring has none.

Traditional home, Astata, 1997

He is called the Lord of Mercy because that is how he appeared. Those who venerate him with their dreams say that the saint said, "I am the Lord of Mercy." Well, that word, mercy, you know what it means? In the Bible that one studies, mercy means something like compassion.

Once the grotto dried. Only small drops of water fell. It never dries, no matter how much calamity there has been, though one time it seemed to be drying. They say that the young people were being discourteous. There are a few who smoke marijuana in the town. What the townspeople did was to ask for a mass to be celebrated. Whenever a mass is celebrated, even if the [officiant] is from outside, they come to say the mass here. They say that the people cried because, when the priest arrived and was at the middle of celebrating the mass, the water began to spring plentifully. By the end of the mass, the pool was full. From that time on it has never dried.

. . . Now it is closed on the Second Friday [of Lent]. Bathing is no longer allowed on the Second Friday, because people perform too much sorcery here as well.

Las rezadores (the mourners), Santiago Astata, 1999

Since soon after the Conquest, the Chontales of the region have been assigned to a few priests, who have had to divide their time to cover the large expanses of the region. Gerhard says that one priest, "probably resident at the port of Guatulco from 1543, visited the entire area, from Tonameca to Mazatlan [Mazatan],[15] for several decades." And after the 1570s there was a priest who visited from Huamelula.[16] This remains largely true among the coastal Chontal. The priest visits sporadically to officiate over services, sacraments, and local feasts.

The original church of Santiago Astata stood where the market is now, but the townspeople saved their money and contributed their resources to building a new church dedicated both to Santiago—Saint James the Moor Slayer—and to the Christ of Mercy from the aguaje. The townspeople tell the story of the priest who came to officiate one day after the church was built. When he finished saying the mass, the priest asked for the keys to the building. The townspeople asked why he wanted them, and he replied that he needed the keys to collect the offerings, since he was the priest assigned to Astata. The people refused, saying that it was their church and they knew what it needed. The priest left in anger and refused to return to Astata for more than two years.

The people are proud of their church and take turns caring for the saints, whose clothing is changed for different feasts. A woman from the Texas border has returned with her daughter to fulfill a promise she made to El Cristo de la Piedad. She is giving herself and her daughter a spiritual cleansing before the altar, using mostly sweet basil.

Two white-haired men, the sacristans charged with the care of the church, are sleeping on the benches. They wake to the sound of footsteps and talk about all manner of things, including where to find doña Celia. Years ago she worked in the old market, selling *panela* [sugar] from the neighboring village while honeybees swarmed over it. The panela, wrapped in banana leaves, was made in Huamelula, in the old *trapiches* (sugar mills). She sold painted jícaras, *bules* (gourds), and other goods. She wore a beautiful flowered huipil and brilliant turquoise enagua. Then the market, damaged by rain, was closed for repair, so doña Celia could be found at her home, selling her goods from there.

There are a few traditionally constructed thatched homes scattered throughout this village. Celia's house is made of brick and mortar with a thatched veranda in the front held up by horcónes, or y-shaped poles. Here she invites guests to lie on her hammocks while customers buy eggs, sugar, candies, refreshments, and other things. Her dog sleeps in the sun. Sometimes, tied in the corner, there's a pig or other animal that she has bought or is about to sell, especially on the eve of important feasts when people prepare tamales and special foods.

Celia is inquisitive and travels as much as she can in her capacity as a storekeeper to the townspeople. She has a satellite dish, and she watches programs about national and international news and events. She jokes with several people about traveling to Egypt and Africa, and she describes what she has seen, to their surprise. She has one daughter who is a teacher in the Isthmus, another in Mexico City, and three sons. Her husband Eloy is dedicated to his land, and he works it every day. He also plays the trumpet and the marimba, and is busy with local festivities when he is not tending his land. He is a quiet man. He and Celia remarried after a long separation. Luckily, it's as though they were never apart.

Celia's son Armando and his wife Lucrecia work at one of the major hotels in Tangolunda. Armando takes the microbus that comes by the village before five in the morning to pick up workers. Lucrecia, who is from the Chontal hamlet of Coyul, goes in a little later. She has an hour or so more time to get the children up and ready for school. The hotel is planning to reduce its staff by half in the aftermath of September 11, 2001. Repercussions of that day's terrorist attacks reverberate strongly all the way here. But Armando and his brothers are also fishermen, and they can work in masonry. They still have their land in Astata and work the fields. Celia says:

I have three sons. The three are fishermen with the union. My sons are lagoon fishermen. They know how to swim, but they don't work in the ocean. They catch plenty of fish and shrimp. They learned out of necessity. That's where they get their food. One lives in Coyul. He goes to the lagoon they call Las Paltas, where there is a rock, close to La Barra at Rosario. He catches pargo and lisas. He takes two coolers with him. Good luck follows him, and he comes home with the coolers filled with fish to sell.

There's a lagoon they call Mascalco. They say that when you are in the lagoon you can hear a bell. There is a bell made of stone that rings on its own. I don't know what mystery it has. It's an encanto, and the bell rings very loudly. You will not see who is ringing it or where it is located. A person cannot go alone to fish there because the lagoon has its mystery. My son says he went in where it's shallower and narrower. He says he dropped a sinker there with about thirty arm extensions of cord. He said, "I

Doña Celia's embroidered dress, 1999

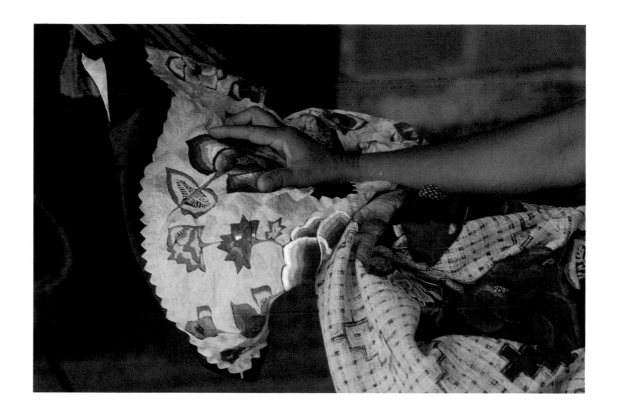

Don Eloy and doña Celia, with their granddaughter Ayari, 1999

touched the mud, and when I brought up the rock that I had tied, it was very hot, but covered with mud. It's possible that there is salt down there. Who knows what's in there, perhaps there is a mine." Everyone says that the lagoon is so deep it has no end. They say an animal, a cow, fell in and it never came out. When an animal dies it floats—first it drowns and stays down, then eventually it floats— but not this one. . . .

There are estuaries and lagoons close to the ocean, virgin lagoons. This is why they now want tourism around these parts, from the Colorado to San Diego. This town is picturesque. A millionaire came, a wealthy man, I don't know what price they quoted him for the hectares. The town told him, "We will sell it to you, but at this price." "No," he said, "I'll give you this price." "Go look somewhere else. Over at the Crucecita you can buy," they told him loudly.

For a very long time, schools punished children who spoke languages other than Spanish. Celia remembers, "I was six years old. The teacher punished me. I was made to stay in the sun because I only spoke dialecto. When that teacher came they took away our speaking Chontal, more than fifty years ago. I couldn't speak to any girl, like I'm speaking here, in Chontal, because they would laugh and they would say, 'They only speak in dialect.'"

Now the language is a source of pride. All the old people who still speak the language ask newcomers if they know Viola Waterhouse, who came to Astata and Huamelula to study Chontal, and translated the Bible into Chontal.[17] People speak about her as though she was here in the last month or two, rather than more than forty years ago. Most people here understand Chontal, but doña Canora, who lives around the corner from Celia, is singled out as a person who can teach the language. She is also a *curandera*, or healer. *Cordoncillo*, known as the tortilla of the deceased, and *albahaca* (sweet basil) grow in front of her home. She is often busy performing *limpias*, or smudgings—spiritual cleansings. She uses an egg, mezcal, cordoncillo, and albahaca. Most people suffer from having someone's ill will fixed on them. People in the region often tie an *ojo de venado*, a doe-eye seed-pod, to a baby's wrist or clothing, much as evil-eye talismans are worn in the Middle East. Canora and others heal the affliction with various herbs, but some also use orange water as a precaution.

Canora is also one of a group of devout women who gather to wail and to pray for the dead. She and several other women from the group have come to the house across from Celia's to pray for the woman's son and daughter-in-law, who died in a car accident that July. The women are in a dark room, and light from a window falls on the cantor, creating a bright silhouette against the darkness. The cantor leads the prayer and intones verses, and the wailing women answer in song. The verses echo 16th-century liturgical music. There is copal incense burning at the cantor's feet and at the foot of the altar, which is vaguely lit by votive candles. On this Day of the Dead, also known as the *cabo de año* (the end of the year), prayers are said for all those who have passed within the year. As Canora and her colleagues finish the prayers and song, family and neighbors assist the mother of the deceased in offering tamales, totopos, and chocolate to everyone present. The cantor and the wailers visit for a little while, then leave to mourn with other families and to prepare their own homes and the gravesites at the cemetery for the return of the ancestors.

Doña Celia, in her sixties, wakes up at five every morning. At about the same hour, people come to buy eggs and other things they need. This gives doña Celia very little time for herself and her family. On festive occasions, such as Todos Santos (All Saints), or as she calls it, Todo Santo, she has the precise hours that will require her attention scheduled throughout the day or the week. Her children will be arriving on November 1st for the

Right: The sacristan of the Church of Santiago de Astata, 1997

Left: The sacristan's grandson, listening to his grandfather's stories

tamales, and she needs to prepare the mole in advance, because it takes time. This year, November 1st falls on a Sunday, and grandchildren and other relations will also come to pay their respects to their ancestors in Astata, and to share in their meal.

While Celia makes sure the souls who return have their food on the altar, she focuses a great deal of attention on her children and grandchildren. She takes no shortcuts with the mole.

I put half the ingredients in at the beginning so that it will be delicious. I have to add hot pepper according to the quantity. Depending upon what type of mole one makes, one has to add pepper, cinnamon, cumin, oregano, garlic and onion. If you want to, you can add a little eucalyptus, some bitter leaves. Then you fry all of this separately and you put it through a sieve, and you fry it again and drain it again. Once you have boiled all of these condiments, you are ready to add the guajillo chile.

You fry it nicely, you grind it with ancho, red, and chipotle chile, a little, but not from a can. It's got to be dry. The ancho chile you add is the dark one, the mulatto or black one you add so that your mole will have a beautiful aroma. You prepare it and you grind it so that your mole is seasoned. Once you have boiled what I just described, you add it in. Then you fry the peanuts, the sesame seed, and the almonds. You fry all of this and the Castile banana [a large, sweet plantain]. You blend it together [in a blender] and drain it in a sieve. By this time your mole has boiled. . . .

This is what I say, because many people make it out of only one chile. In order for your mole to be delicious, you have to season first, as I did, and then boil it in your saucepan. It turns out so delicious. If you don't add all of the ingredients, how will your mole have a flavorful aroma? This is mole poblano, or mole Oaxaqueño.

At the moment, Celia is adding the peanuts, sesame, and Castile banana. "You can't use an ordinary banana," she cautions. "This is special for the mole." There are other ingredients, such as raisins, chocolate, bread, chile, garlic, cloves, and tomato. The cooking lesson continues.

We have two types of tamales that we eat for Todo Santo. We eat chicken tamales with mole poblano, and we have iguana tamales made with pumpkin seeds. You toast the seeds with a little corn, and you add green tomato. You prepare it well. This little mole is plain, but it is well liked. It takes pumpkin seed, a little corn, plenty of tomato, and then it is mixed well. I'll make it on Monday, because the second [of November] is the day of tamales. On Monday by two o'clock, I will have made the tamales. I'll be finished. I will have prepared the iguana, and I'll have many of the tamales already made. I prepare the iguana at five in the morning.

I always say, as I'm saying right now, "I am going to take my time." I am going to make my bread at about five in the afternoon. I made the leavening last night. This morning I mixed it. The majority of people make good bread. One can make two types of bread with decorations. One they make is in the shape of a doll or in the shape of a skull. But I don't do it that way. I don't add designs to my bread. Since this is the custom of my village, I make it. I don't make the pan de muerto [for offering to the dead]. I buy inexpensive bread for the santo [soul]. I make the bread we eat—all the children rush to eat it.

Celia prepared the bread a few days ahead in anticipation of the "day of the tamales," as she calls it. After preparing the leavening and letting the dough rise overnight, she made arrangements to use a woman's *horno* [oven] down the way, close to the river. Celia makes other dishes, as well, such as a delicacy made with squash, sugar, and almonds. She speaks about how the townspeople prepare for the vigil for their ancestors' return.

The entire ceremony begins almost a week in advance. Some men, including the cantor—which is what we call the vecinal [local person] who attends to the church—go to pray. The cantors are mostly men, and they seek out the women and men who pray. They pray outside the entrance to the cemetery. We call those who pray outside the cemetery las Animas [the Souls]. They pray there for two days. They say that this is for the angelitos [little angels, the children who have died]. The 28th and 29th of October are the days of the angelitos. . . .

Whoever wants to pray for their child gets the people who pray to come to their home. Yesterday they had fireworks because they were remembering a child's death. Fireworks are not used for the adult muertos. Around there [signaling up ahead], they pray and they light one, two, or three fireworks. They have tamales. They have chocolate and bread where they are praying. . . .

For the adults they will pray without fireworks. They use bells. When they pray, the bells start ringing. For the adult dead, for the muerto, the bells make a sound like this, deen, don. For the angelitos we call the sound tequila, because the bell rings like deen, deen, deen, deen, deen, and we say, "A child has died, they are telling the village." The bells are so loud, the entire village hears them. But when we hear them at midnight, the sound of the bells for the grown-ups is very different.

On the first, Todo Santo, we do nothing but pray. Everywhere, everyone prays. But all through the week, all of the people go to the cemetery to leave flowers and candles. This is a little funny, because they leave flowers and candles now and the rest of the year it is the rare person who goes to see the deceased. But on the day of Todo Santo, the whole world eats their tamales. The fact is that one has to spend [money], and that's just the way it is. It's the same thing with the offerings for Todo Santo. We place [on the altar and gravesite] those flowers [pointing] and the yellow flowers. We call those cresta de gallo [cockscomb] and we call the other one flor de muerto [flower of the dead]. Who knows what they are called elsewhere? Sometimes we wonder how it is that God left us all of this at this season, that these flowers are just here at this time.

The custom is that one sweeps and cleans the home because we are waiting for the dead on the day of the tamales, the second [of November]. . . . Here we have this custom that the day of the adults is the

Lucrecia's sister, reading at Lucrecia and Armando's home in Astata, 2001

day of the tamales. Now then, at eight o'clock in the morning there is a celebration in the church. All of our people gather together, and we unite spiritually. Once this celebration is over, the bells begin to chime. It starts at eight in the morning and they continue to ring all day, so much so that you start getting bored with the sound. At night they call men's names, young men, who will take turns ringing the bells. This is the custom around here, including in Huamelula. They say that it is the custom to continue ringing the bell to announce all of the dead who are arriving.

At eight o'clock in the morning at every doorstep, on every threshold there is incense. You stand at the door with your family, and you begin to pray, "Our Father, let those pass who want to come in." You leave the copal burner, and the incense is smoking for the saint [the dead soul]. . . . For example, we mention the names of our family or others we know who will be returning, such as my great-grandparents. I say, "Grandfather, great-grand-father"—well, here we don't say great-grandfather, we just say, "Grandfather, come in." My [great-] grandparents' names were Nicolás de los Santos and Francisca García. Then there is my grandmother Norberta Santos, Sebastián Piñon, brothers, uncles, so and so, and what's his name. . . .

In this house, I will not eat the fruit or bread [on the altar]. I tell the grandchildren to take the fruit. I know they are needy, and my granddaughter already knows that on the last day they gather all of the fruit. After all of this, on the third, all neighborhoods gather the fruit, because as we know, by that day all of the dead have left. The principals of the church go to pray at the cemetery. They take their baskets to the graveyard and to the gravesites. There is fruit there. They gather all of the fruit and return with the full baskets to the church, and they pile all the fruit and divide it up and give it away to the children, to the people—bread, choco-late, and fruit. . . .

In the morning one awakens to the gathering of the food. A man comes out of the church and the bell rings, din, din, din. It starts at about nine o'clock. The notes from a sad bell can be heard. The sound for the bell of the dead is thin. They go to the homes of the families of the most recently deceased. For example, if there are ten men and women who have died throughout this year, they visit the homes and pray there. . . . This is a very ancient custom. . . . They gather the fruit of the newly deceased. Those who wish to have prayers said for the santo in their family on the second anniversary of the death ask the cantor and the men who pray to do so, and then they gather their fruit as well. We have this custom for the newly deceased, since we are a small town and we all know one another. There may be four, five, six, eight, or ten [deaths] a year, but we know who they are. They have never been here to this house because I don't have any people who have died, God forbid, but they pass through on the way. At night when we're sleeping there is a procession of men, a pilgrimage. This is the tradition, that the men are charged with gathering the fruit. By the morning of the third they will gather it all from the cemetery. They divide it all, and this is where the ceremony ends.

San Pedro Huamelula | The Place of the Seeded Trees

The main highway bends gradually to the north along the river, about one kilometer southeast of Santiago Astata. The road edges along rock walls. Legend has it these mountains contain a system of caves that reaches all the way to Oaxaca City. The 19th-century priest and historian Brasseur de Bourbourg and others recorded this story.[18] There are several enchantments here at El Boquerón, among the caves and cliffs, and beyond, in the ocean and the small valley that holds the town of San Pedro Huamelula. El Boquerón, called Cocogua in Chontal, meaning "where the wind blows," is the name of the two cliffs that guard the entrance to the village. At certain times of the year, a snake that can be seen in the rock formations of this encanto drips the blood of the Passion. The snake is next to the mouth of a cave that was closed off by the people of the town of Huamelula, after, they say, the priest and some gringos went in and took gold and idols that were hidden there. The cave is sealed, but the snake still guards it.

Here people tell a story about how the Huaves from the Isthmus once threatened to take the church of Huamelula away from the Chontales, to San Mateo del Mar, where the Huaves lived. One day they arrived at El Boquerón and blocked the entrance to the town with a great serpent. This took place around the time of the rainy season, in mid-July. With their magic they built a type of dam, so that the heavy rains would flood the area and wash the church to their community. The Chontales, wise to this plan, went down to the seacoast by the Huave community and, through their own magical ceremonies, caused the ocean to swell. This frightened the Huaves, and they asked for forgiveness. The serpent returned to its nest. This is also the reason why, as Armando says, San Mateo del Mar now has its "dead sea," and the serpent's head still guards the entrance to Huamelula.[19]

Across the way are limestone caves where the people lived long ago. At the very top of the cordillera you can make out the head of a reptile, followed by the body and tail. During the dry season, when the mountainside is bare, it can be hard to see the animal's shape, but during the rainy season, the green of the bushes and trees adds more depth and delineation to the formation. Some people say it is the snake from long ago, but many see an alligator. Eugenio and others say that if the water reaches the alligator's head, it will signal the end of the Chontal people who live along the coast. That seems an almost impossible turn of events, but the community of Santiago Astata, situated near the alligator's hindquarters, has already moved at least twice, most recently during the 1600s. The reptile faces toward the oldest community here, Huamelula, the seat of the coastal Chontales. These two communities have always been at odds with each other over lands. At the same time their citizens come from the same families and are united in protection of the uses and customs of all Chontal peoples, those in the mountains and along the coast.

Recently, doña María Escamilla and don Manuel Zárate's son Graciano was killed in an automobile accident on the highway heading toward San Pedro Huamelula. He and his wife, a schoolteacher from nearby Tapanala, were married in a large ceremony just a year and a half ago. Graciano, or Chano, was returning from working in Salina Cruz. He was in a taxi along with several others, who were also killed. The driver had little time to stop before a herd of cows ran out onto the roadside. Hundreds upon hundreds of people came to the funeral for el güero (the fair-skinned one), who often stopped by to see how his parents were doing and ask after what they might need.

Doña María and don Manuel, who was orphaned at a very young age, have been exemplary leaders of San Pedro Huamelula and are highly esteemed. Don Manuel has held sev-

El Boquerón, the cliffs guarding the entrance to San
Pedro Huamelula, 2001

Alligator formation at the top of the cordillera, 2000

eral positions of authority. They added three sons and four daughters to the Chontal community. Elizabeth (Eli), now in her mid-fifties, is the oldest and lives in México City, working for the Instituto Nacional Indigenista. She loves her *pueblo*. But after teaching in the village, she moved to Mexico City and worked as a housekeeper for many years, saving to help her parents and her siblings, and to study as well. Her sister Josafat followed, as did her brother Jaime, and another sister, Naomi. Josafat also worked and saved and studied. She returned to Huamelula as a young doctor and got the first x-ray machine for the community. Later she headed up large clinics in Salina Cruz and Oaxaca City.

Jaime, the eldest of the sons, is near retirement from his job in the athletic department of a university in Mexico City. Jaime is a singer and composer. His music echoes his love for his people and the land of his origin. Another sister, Pina, lives in Huamelula, around the corner from her parents. Agustín married a young woman from Astata and lives and works in Salina Cruz. The Zárate Escamilla family is dedicated to the Chontal people. Most importantly, they want to make certain that the traditions of the community remain intact and that children learn the language and pass it on to future generations. Little José, Pina's son, studies Chontal at the Escuela Indigena (the Native School) and with his grandparents. Many young people from the Chontal hamlets and villages and from other parts of Huatulco have studied in the secondary school in Huamelula. Esperanza from Copalita stayed with a member of her family for several years while she studied there, for example. Despite its poverty, Huamelula continues to be one of the most prominent villages in the region and a beacon for Chontales who insist on maintaining their culture.

The Chontales of this town conserve their cycle of rituals more closely than do communities in other areas along the coast. Their relative isolation, in a small valley fortressed from the rest of the world, allows them the freedom and autonomy to practice their "uses and customs." Vantage points along the cliffs make it easy to see who is coming to the village, and its people have learned through centuries of resistance to protect themselves from invaders. The Spanish conquistadors had to be led to this place by their Native allies, it is so well-hidden.

The origin of the name Huamelula—on 16th century maps it appears as Guamelula—is still to be unraveled. The Nahuatl language offers two possible derivations: from Huaumimilollan, meaning "the place of the ancient seeded lands," or from Cuauhmilolan, "the path of planted trees."[20] While the old derroteros show the encomienda of Guamelula as a town surrounded by large trees (perhaps those seeded trees), trees are now notably absent from the town's landscape.[21]

The origin of their people and language is a question the Chontales often ask themselves, perhaps because they have been asked many times by others. They know they have been here for a very long time. Chontal stories of heroes and deities date to as early as the 4th century C.E., according to Avendaño from Astata.[22] Many Chontales want to know their connection with their Zapotec, Zoque, Huave, Mixe, and other neighboring peoples, including the Maya farther south. The Chontal language, unrelated to those of the surrounding ethnic groups, has been linked to the Sioux Hokan language family, one of the oldest in North America, and is the subject of much conjecture. Other peoples belonging to this very ancient language family live in Southern California, Baja California Norte (the Seri of Sonora), Arizona to the north, and Honduras and Nicaragua to the south (the Jicaque-speakers).[23] There is little knowledge about the migration of the Chontales, probably because it happened so long ago, but they think they may have come from the ocean, farther south. Certainly they have a great devotion to water and to the sea.

Doña María Escamilla Zárate, 2000

Scholars used to believe that the Chontales of this region might be tied to the Maya Chontal of Tabasco—that they migrated from farther south using a route across the mountains, where many Chontales still live—but linguists have discounted the connection to that language. The word Chontal, Nahuatl for "stranger," is used for several groups with no apparent connection to each other. Archeologists, however, still see a link to the Maya in some early ceramic styles, although not enough work has been done to offer more conclusive evidence. This much, perhaps, can be said: the dominion of these Chontal appears to cover a larger area than has been widely recognized. Based on regional narratives and practices, it is reasonable to believe that Chontal lands encompassed much of the region that in the early days after the Spanish Conquest was under the jurisdiction of Huamelula—from present-day Huatulco (both Santa Cruz and Santa María), San Miguel del Puerto, and most of the region covered in this chapter, to lands that are now part of San Mateo Piñas. Don Cástulo García García, of San Mateo, concurs with those who believe that the area of Chontal influence was quite extensive. He says that the Zapotec spoken in his village maintains some traditions and words from the Chontal language.

There are few Chontal villages along the coast. Many more are located in the mountains, for several other groups, including the Nahua and Zapotecs, had pushed the Chontal away from the strategic trade areas before the Spaniards arrived. In 1529, Huamelula was made an encomienda, and its people were assigned to pay tribute to Juan Hernández de Prado for two years, after which the town was taken back by the crown.[24] It is believed that most villages that were made encomiendas were formidable in size and important long before the Spanish Conquest,[25] and both Huamelula and Astata were encomiendas

with relatively large populations. They are still large communities, with Huamelula the larger of the two.

Many families from Huatulco and the mountains have never stopped making the pilgrimage to Huamelula and Astata, and people continue to observe the most important market days of the dry season. For people from Huamelula, wherever they may live now, the pull of the community is very strong. The Zárate children, like others living elsewhere in México and the United States, make it a point to return to Huamelula throughout the year to see their aging parents, pay homage to the principal saints, and attend the most important celebrations, such as the Feast of the Virgen del Rosario. Elizabeth Zárate says that she was childless until she prayed to the Virgin. Elizabeth's dream is one day to be the mayordoma of the Virgin's feast, which lasts from mid-September to October, to pay her debt of appreciation for the son she bore, now a teenager.

The Virgen del Rosario first appeared in ancient Zimatan, in a grotto. People say that she was a *ranchera*, a ranch woman who cared for cattle, and that she married St. Anthony, one of the saints in the Church of San Pedro. St. Anthony turned out to be a drinker and good for nothing, but she was a model wife who remained faithful to him, and in so doing she became the Virgen del Rosario. For almost 500 years, a hacienda has been dedicated to her honor, the old land titles specifically stating that its income is to support her yearly fiesta. Although these lands were the subject of years of conflict between Huamelula and Santiago Astata, the custom of using their income to support the Virgin's feast has been closely guarded.[26] The titles also declare that the salt marsh of El Rosario is to be shared by the towns of Huamelula and Astata, and the salt to be sold to pay for the Virgin's feast day. El Rosario is now a concession, but the people of the region still use the income from the cattle on the hacienda to venerate the Virgin.

Don Valentín Rey has been named to the *cofradía*, or brotherhood, charged with watching over the chapel where the Virgen del Rosario is venerated, an honor bestowed each year by the municipal president. The only road to her hacienda appears to be a dry creek, and thickets of mesquite and cactus grow along the way. The chapel sits on a rocky mound. There are pastures for grazing cattle and a few scattered houses in the distance, but the entire area is a sanctuary. By 1702 the old town of Santiago Pijutla had been deserted for at least twenty years, abandoned in order to consolidate the Chontal in other villages. Some of its citizens tried to make their way back to the hacienda, but most joined other communities nearby.[19] The chapel that houses the icon of the Virgin is small and lighted by candles.

It is mid-September, and the procession carrying the Virgin from her hacienda to the church at San Pedro Huamelula has snarled traffic on the main highway, the only road connecting the ocean communities north and south. Buses, SUVs, taxis, trucks, and cars—all are honking. The long procession is making its way from the hamlet of Tapanala to the hamlet of Santa María Huamelula, or as it is known here, Santa María Pueblo de las Ollas (Saint Mary Town of the Pots). Doña Celia, who is following the procession, explains Santa María's local name: "The women there make comales and other everyday pots. They don't use any special techniques or apparatus, just their hands. . . . They use a piece of gourd for the burnish. When a comal is finished, they let it dry in the shade, and once it is dried, they fire it. It is the town of potters, the Town of Pots."

Many of the men, women, and children taking part in the procession are singing as they walk. A few women carry umbrellas to shade them from the hot sun. Others are talking and visiting. Some are on horseback, and the mayor is driving his family in a truck. Leading the procession are those who carry the painting of the Virgin, wrapped in a *petate* (woven palm mat). It is considered an honor to carry the Virgin, and men and women take turns. The palm mat was used by the ancients as a throne and place of honor. This is where they set their feet, so as not to stand on the dirt. Important individuals are often depicted on the old codices seated on petates, drinking chocolate from gourd cups. In many traditional weddings of the region, newlywed couples stand on petates, as in ancient times. The Virgin is honored in much the same way. Her petate is adorned with flowers, and many women and children carry more flowers and other gifts to offer her once they arrive at her next resting place.

Procession of the statue of the Virgin Mary to her reunion with Christ, Holy Week, 1999

Virgilio, the municipal policeman, is controlling the traffic. The members of the procession ignore the honking horns of anxious travelers. Virgilio says that the Chontales of this area know that the Virgin cannot be rushed as she dispenses her blessings in hamlets and villages along the way to San Pedro Huamelula. He says that there have been several attempts to bring her hurriedly to Huamelula. People have even tried bringing her in a vehicle. But the faithful know that if she is not venerated properly, she will disappear and go back to her hacienda, and then they must begin the procession all over again. As Virgilio tells it:

They brought her to San Pedro Huamelula, to the church. The next day she was not there. They went to look for her in the same place where she had appeared, and there was nothing. One day a man brought with him the knowledge that a young woman had arrived seeking shelter for the night. She did not want to stay in Huamelula. The man then offered, "Stay here." He says that the following morning at daybreak the young woman was on the altar, but as an icon. So they lifted her from there and brought her to the Church of San Pedro Huamelula.

When they arrived to the town's square, she wouldn't stay. The following day, they found her in the same place where the man had seen her. She was there in the same place in Zimatan. She was in Astata another time. They kept bringing her back to San Pedro Huamelula. Again, the following day she was not in the church. She was once again in Astata. So they said, "Let's see where she's going to stay this time."

They built her temple in a place known as El Limón. There she has stayed, and that is why she is at the hacienda del Rosario. She has eighty head of cattle. They come walking from there. Because, look, I don't believe it, but up until now, if they travel with no haste she arrives happily. But if people try to rush her, she appears black the following morning. She changes color, and the following day she's not there. She will return to her chapel. And they have to go back for her. This is why they take their time.

Within a couple of hours the Virgin arrives at Santa María Huamelula, and the procession heads to the house of the person whose privilege it is to host her. She will be here for several hours. The painting is unwrapped, and the petate placed beneath it. Many rush to

touch the Virgin's image, and prayers are said in her honor. Songs are sung, and food and drink (chocolate) are distributed to everyone under the thatched *enramada* (resting place).

The feast lasts at least fifteen days. The *octava* (the eighth day) is celebrated with a fiesta and dance. Then the procession reverses itself, and St. Anthony accompanies the Virgin back from Huamelula to El Boquerón, where she is once again covered. The statue of St. Anthony and many pilgrims from town will go back to San Pedro Huamelula. Others will accompany the Virgin back to her hacienda, where she will rest until next year.

In December the new mayordomo is presented with the charge for the coming year. The *fundador* (founder) oversees the rituals that will ensure the health and safety of the cattle from the Virgin's hacienda, making the necessary offerings to the earth, and to the devil, who must also have his due. In a ritual, the fundador offers food to the devil in the form of water and fire, then awaits the sign that the devil has given his compliance, or *cumplimiento*, and that all will be well for next year. The fundador is one of the most important positions on the village council, serving for the good of the entire community. But he is also someone who has knowledge about healing and curing. Don Manuel says that he might be considered by some to be a *brujo* (sorcerer) because of his strong magical powers, but he is foremost a wise man.

Holy Week is celebrated elaborately in San Pedro Huamelula as well. Many communities in México reenact the passion of Christ. Here the people make a point of venerating the old saints, from the churches that date to the 16th century or before. The Church of San Sebastián and the Church of San Pedro Huamelula, both dating to the late 1500s, are at the center of this ceremony. The Holy Week ceremony is important to Chontal people from throughout region, who make it a point to take part in it. Doña Celia says:

Those people from Huamelula do the encounter of the Virgin and her Son very well. In Huamelula, Jesus of Nazareth comes out of the Church [of San Pedro] through the side door. They bring the Virgin out through another door, while they take the Christ around the side of the hill. One man plays a trombone that goes toooommmb, toooomb, toooomb, and everyone goes down to the other church [San Sebastián]. Only men follow through the street, not one woman can be seen there. The women walk all the way down the hill, and that's where the encounter takes place, They cry, they grab the mantle where Christ's face appears, they place it where it goes. They do it beautifully.

These are ancient practices that persist. At the hour of the encounter, a woman screams and cries. She cries because she is encountering her Son. After this they go back to the church to pray. In the afternoon they have a meal they call cena [supper] where they distribute things. The sacristan dresses and takes two donkeys with him to the burial. They act out Christ's death. They carry the cross. And they have a vigil all night for Christ after he is placed in his casket there in the church. They do this all night as though it was real and happening at this moment. They do it beautifully.

Many of the townspeople, most of whom participate in the event, say that their favorite part of the drama of the Passion is the moment when Jesus the Son meets his Mother during the enactment of the Stations of the Cross, the path Christ takes while carrying the cross. Women follow the Blessed Virgin of Soledad, dressed in the purple cloth of mourning, along a road that leads out from the Church of San Pedro in one direction. Men follow behind the statue of the Nazarene Christ, also in purple robes, along another way. The Chontal orchestra follows behind the Christ image, and men follow the procession, walking to the sound of the dirge. Most women sing and pray with their heads bowed and covered. It is a large and somber funeral march. Finally, Mary meets her Son at the fork that leads to the Church of San Sebastián. After the Crucifixion, Christ's statue is taken down from the cross and placed in a coffin in the church of San Sebastián. As he is laid to rest in this small sanctuary, the townspeople take turns keeping the vigil through the night. The Church of San Sebastián is lit with tiny electric lights around some of the saints on the altar, but most of the light comes from hundreds of votive candles. They cast shadows of everyone there, the people and the ancient statues of saints with no faces. Women wailers, the rezador who leads the prayers, the cantor, the band, and all who pray are accompanied by hundreds of shadows until daybreak and the Resurrection.

Catholicism, with its saints and religious hierarchy, was superimposed onto the Chontal religion, and Chontal beliefs survive to this day. Early chroniclers describe the Chontal religion as polytheistic. The deities were associated with the elements, with the main sources and events of life: water, wind, hunting, planting, fishing, childbirth, war, and peace. Some of the saints venerated in Huamelula have many of the same attributes as the old deities.[27] At the same time, the old deities persist as well—some are encantos—sources of strength for many of the people of Huamelula.

At the Church of San Pedro, the statue of St. Peter, holding the keys to the kingdom of heaven, sits directly above the main altar. For many in the community, the saint they call by the endearment San Pedrito is synonymous with God. Through St. Peter's intercession, the community observes some of the most important practices from before the time of the Spanish Conquest and the people's evangelization by Spanish missionaries.

One of the most important events takes place on May 1st, the day used to mark the beginning of the rainy season and a critical time for people who live off the land. On the first day of May, the fundador calls together the municipal president and all of his authorities, as well as the council of elders, or asesores, those beyond

sixty-five years of age. They go to the designated site and begin a ritual for the benefit of the entire municipality of Huamelula, with all of its lands and agencies. The devil is summoned, as well, because, as don Manuel says, an offering must be made to appease the demonic forces. The fundador offers the devil copal and fire to ensure that he will be satisfied and will leave the community alone. As don Manuel narrates:

The fundador lays the foundation for things. He is here to ensure that all works properly, that the president works well the three years he will be in office. Each authority must go and ask the permission of the earth. They say: "Mother Earth, we come to ask your permission to grant us space. We are going to work the land where the generator will bring us the most water. The authorities have arrived, all of whom must resolve the problems of the community. The municipal president, the syndic (trustee), the municipal judge, and all of the aldermen have arrived. They want to work honorably. They want to work for the benefit of the town. They come to ask for what they will need."

Then the president speaks. He asks Mother Earth to keep in mind all the services he will perform. He asks for consideration for the municipal palace. He asks for consideration for the people, the campesinos, the teachers—that they be received in the schools; that the children do what they can to take their lessons as they should; that they not give any problems to the teachers. He asks that there be no problems with the citizens; that when there is a general assembly the people be united, and be treated in good faith; that they not fight; that there not be any discord; that they be united to speak and to ask to speak—whatever is of benefit to the town.

Then the same president says: "We come to ask that the masses said by the priest benefit the people. We want the people to go to church, that they are united in their prayers at church to ask God for what they need. We want all this to come to pass. We come to ask that in God's time and in the season of water, that it rain tranquilly and well; that there be plentiful and good harvests, such as of corn, beans, squash, watermelon, all the important trees, bamboo, all that we want to have grow.

"Mother Earth, may God serve you in your path. God St. Peter, we come to implore you, with all our hearts. We want to work together. We want to fight together with you. This is why we come to make our offering. We want to pay our respects, to fulfill our obligations properly. We are the authori-

Left and opposite: Offering incense to St. Peter
and the four cardinal directions, 1999

ties. Give us courage, strength, and a great heart, so that this may be fulfilled. Let there be no disgrace
in the town. Let there be no illness. May all sickness be gone. Take away all the evil so that here in
Huamelula there be no difficulty, so that all humanity be content and fight for the good. Let the meetings held be beneficial for a particular task, that the town accept it or revoke it; that they not fight; that
all be peaceful."

Then, the representative who is going to burn the copal asks: "Lady Juana de Agua, just as the
municipal president is asking, you, who are the Mother of the Ocean, we want you to have enough
water, so that there will be good rainfall; that there not be too much rain; that there be enough for cultivating, planting, and processing; for the corn to give abundantly; for the harvests not to be damaged.
We don't want flooding. Just as you are the Mother of the Sea, let the atmosphere that you give be given
with patience. Give it to us so that the rain that falls makes everything productive for all of the depend-
encies—for Santa María, Tapanala, Río Seco, Coyul, Playa Grande, La Barra de la Cruz, Río Papaya,
El Bejuco, San Francisco, El Gavilán, El Caparosa, Zaachila—all those places that are part of San
Pedro Huamelula. Enclose these lands that are part of Huamelula. We want there to be good rainfall
that there may be good harvests and all farmers profit from their harvests. That is all that we ask,
Mother of the Sea."

Some older campesinos observe a similar custom or ritual in the corn and sugar cane
fields, or what they call la labor, around the time the land is cleared before planting. The
farmer abstains from eating certain foods and from sexual activity for a prescribed period
of time. Before he begins work, he burns copal and blesses the land and the tools he uses.
The ritual sometimes includes other offerings—in the past, it included small animal
parts, such as turkey heads.[28] The offering is made to the elements, principally those
ensuring fertility—Mother Earth, Juana de Agua, the encanto of the ocean, and the other
elements. On the whole, these are private rituals, not public observances. It is true, as don
Beto says, that farmers in the region often find small figurines as they cultivate the land—
clay heads and torsos of women, or sometimes breasts. Clearly, the practice of making
offerings to ensure the fertility of the fields is ancient here.

Above: The cofradia prepare to take the Virgen del Rosario from her hacienda , 2001

Right: Procession of the Virgen del Rosario to the Church of San Pedro Huamelula, 2001

The ocean is one of the main encantos throughout the coastal region, but the name Juana de Agua, Mother of the Ocean, is still used only among the Chontal. Juana de Agua and Mother Earth go hand in hand with St. Peter, who is the patron of fishermen. The sirens, or mermaids, and Juan Diego are important encantos as well.

The parish church of San Pedro Huamelula is one of the oldest in the region, and some people call it a cathedral. An assistant at the rectory offers a summary of old documents once located in the parish archive. The summary offers insights into how the church saw its mission to indoctrinate the Native population. The earliest document listed is a royal letter of 1608 reminding the clergy that the "Indians are not to be dominated. Instead they are to be loved like sons and brothers." In another letter, dated 1645, ministers and priests are urged not to seize the wealth or possessions of the Native people, and they are reminded to provide for the poor. On the other hand, in 1737, the parish holds a record of the confraternity of the Virgen del Rosario and notes an inventory of animals at the hacienda, as well as the costs and sales associated with the "cult" of the Virgin.

A letter dated 1782 urges the teaching of Castellano (Castilian Spanish), and another refers to a royal decree issued in 1789 for the establishment of cemeteries outside the towns. A document of 1802 describes the practice of "pastoral visits" to the Church of San Pedro Huamelula and evaluates the condition of the church, suggesting the use of the monies from the confraternity of the Virgin to cover the costs of its repair. Apparently the church is in such poor condition that it might prove dangerous to the parishioners. Among the many instructions for those who observe the cult of the Virgin, there is an added solicitation that the devout should have a Christ made that could be taken down from the cross and placed in a coffin for the Good Friday ceremony. At the same time the letter chastises the people for the "improper" and "ridiculous" manner in which the saints are dressed and strongly urges that they be taken from view and "re-dressed" with

decency, "seeking that Indians and crude people form a better understanding of the Dignity and largess of the religion."

A year later, in 1803, a document to be broadly disseminated to all parishioners urges vaccination against smallpox. Another letter recommends the use of the *Dictionary of Agriculture* written by Abad Rozier. Then in 1805, there is an announcement of the investigation of monuments that date prior to the Conquest. By 1806 there is a general announcement of the presence of revolutionary people, and the church asks for donations in support of the troubled Spanish monarchy. There is also an announcement related to the establishment of a special Spanish Supreme Junta of the Indies. Later, the church, through an edict of excommunication, lets parishioners know that leaflets, the Constitution, and other decrees relative to the new republic are to be ignored, and it lists the revolutionary insurgents from different parts of the country. In 1822, the parishioners are notified that the new Constitution has elected don Agustín de Iturbide emperor of México. In 1833 there is a tally of the amount in the offering box from the Señor de la Piedad (Lord of Mercy) of Astata. In the last entry, the newly designated priest has taken charge over the offerings at Señor de la Piedad, and he establishes that he will hold one key to the offering box, and two others will hold a second and third key.

These *Relaciones* of various pastoral letters are described as recalling the "truths and doctrines of the Church."

Feast of San Pedro: The Path of the Alligator

For the Huamelulences (people of Huamelula), one of the most important events of the year falls between the the summer solstice, which usually occurs around June 21st, and June 29th or 30th, the date of the Feast of San Pedro, the patron of the town. Through performance and rituals, the history and beliefs of hundreds of years are collapsed into this week, and the day after the feast, and the final day, when the pots are washed and returned

Procession of San Pedrito from the Church of
San Pedro to the mayordomo's home altar,
Feast of San Pedro, 1999

to their owners. Events take place in the rivers, in houses, in the central part of the village, in the churches, at the edge of town—basically, everywhere. The entire village is a living stage set for the performance.

At the Feast of San Pedro, the encantos are invoked. The feast is usually sponsored by a mayordomo. There are some years, however, when a single individual or family cannot carry the burden of the expense. Then, the municipal president and other authorities must find a way to sponsor the festivities. The municipal president must always show respect and leadership.

The fiesta involves several weeks of work before and after. In anticipation, some women order special huipiles and enaguas from doña María, who goes to visit her sister in Tehuantepec and has beautifully embroidered blouses and skirts sewn by the women there, the Tehuanas. Very few of the women of Huamelula wear the old *enredos*, the wrapped-style skirts, dyed with *Purpúra* and indigo. Instead, they have adopted their own version of the dress worn in the Isthmus by the Tehuanas. Some of these festive huipiles and enaguas are embroidered with geometric motifs. The most expensive and most coveted, however, are decorated with beautiful floral embroidery, the colors of the flowers graduating from dark to light against a background of dark velvet. These floral motifs are reminiscent of the beautiful shawls, the *mantón de Manila*, worn by women in Seville.

The mayordomo's house during the Feast of San Pedro, 2000

There is no doubt that the embroidery style was influenced by 250 years of the Manila Galleon trade (1565–1815), from the Philippines to this littoral, then on to Spain. From small girls to the elderly, townswomen have their hair combed in a special hairdo, and they get out their finest jewelry, especially their earrings and necklaces, for the Convite de Flores (Feast of Flowers) that will soon take place.

The men will slaughter a cow or two for the mole to feed the whole village; often, they will prepare venison mole. The women will make mole and soup, chocolate and bread. There will also be chicken on one day of the festivities. Everyone knows that any animal (mostly chickens) left in sight will be taken by members of the cast of the enactment and cooked for the village. This is part of the performance of their history, and at the appropriate time children and women scurry to catch their fowl before they can be taken away.

But first the men must capture the main animal protagonist of the drama, known as La Princesa (the Princess)—the lagarto, or alligator. The men go to the Huamelula River, to the Río Papaya, to Garrapatero, or to Mascalco to find an alligator. In the meantime, the members of the cast, which includes the Christians, the Muhú (blacks), also known as the Negros or Negritos; the Pichilingües (pirates); the Caballerangos (Spanish lords); the Mareños (sea people); and the Muliatas (men dressed as women), prepare to play their roles. Traditionally, each of these groups is made up of twelve individuals, in addition to their captains or leaders.

The Muhú wear dark sport jackets over their trousers, red bandanas over their heads, and black masks. They carry a rattle in one hand and a stick, representing the traditional indigenous staff of authority, or a rope in the other, depending on their rank. Their captain is an elderly man who has mentored all of the younger dancers. He represents the character of José Lachimir. This man says that he started dancing as a child and danced for a long time before he became captain, and that he has been captain for at least forty years. His father and grandfather were both captains; he took over the role when his father died.

Right: Young man dressed to dance the part of the Muhú (blacks), 1999

The captain carries a permit, notarized with the town seal and the mayor's signature, made out to the Danzantes Muhú (black dancers). It states that the dancers departed on the 17th of the month from the City of Montero, neighboring Jamaica, and that at twelve midnight they viewed from the Cerro Jamaiquero (Jamaican Hill) the enemies, the Turks from Champerico Roma, with their emperor the Rey Mahoma, who are approaching from a far distance of 27,000 leagues (130,000 kilometers). The captain of the Muhú, José Lachimir, signs the document, as do his second-in-command and the other dancers. The character of the captain's second-in-command is named Aladino Torrencín, and all the other Muhú have names that rhyme with Torrencín, such as Perriquín, etcetera. It is interesting to note that these names echo the honorific Nahuatl form *tzin* (lord).

One role of the Muhú in the festivities is to deceive the people. They act as owners of the land at times, and try to become go-betweens in some of the land negotiations and disputes. Some of the townspeople see them as the poor, who do not have papers, like many present-day comuneros. The Muhú also represent an incursion into the community. The captain makes certain to tell the dancers the significance of their part in the drama. There are usually twelve lead dancers, but this year they are training more, ranging in age from six or seven years old to the captain, who is in his seventies. The captain teaches the others what they must say and what it means. He takes great pride in what he does and is stern, making sure that the children take their role seriously. They have kidnapped La Niña, a Chontal princess who is seen as their accomplice in the enactment. She is carried as one of their standards of identity, dressed in her best clothing, which changes every year. In fact, she is a very old wooden effigy, whose features have been worn away by time, except for the ones someone has drawn with a little ink. Most importantly, she is made of local wood, thus she is a native of the Chontal community.

There are twelve Pichilingües (pirates), as well as their captain, Alférez. The Pichilingües are the same as the Turcos (Turks) and Moors (from the Moors and the Christians), words synonymous with pirate in the 17th and 18th centuries.[29] The word "Pichilingüe," from a later date, has a similar significance, though only along the Pacific coast, where people use it to mean robber as well as pirate.[30] It may well be tied to a local Chontal word. The Pichilingües are the elite of the conquerors, for the drama says they come on well-appointed ocean vessels. They are traders on their way from Champerico Roma, Panama, a place not yet identified but very real to the performers. Panama was an important part of the trading route that extended down the coast beyond Perú, and the Pichilingües play the part of merchants.

The Pichilingües wear all that is symbolic of wealth to the Chontales. They wear two long strips of purple cloth, originally woven on backstrap looms, crisscrossed over their shoulders. Purple cloth dyed by the Chontales was always given the highest value.[31] Zelia Nuttall documented the importance of purple as one of the pigments with which the pre-Hispanic Mixtec Codex Zouche-Nuttall was painted.[32] The Pichilingües also wear conical hats wrapped in red handkerchiefs, symbolic of the red dye extracted from the cochineal, another highly valued product harvested by some of the mountain Chontal. These hats are decorated with mirrors that reflect the sun and bewilder the enemy; ribbons of different colors; tiny bells; and, at the tip, *topfques*, or small bunches of flowers. Old codices depict scenes of pre-Hispanic warriors wearing similar pyramid-shaped headdresses. Each pirate carries a machete in one hand and a kerchief in the other, and has with him a passport, saying that he has come from Champerico Roma, Panama. Both the Muhú and the Pichilingües are well versed about where they have come from to this Chontal land. The

The Pichilingües (pirates), dressed in symbols
of wealth, 1999

Pichilingües' standard is the Virgin of Guadalupe, and their captain, Alférez, is one step
below their emperor, El Rey Mahoma (the King Mohammed).

In their passports the Pichilingües request the right to disembark. They go to the
municipal president, who represents the King of the Chontales, asking after the Muhú
who have boarded their vessels and stolen some of their goods. Alfredo Jiménez López,
one of the Muhú dancers, says the Pichilingües carry with them things of great value, such
as "petates, gold, silver, blankets, pearls, necklaces, and *chapulines*" (grasshoppers, considered to be a delicacy). These were among the treasures paid as tribute by the people of
the coast to the Mixtecs and to the Mexica capital.

The Christians also come to claim the land—although many townspeople say that the
land of the Chontales became Christian, and that the Christians are actually witnesses to
these attempted conquests. The Caballerangos are the Spanish owners of the haciendas
who rode horses (*caballos*). They also represent the time of the conquerors Pedro de
Alvarado and Juan Bello, when the mountainous Chontal lands were dominated by
Spaniards on horseback, with multitudes of soldiers in assistance.

The Muliatas, from the Chontal words for male (*mulyi*) and female (*áata*), are men who
parody women. All of the actors of the yearly drama are men, but the Muliatas are also the
town's homosexuals, who enjoy a bit of dramatic license on this festive occasion. All are
known to their fellow townspeople, although many of the actors keep their heads covered.
Some help prepare the food for the feast, but the Muliatas also have a designated place

and time where they perform. They come with the Pichilingües, and the townspeople say that they are spies who have disguised themselves to learn what their antagonists are planning. This masking is in keeping with other stories of men impersonating women to act as spies, as in the Codex Chimalpopoca.[33]

The Mareños (sea people) are also called Huapis, from Huaves, long-time rivals of the Chontal living along the coast of the Isthmus. Chontal tradition holds that the Huapis, like the other actors in the drama, came to this place from other lands. They, too, come in a group of twelve and are played by Chontales. Across their shoulders they carry atarrayas, round nets used for fishing. Most of them wear light clothing and straw hats and have covered their faces with ash. Their primary role is to care for La Princesa, the alligator princess whom they bring with them and who will bear the name of the mayordomo, or King of the Chontales, and his wife.

In the church, people dress the statue of San Pedro in preparation for his feast. In the municipal building, a tank holds last year's Princesa, now getting too large to carry. The townspeople have decided to catch a smaller, more manageable lagarto. This year, because there is no mayordomo, the municipal authorities prepare an altar in a room at the municipal president's house, where Saint Peter will visit for part of the ceremony. They must also prepare official documents for the Muhú and the Pichilingües, and the other things required for the enactment, including the food and drink, and the sound system.

There are two musical groups. The musicians who play the traditional flute and drum are known as the *chicanteros*, from the Chontal for drum, or *ahuag chicante*, used in the ceremony. The very important *pitero*, or reed flute player, always accompanies the drummer. They usually follow the Muhú and Pichilingües as they try to invade the Chontal lands. The orchestra from Huamelula, which performs throughout the region, is very busy, and sometimes splits up into trios or quartets to accompany other protagonists of the drama.

On the first day of the fiesta, the dancers prepare themselves in the homes of their captains or in a public space. They perform their act of reverence, or reverencia, before the churches of San Sebastian and Saint Peter and before the authorities at the municipality. They dance on the main street to the rhythm of the chicanteros' flute and drum, the oldest music in the village.

The Muhú visit every house to dance for the people there. The dancers introduce themselves in character, saying who they are, where they come from, and the history of what has occurred. Some Chontal say they identify most with the Muhú because, "they are poor and dark like us." The Muhú represent the Huamelulences. They are the popular army, defenders of the original people.

There are Negrito dancers in other parts of México—in Michoacan, Guerrero, and other states—but none are Muhú. African peoples came to New Spain at the time of Conquest, and a large number were brought immediately after. That they had an impact on the indigenous population, intermarried, and became part of some of the longstanding and prominent communities along the coast and inland is evident, and the enactment in Huamelula bears witness to this history. Those who escaped the slave ships in Oaxaca found refuge in a place known as Tonameca, northwest of Huatulco and Huamelula. There were also runaway slaves in Coyula, where port authorities feared they were destabilizing the Native population. Mulattos were scattered throughout the region.[34]

This dance of the Conquest varies from dances in other parts México that incorporate the characters of Cortés and Moctezuma in their performance.[35] The dance in Huamelula mixes elements of the Spanish dance of the Moors and Christians still performed in Spain

Above: Through ritual ceremonies with the alligator, the Chontal reaffirm their relationship with the land, 1999

Right: A Mareño carrying La Princesa while musicians serenade, 2000

The Pichilingües' ship, 2000

and throughout the Western Hemisphere, representing St. James the Moor Slayer (Santiago on horseback, the patron of Astata and of the old abandoned town of Santiago Pijutla). The performance in Huamelula incorporates elements of this medieval dance, and of other dramas imposed by the missionaries to indoctrinate the original Chontal townspeople.

Mesoamerican themes are pervasive in the enactment, though adapted to the Chontales' specific regional history. Nuttall, who first deciphered the Mixtec Zouche-Nuttall Codex, pointed out in 1902 that the codices are almost like dramatic scripts. John Pohl, another expert on the Mixtec codices, writes:

> The Mixtec codices were not meant to be read simply as books, they also served as scripts for the celebration and re-enactment of historical events. The codices could be displayed as "storyboards." A poet recited the text from the codex to musical accompaniment, while actors performed parts of the saga in costume. The setting for these literary and theatrical presentations was the royal feast. Imagine a banquet in which the participants were literally part of the art of the performance. They

attended wearing garments painted with figures of culture heroes and gods while drinking and eating from polychrome pottery decorated with scenes from the codices, and exchanging gifts of gold, shell, bone, and turquoise engraved with images of the founding ancestors of the highest ranking dynasties.[36]

The Chontales are unrelated to the Mixtecs, but they did pay tribute to them before the Spanish Conquest. In any event, throughout Mesoamerica the performance of history was not unusual. In Huamelula, where original papers and land titles have been missing, in some cases for centuries (as they are in much of the region), the Feast of San Pedro is unequivocally the oldest continuous oral and aural documentation of the history of the region, of what has transpired through the centuries on lands originally dominated by the Chontal.

So many incursions took place here before the Spanish Conquest that, in order to follow the narrative, you must understand the histories of the neighboring peoples, their languages, iconography, and other related glosses or symbols. Each incursion and land sale is depicted in the performance. The Muhú, hiding in the mountains, ward off the aggressors each time—other Negritos escaping from their slave ships; the Pichilingüe pirates, well dressed in their ritual paraphernalia, coming from their own ships, followed by the Mareños on foot, with the alligator, the captive princess; the Christians and horsemen.

Hector López Ramírez comes back to Huamelula every year to play the role of the Rey Mahoma. As he tells it, all the characters want to dominate the land, but his character, the Pichilingüe King Mohammed, is the rightful owner of everything, the ocean and the lands. While the performers playing all of these roles are Chontales of the village, the Chontales also witness the drama of re-conquest year after year. They often explain the plot according to their own experiences in real life. For example, people say that they are often asked to show property titles that have never existed, since they have always lived as comuneros on their land. Because so few Chontales could read and write Spanish, others defined the legality of ownership on paper, and thus became the title-bearers of the land.

The Muhú perform their parts for several days, each time repeating their history, allowing for the newer dancers to follow along and learn. Townspeople offer them food and drink and a few pesos here and there, and the dancers collect from as many as they can, helping to offset their costs for participating in the feast.

The Pichilingües join the drama by paying their reverences at the Church of San Sebastián. Then they move toward the muralla, or town wall, a symbolic barrier made of a simple rope tied across the main street, from a post at the school to another by a store. There they are met by the Muhú, who hold them at bay. The pirates make several attempts to penetrate the town before they succeed. People line the streets as the Muhú and the Pichilingües perform and dance. Women laugh at their antics, for the Muhú try everything in their power to hold the pirates on the other side of the wall.

Throughout the days of festivities, people have been decorating ox carts with palm branches, bamboo stalks, greenery, and flowers. All the women and girls, dressed in their finery, carry flowers in a procession to the church, where they leave them before the image of St. Peter. Later there is a dance, part of the Convite de Flores. Women, still proudly wearing their regional dress, dance with each other, with their husbands or boyfriends, and with the Muhú. Men and women must also dance with the statue of La Niña, an ancient wooden effigy, or be charged a penalty, in the form of a fine of money or time in jail.

Left: Crowd watching the performance, 2000

Opposite: Young Muhú in jail, 2000

Over a loudspeaker, the municipal president acknowledges the entire community participating in the event:

Today, the honorable constitutional town of San Pedro Huamelula repeats the great satisfaction that makes us feel truly Huamelulences. Today . . . we relive moments that are of incalculable value for us as a town—the value of the dancers, the value that we place in continuing to conserve our customs, our traditions. . . . Today, as a village of 1,549 people, we have occupied this Chontal territory for more than 550 years. It gives me pride that our compatriot of San Pedro Huamelula, Jaime Zárate Escamilla, has made such an effort for us.

We should all feel proud that we live here and occupy this land of San Pedro Huamelula and all of its agencies; that we continue to conserve the traditions and customs that make us feel each time more Chontal, more Huamelulences. I infinitely appreciate all of the residents and the public, because you have dedicated part of your work and labor so that on this occasion we may all congregate here. Your work will not go unnoticed. Year after year you have constructed the boat. I also appreciate all of the Muhú dancers who have collaborated in the festivities, and in addition the Christians, the Muliatas, the horsemen, and all you men and women who make it possible to continue conserving this tradition.

It is the 28th of June, and the municipal president, this year's King of the Chontales, is heard over the loudspeaker again. Jaime Zárate explains: "The president is calling the captain of los Negros, José Lachimir, who must answer the accusations the Turcos have made that his people have boarded their boats and robbed them. But the captain ignores the announcement because he has a permit to continue to dance. He continues to dance with his group until the Pichilingües come after him." The president, the captain of the pirates, and Aladino Torrencín, Lachimir's second-in-command, act this scene out. By this time, almost every individual in town has taken part in the festivities. A fenced space, symbolizing the Chontal lands, is created on the courtyard in front of the municipal building. Many

people from neighboring villages and Huamelulences from the United States and México are here, not as outsiders, but as relations of the townspeople.

On the morning of the Feast of San Pedro, before, during, and after the mass, many women go up to the altar to bless and cleanse themselves with the flowers. Toward the end of the mass the orchestra plays as the Mareños walk into the church with the alligator in their arms. La Princesa, dressed in a christening outfit, is baptized and given the name of the mayordomo, this year the municipal president, and his wife. The mass is ended and the congregation walks out, following the men carrying the alligator. The orchestra plays "Las Mañanitas," the traditional Mexican tune of welcoming played on the morning of a person's birthday or feast day. The mayordomo leads the procession, carrying the statue of San Pedrito to his home altar, where the saint will stay for the remainder of the fiesta. Copal incense and confetti fill the air. As the procession arrives at the mayordomo's house, copal is used to bless each of the four cardinal points. Songs and prayers continue before St. Peter on his altar. Outside the house, a feast has been prepared and tables set, and soup, totopos, and chocolate are served.

In another part of the town, the Pichilingües have already captured the Muhú and put them in jail. The municipal president continues the inquest against the Muhú. Then the Muhú are taken to the *barca*, the pirates' boat—*ashniunma* in Chontal—created for the ceremony by putting two ox carts together. A long pole representing a ship's mast is lashed upright in the center and flies a red flag. Here the Muhú are hanged, one by one, in punishment for their acts. La Niña, their accomplice, is hanged as well.

On the morning of the 30th, all the groups go throughout the village and dance in the homes of the townspeople, collecting food and money. La Princesa, the alligator, is dressed in white, and as many people as possible dance with her. The Muliatas, too, dance with everyone, covering their faces with Moorish shawls and exposing only their eyes.

Later, the sides of the Pichilingües' boat are covered with petates, and the boat is dressed with sails of purple fabric. The Pichilingües are aboard, and one in particular is sounding the trumpet, as hundreds of the town's children pull the boat by ropes toward the municipal building. All of the other characters meet them at the town square. Some years, they carry Native women they have captured as "slaves." The alligator is taken to the town hall to marry the mayordomo, the Chontal king, and to be introduced as his wife. At the same time, the Pichilingües, Caballerangos, and Christians are outside, attempting to purchase Chontal lands and labor. The Muhú are involved in the negotiation of these purchases, using bottle caps for money, while the others use shells. Now that the municipal

Above and right: Pichilingües, 1999

president and the Mareños are related through marriage, they act as allies. They step outside the municipal building, and the sale of the land is forfeited.

According to Leandro Martínez Machuca, this is what is said during the negotiation of the sale:

In the name of my God, you rich and valued merchants who have crossed oceans and mountains, I ask you: Are you capable of buying all of the mountains of this rich region in exchange for all of the riches of the seven seas?

A Huapi answers: I, the Huapi, fisherman of the seven seas and descendant of the Huave race, buy the lands from King Mohammed and the liberty of the Chontales in exchange for our Huapi princess, who has been held captive for thousands of years at the point known as Arco Iris (Rainbow), by the will of our lord the Huave king.

Later, the Muhú captain states: I, the Muhú captain of the army of the town and defender of San Pedro Huamelula, declare in the name of God and our king, Amashi Tlapique, and of the valiant army of the people of San Pedro: We accept the correctness of our battle with the Huapis. This is as it was. Leave the agreed with the King Mohammed so that in that moment the princess be set free.[37]

The money—shells and bottle tops—is tossed in the air. All are dancing and performing. As mezcal is served to the public, the alligator dances with men who are then accused of violating La Princesa. They are forced to marry her, pay a fine, or go to jail. As all this is happening, those Mareños who are not dancing cast their nets over many of the unsuspecting townspeople watching the performance.

The conquest dance comes to a close for the year. All the performers on the town

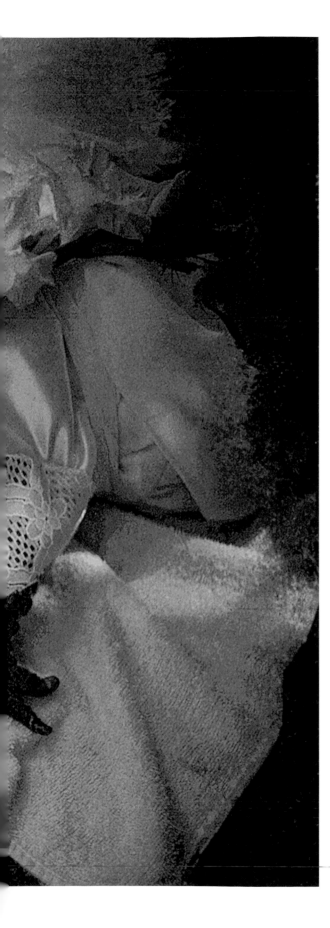

square pay their respects to the community and add part of this year's history to next year's spectacle. The performance is complete. Their marriage to La Princesa has allowed the Chontal to keep their lands. In the end, she is the rightful owner of the land. Aymóo, the alligator, is the symbol of the first day of the Mexica calendar. She is also Cipactonal, the primordial female.[38] She is the monster of the earth, the cave. She has the power to swallow us, to carry anyone away to the middle of the ocean, to the land of the thunderbolts and other encantos. Now, after the solstice, it is summertime, when the alligator is most fecund and the land she inhabits most fertile. And she is fearless in protecting her progeny in the face of encroachment from all sides.

The dance brings us to the present. The Chontal, like indigenous peoples around the world, continue to fight against all odds to maintain their lands and practice their uses and customs. No one really knows how long the Chontal have had to repeat this struggle, or how far and from which direction they have traveled—or been pushed back—to come here. But one fact is certain: the Chontal of the coast are an ancient people who dance with the most ancient of all animals and follow the path of the alligator.

La Princesa in her gown, outside the Church of San Pedro, 1999

El Encanto del Norte
The Enchantment of the North

Baja California: The Peninsula and the Border

The peninsula of Baja California divides the Pacific Ocean and the Sea of Cortés, once known as the Mar Bermejo (the Red Sea). Along the Sea of Cortés, on the eastern side of the peninsula, desert panoramas with deep hues of red and brown earth and occasional mountains stand out against the backdrop of the deeply colored skies and ocean. Ocean currents allow for a somewhat cooler and less severe environment along the Pacific, and the lands there, while still dry, have become a veritable garden.

Indigenous people from all parts of the Mexican Republic have migrated to the state of Baja California Sur, which occupies the southern half of the peninsula, to work in the fields. Many of these people barely speak Spanish, favoring their languages of origin. They make and sell some of the same crafts they made in their homelands, weaving beaded belts on backstrap looms, or making the embroidered clothing they continue to wear in the traditional manner. Some live in enclaves of small houses in the middle of the desert, others in old campers and railway boxcars. There are colonies that include pockets of Nahua from Guerrero, Purepecha from Michoacan, and Oaxacans of different ethnicities. People also come here to work at one of México's most popular tourist resorts, Cabo San Lucas, where the landscape has been overwhelmed by hotels, businesses, and other buildings that look more like the temporary façades of a movie set than permanent structures. Tourist development has been underway much longer here than in Huatulco.

Silverio Lavariega followed the path north that so many from Huatulco and Huamelula have taken. It is almost the same route that Fernando de Alva Ixtlilxochitl wrote that the Toltecs and Quetzalcoatl traveled. At Guaymas in the state of Sinaloa, there's a ferry that takes people across the Sea of Cortés to La Paz, Baja California Sur. After working for a while in the sardine industry in Sinaloa, Silverio crossed over to the peninsula, to a bay whose name has a familiar ring, Pichilingüe Bay, close to La Paz. Huatulco and Piedra de Moros may be three thousand kilometers away, but they share with this place a history of pirate raids. For some migrants, this place is a stop en route to the United States, a way north that bypasses the long Sonora Desert. Others stay and make their living here as fishermen or pearl divers, or by gathering abalone for their shell. Silverio spent several years here working on fishing boats before he returned home. He says, "In Ensenada, Baja Cali-

Left: Desert road and salt lands on the way to Pichilingüe Bay, La Paz, Baja California Sur, 1998

Above: Oaxaqueños planting the fields, Guadalupe, California, 1999

fornia, we belonged to a cooperative for a small bit of time. In Baja California we also caught shrimp. At that time we were on Don Aarón's sardine boats—he had twelve of them. Then we went to Puerto Madero and to Guaymas, to fish for shrimp. I fished for sardines as well."

A few kilometers from the cathedral and the central square of La Paz, the Simeón Martínez family runs a store. The daughters, out of classes for the day from the local university and secondary schools, serve customers shopping for their evening meal. In their house behind the store, Gil Simeón Martínez, a Chinanteco from the northern part of Oaxaca, and his wife and family are preparing dinner as well. Señor Simeón is one of the leaders of the Oaxacan community, a community that continues to grow in this coastal city at the southern tip of the peninsula.

Señor Simeón moved north in search of work, and studied and worked in Mexico City. He eventually arrived in Baja California Sur to help organize some of the campesinos. With others, he has worked together since the 1970s to forge a structure to support many of the indigenous laborers who come from Oaxaca and other parts of México to this state. The Asociación de Oaxaqueños (Association of Oaxacans), in which Simeón plays a leadership role, and the Instituto de Cultura provide a base through which Oaxaqueños in La Paz can maintain cultural activities revolving around their feasts and customs.

Oaxaqueños, working on contract for very little, cultivate and harvest the tomatoes, squash, onions, Brussels sprouts, strawberries, and chilies grown here and exported by truck or ship to the United States. Simeón says that 5,000 to 7,000 contract laborers come from Oaxaca to the area each year, and that a number of Maya travel here to work as well:

They bring their families, including uncles, aunts, and grandparents, to work in this desert land. The money here is almost twice as much as they would make at home. There are also agricultural journeymen who come for the season, but they usually move on to the next harvest. About half of those who

Gil Simeón Martínez and his family, La Paz,
Baja California Sur, 1998

come to harvest stay in this state. Some become
independent of their original group contract.
Some continue going north, to Tijuana, on the
border in the state of Baja California Norte.
Those who eventually want to get to the United
States must first pass through the valley of San
Quintín, where the associations are much better
organized. The costeños [people from the
coast] and others are indigenous groups from
Oaxaca, including the Mixtec, Zapotec, Chi-
nantec, Triqui, Mixe, and Chontal, who come
from close to Salina Cruz.

Simeón says that the Oaxaqueños
speak at least nineteen distinct dialects
and languages. He says that his association, which has received state and
national support, provides different types
of assistance, based on his own experi-
ence and the experiences of others. It emphasizes the "preservation and respect of our
cultural traditions," he says, in part through the establishment of commissions responsible for traditional crafts, culture, sports, youth, health, justice, and special events. It also
promotes solidarity with human rights organizations of indigenous peoples throughout
México and from other countries, and represents the voice of the indigenous workers in
this part of the world.

Baja California Norte

In the distance, one sees men, women, and children working in a field, their backs bent.
They have been working since the early hours of the morning. A truck holds large ther-
moses of water, and they gather there for a break and to joke with one another. Then it is
time to get back to work. The sun is bright overhead. It is barely eleven, and already the
heat and dirt are adding to the strain of their work. They all wear large bandanas over their
heads, and many cover their mouths as well, against the dust and whatever is sprayed on
the crops. The tomatoes, grapes, cucumbers, and other vegetables and fruits they are
picking will soon garnish the plates of people in the United States. Many of the workers,
too, are on their way to El Norte.

Maneadero is three or four hours from the border, south of Ensenada. It is one of the
way stations where so many migrant workers stay on the way to the crossing. They have
come up from Baja California Sur, or perhaps through the mountains and desert of the
Mexican interior, to this place where there is work. Many who come with the intention of
continuing northward stay in this makeshift town, in homes made from found materials,
anything that will provide a roof overhead—wood, cardboard, tin, plastic. The children go
to school, and many also work to help their families. Within the town there are colonies
separated by language and culture.

After they leave the fields, many people make the crafts vendors sell to tourists in the more pleasant surroundings of Ensenada. They create what they can with the materials they can afford, using skills they learned at home. Those who are a little better-off do weaving and embroidery, paint rice, or make vessels or reproductions of clay and plaster.

A woman from Oaxaca weaves under an enramada made from a few timbers found in an area where there is little vegetation. Children bathe in old washtubs, happily squirming or screeching as the cold water is poured over their hair. A young mother from Oaxaca takes the embroidery she is working on from a plastic bag, holding the needle and multi-colored yarns, and proudly shows it off. Before she can work on it, she must prepare a meal for her children. They have all just arrived from the fields. They will help their mother with their chores before they go out to play with the other children.

California

The Oaxacan restaurant, the mercado in Santa Monica, and the Oaxacan newspaper all announce the Guelaguetza, a Zapotec word meaning gift or reciprocal exchange. This part of Los Angeles, near Loyola High School, where some of the city's oldest families used to live, is now home to thousands upon thousands of Oaxacan immigrants and first, second, and third generation children. Today, in mid-August, above the hum of English, Spanish, Zapotec, Mixtec, and the many other languages spoken in their home state, the governor of Oaxaca is on-stage along with Los Angeles politicians to greet them. People have come by the thousands to celebrate the Guelaguetza as it is done in Oaxaca. Harvest bounty—mostly fruits like pineapples, bananas, and papayas, and vegetables, such as squash and corn—is presented and, literally, thrown into the audience after dancers from various parts of Oaxaca perform. Because this is the United States, the festival also includes civil rights workers and volunteers coming to get signatures for a legal claim against the telegraph company. The company has been accused of exploiting millions of dollars from poor Oaxaqueños who wire their money home to their families.

The dancers in the *folklórico* group are children of parents who yearn for their place of origin, and who have ingrained in their own children a love of their culture. It is estimated that there are at least 80,000 indigenous Mexicans residing in California alone; Los Angeles has the second largest population of Mexicans outside of México. The Oaxacans at the Guelaguetza—who represent all of the indigenous ethnic groups and villages of that state—comprise only one small portion of the total Mexican and Latino population of the United States, and the costeños from the Mar del Sur, far removed from their encantos, are just a small part of this larger group of Oaxacans. Most Oaxaqueños here, like the majority of Mexicans in the United States, work in the fields, orchards, and hot-houses. Others work in service—cleaning, busing dishes, caring for children. Many of the women, like Leticia, who is Elizabeth and Jaime's cousin from Huamelula, work in the clothing industry, sewing for a living, at home or in factories.

Leticia is doing well in the United States and is a permanent resident. She has the assured bearing of the Chontal women, and the same pride in what she wears and how she looks. She grew up in Huamelula, and both her mother and father were from Chontal villages, but when her parents separated, she moved to the state of Veracruz. Though she rarely visits Huamelula, she remembers it well, and keeps in close touch with her cousins, speaking to them frequently over the telephone. She has no children, and she wishes that some of her family would come to live nearby. She says:

Oaxacan woman weaving on a backstrap loom, San Quintín, Baja California Norte, 1998

Bananas, part of the harvest bounty tossed to the crowd at the Guelaguetza in Los Angeles, California, 1999

The adobe house that is in front [of my Tía María's] belonged to my grandmother, and it was very beautiful. It's almost about to fall. My aunt doesn't want anyone to knock it down. It's like a relic, because this is where my Mamá Juana lived. My grandparents spent their childhood there, my grandmother, Juana Robles Alegría, and my grandfather, Agustín Escamilla. I never addressed her as grandmother. For me, she was my mother.

My uncle Abraham Escamilla visited once. There are two uncles. When they arrived, I thought I was seeing my two cousins, sons of my mother's brother, the oldest brother of my Mamá Juana. They looked just like my cousins, but they live in Santa María de las Ollas, near Santiago Astata, and San Pedro Huamelula.

There are so many rich things [in Huamelula]. Many people have gone to the caves, to explore, as they call it. They say that these people just don't come out. Some people have come out, but when they do, they're crazy. They say the place is huge, and it has only a small opening through which they enter. My grandmother would always tell us that it was a bad, malign place because it was a place having to do with the devil, according to some of the legends that are told. There are beautiful things as well that I don't recall. It is just that the entrance to Huamelula has left me with such an impression, mainly because of those large mountains that have figures of things at the entrance. I haven't really seen the figures, although I made a video of the entrance when I went there. These figures cause fear because as one walks along the path to that place, the mountains make a very strong echo. A river runs between the two mountains, and they are so impressive. I was very frightened at night. I wouldn't pass through there at that time. My grandmother said that the place was enchanted, that it was an enchantment. She said that many gringos had gone in and that there were people who never came out, and those who did said they had seen the devil. When they came out they were crazy after what they had seen inside.

But this is what I remember most about Huamelula: I remember the small cathedral there. I remember its river. I have so many anecdotes about the river. Then it was a huge, beautiful river. I would jump in to swim. Now I think it is dry, but it used to be an enormous river. I loved to climb up the mango trees to cut mangoes. My grandmother, who was a very strict woman, would say, "Come down, child." I would climb up the mango tree, and my grandmother would come after me, behind my back with her belt. "Come down from there, my love, come down from there, my little queen, or you will fall," she would say with so much affection. When we got down, she'd really give it to us!

Once she was after me with the belt because I loved to go swimming. She would tell me I was a tomboy. I loved to dig for those large shrimp known as chacales. I liked to get them from the rocks. I also loved to go through all of the hill-sides. I loved to run. I would find fruit, and I loved to cut fruit, fresh mango, papayas, guavas. There was a young gringa in Huamelula, as well. She stayed there. I just remembered her. Miss Viola, they would call her. She was very nice. I don't know where she is now. We would visit her at home, and she would preach "the word of God" to us. My Mamá Juana belonged to her religion. That's what I remember about my childhood.

Several hundred kilometers north of Los Angeles, along the fields of the central California coast, Oaxaqueños are planting broccoli and other green vegetables. Men and women plant seedlings, following a large tractor. These fields, in Guadalupe and Santa María, California, are as familiar as the fields of Baja California and Oaxaca, but the machinery is new. Depending on the time of year and the type of harvest, workers are paid by the hour, sometimes as little as a dollar an hour, or by the number of crates they can fill in a day. Some work for as long as sixteen hours a day. Few people will do this backbreaking labor for such substandard wages. Even so, most employers prefer to hire Oaxaqueños because they work hard, pay their bills, and save. These farm laborers are of all ages and from all parts of Oaxaca. They share apartments or live in camps operated by the farms. There are other labor camps, where the waiting list is long. Some are old trailer camps. Others have nicer homes available at affordable prices for the laborers and their families as long as they follow camp policies.

Those who identify strongly with their Native origins keep home lives much like the ones they lived in Oaxaca, with relatives all around, and find the resources to practice their customs and traditions. Activities for Oaxaqueños are announced over the Spanish-language radio stations, such as Radio Bilingüe, run by Hugo Morales, of Mixtec origin, who studied at Harvard and received a MacArthur "genius" award. Radio is a primary source of information, since there are many people who cannot read. This station and others reach broad audiences of indigenous laborers with news and music from home, and programs designed to inform people about social services and cultural events.

Sonoma Valley is one of the last stops for many Oaxacans, though many continue up to the states of Oregon and Washington, as well. Many are Mixtec and Zapotec. Others don't know their parents' language. Many of their children speak only English. Some people take years making their way this far from home; others come directly to Sonoma, after relatives have assured them that there will be work.

Over half a century has passed since Señor and Señora Morales left Oaxaca, time

Oaxaqueños stopping for a break from planting, Guadalupe, California, 1999

enough to raise a family of accomplished children who are now prominent and influential in Northern California. Señor Morales's hard work and keen ability won the confidence of the owner of some of the vineyards where he worked, and he became a foreman, able to hire many other Oaxacans who wanted to work. Now that he has retired, he tends his own garden, growing delicious fruits and vegetables. Señor and Señora Morales are proud and knowledgeable of their Mixtec heritage. He has built an oven on his patio, and likes to make bread for Día de los Muertos and for community events in which he and his wife participate. Between them, the Morales have helped many people make the transition between their home villages and Northern California. But time has not erased the memory of the pain, struggle, and loneliness that señora Morales felt as a young wife far away from her home, and tears still well up in her eyes when she thinks of it.

The immigration of Native Oaxacans and other indigenous Mexicans is on the rise, although the number of people in the United States from the region along the Mar del Sur is not as well-documented as it is for groups from other parts of Oaxaca. Expropriation of land and tourist development began to displace these people as recently as the late 1980s. But the Mixtec labor force in California alone is estimated to be between 20,000 and 30,000. The Zapotec labor force in Los Angeles and San Diego is estimated to be 15,000 to 20,000. A recent study shows that México's economic crisis, combined with the need for labor in California, has sustained the "recurrent cycle of ethnic replacement that has characterized California's farm labor history."[1] Mexican Natives have followed such other groups to California as the Chinese, Japanese, Filipino, "Okies," and Mexican mestizos. And once here, they maintain strong social and familial networks across a border that remains permeable to the first peoples of the continent.

New Jersey

A young Chontal man from along the Pacific coast of Oaxaca walked into the desert with only water and a change of clothing, not knowing what to expect. The young man next to him carried less water and no extra clothing. They walked for three days, seeking the shade of cacti and rocks, anything that would allow them a moment out of the scorching sun. The "coyote" who "arranged" their passage did not prepare them for the worst. When the second man fell behind, with almost no water left to drink, a parched throat, chills, fever, and leaden feet, the young Chontal slowed his pace and shared his water. They made it to the Río Bravo (Rio Grande). For a moment it seemed that one of the requests the young Chontal had made at El Pedimento was about to be fulfilled. Then he was caught at the river and returned to México. This is the experience of many young Mexicans. El Norte has its mystery, its enchantment. Coming here has become a rite of passage for a large number of mestizo and indigenous youth. And it is not just the youth—adults, too, seek a better life, and opportunities not offered at home. Entire villages are left with only grandparents caring for grandchildren. The generation between has had to leave, to find a way to support their families when the soil becomes barren and there is no other recourse.

The tourist economy and the presence of tourists in places such as the coast of Oaxaca are also partly responsible for an exodus not seen in other regions. When tourist development first started along the Mar del Sur, many of the entrepreneurs from outside the region said that those they hired locally "were lazy and did not want to work." This drew workers from other states in México. But the tourist hotels failed to attract as much business as investors expected. Hurricanes, earthquakes, and other natural disasters were crippling both for local farmers and workers, and for the tourist industry, and political conflicts and guerrilla uprisings contributed to the slowdown. In the last few years, things have improved for the local population. As international tourism ebbed, more Mexican visitors began to vacation there. Better roads also helped. All this has slowly worked in favor of the local people, who are being trained and hired more often. Many who now live in El Norte have plans to return home. Others continue to come north, if only for a few years, to earn and save money that will allow them to help their families, or build small houses or businesses in Oaxaca. The communities in which they live have changed from small hamlets of humble adobe and thatched homes, where people use wells for water, to large cement-and-cinderblock developments. So the young people of Huatulco and Huamelula—Chontal, Zapotec, Huave, and Chatino—look for work in California, Arizona, Texas, Oklahoma, Illinois, North Carolina, Michigan, Florida, New York, New Jersey, and many other states.

Yadira, a young teacher from Huatulco, who taught preschool in La Crucecita and took her laundry to the wash lady who lives behind Tío Nacho, now lives in New Jersey, where her own child was born in the spring. She and her husband decided that they, too, wanted to make their dream come true and that the time to take the risk was when they were newly married. Her husband now works at a restaurant in a mall. Yadira worked at McDonald's for a while, but her husband says that she would come home crying because she did not understand what people were saying. They are lucky, compared to many of their compatriots. Yadira's husband says that his boss is very good and remembers what it was like when he first arrived from Greece.

This comfortable town, a bedroom community to a larger township, has its own Oaxacan market. The Huatulqueños here are all interrelated. Felix, the young man who crossed the desert, now has a job at a deli just across the way from Yadira's husband. Yadira's brothers, Carlos and Emanuel, work in the fields and in landscaping with Ulises, Francisco's brother from Rancho Tangolunda. Felix's cousin and Yadira's, who are married, left their sons with her mother in México; they both have two jobs. At least eight people share a formidable Victorian house. The large parlor and sitting rooms have been subdivided into bedrooms. Some of the housemates leave for work at four o'clock in the morning. They all rotate in and out between their first and second jobs. The women work as maids and housekeepers, or in the service industry alongside the men, who are often waiters and dishwashers. Their large dining room has become the place where all congregate comfortably during the little time they have off from work. They watch soccer, novelas, and the news on Spanish-language TV. The landlord charges them $1,500 a month for the downstairs space, where they live, and about the same amount for upstairs, which is rented to migrant workers, as well.

These husbands and wives, brothers and sisters, friends and cousins have come farther perhaps, than most people who leave the Mar del Sur, but there are many others from home in this part of New Jersey. The names, stretched over a large region of the Mar del Sur, cover different topographies. Some of the young people are mestizo, others identify strongly as Chontal, and others are Zapotec. On Monday evenings, a soccer team made up of players from Huatulco competes against teams of players from Pochutla, the Isthmus, and many other places in Oaxaca. Centuries of ethnic rivalry along the Mar del Sur— echoes, perhaps, of ball games played by the ancients—persist here on a friendly field.

From right: Yadira, her husband Carlos, and her brother Carlos in New Jersey, 1999

Epilogue

Throughout Huatulco and Huamelula, boundaries have been contested since before the Spanish Conquest and have been the subjects of litigation from 1539 to the present. Many factors account for the importance of these lands, including control of a great wealth of natural resources and the strategic significance of certain locations to war and trade. Pre-Hispanic codices illustrated with symbols of riches show that this region was an important source of tribute to Zapotec-, Mixtec-, and Nahua-speakers. Most important to the original peoples of this place, however, are the security and continuity of community sovereignty and identity, the tie to their place of origin. The historical narrative performed in San Pedro Huamelula celebrates the tenacity with which they have held onto their lands. Yet most of the stories of place, time, and migration recounted here contain an *añoranza*— a lament or yearning—over the absence of a past, and a sense of imminent loss that seems constant. This yearning transcends time and places all loss in the present, although the loss may have taken place long before the Spanish Conquest.

The narrators who tell many of the stories in this book weave metaphor with fact. In addition, they raise themes that have endured throughout Mesoamerica, such as the origin of corn or the story of the flood. Communities have long maintained their niche in the world as sacred. Note that Cerro Isla, or Cerro Huatulco, a hill surrounded by water, is a garden paradise that must not be violated. Note, too, that this encanto is one of the most salient boundaries of the region. Many groups tell stories of giants or gentiles who lived on mountaintops. And indeed, there are many ancient settlements on precipices throughout the region, with evidence of old terracing similar to that practiced elsewhere throughout México and other parts of Mesoamerica. Brockington noted some of these similarities in the late 1960s and early 1970s, when he worked in the region.[2]

Pre-Hispanic codices describe the conquest by heroes of territories in lands adjacent to this region, yet many of the important places recorded in these documents remain unidentified by scholars. There may be several reasons for this. For one thing, this part of the Americas is prone to earthquakes, hurricanes, and other natural disasters that can erase whole chapters from the story of the land. Historically, there has been a great deal of movement within the region, in addition to devastating epidemics of smallpox. Strategies for survival included hiding in remote caves and natural fortresses in the mountains, or joining less vulnerable communities. Finally, as we have seen, each ethnic group, sometimes each hamlet, has its own names for the same places. All this makes the challenging task of reconstructing an early picture of the region even more difficult.

The story associated with the encanto near Astata is a narrative we heard many times. The encanto is a grotto where beautiful gourds appear to be floating in the water. Anyone who reaches for them is swept away, to return only after everything has changed. In a footnote in *Crónica Mixteca*, Anders, Jansen, and García discuss the pictographs related to those places conquered by the Mixtecs. They say:

> The names of the places conquered during this campaign do not appear
> in the codices as names of the Mixtec señoríos. This is why we think
> that they deal with a campaign outside the Mixtec territory that took
> Lord 8 Deer away from his land of birth, accompanying the Toltec chief.
> [In the Codex Zouche-Nuttall] as well as in the Codex Colombino . . . a
> great deal of importance is given to the scene where the conquerors
> cross an extension of water. It is clear that it is not just an ordinary river.
> The Colombino adds many multicolor waves and illustrates that some
> [individuals] crossed on canoes, while others swam with the help of
> gourds. The column that supports the sky probably signifies that there
> one can see the extensive horizon. The sky rests over the water.[3]

The authors go on to say that "by all indications, it appears" that the conquerors "had reached the ends of the earth," by a lagoon that was next to the ocean. The place was in a tropical location to the east, and the narrative deals with the journey of Quetzalcoatl. Anders, Jansen, and García pose Yucatan as the setting. However, that idea has not been firmly established. From Tututepec, where 8 Deer was the sovereign, Huatulco and Huamelula are to the east. The region had not yet been conquered by the Chichimec Toltecs at that time, and certainly not by the Mexica, who came much later. The coast of the Mar del Sur could possibly be one place shown in the Codex Colombino.

Native peoples throughout the Western Hemisphere never discount their stories. They know that the word of their elders is sacred. Recent work by Heather Harris comparing the stories in oral tradition with geologic time lays to rest the idea that these stories are myths with no credence, or that they are allusions related solely to cosmology.[4]

The story of the grotto can be heard as a metaphor for migration. Migration poses a longing for those absent and for those left behind, even when the loss is temporary. And people have always migrated, throughout time.

Mixtec transnational migrants and migrant workers of other ethnicities in México have been the focus of a great deal of attention during the 1990s and continuing into this decade. Scholars in the United States and México argue that the recent migration of indigenous peoples has brought a very different and complex set of relationships into the global economy, as more and more migrants see both countries as home, both as temporary and permanent.[5]

The impact of increasing numbers of people, especially the youth, migrating north has yet to be measured in places like Huatulco and Huamelula, where the forces driving migration are new. The people we spoke to seem to have maintained a strong sense of identity, thanks to their close ties to their families in their Mexican hometowns. Although migrants from Huatulco and Huamelula have been relatively isolated in the United States until very recently, they phone their families as often as possible, in some cases every Sunday. They keep up with their roles within their families, and they return to the Mar del Sur. Often, they arrange their visits to follow the ritual cycle of the region, returning to fulfill a charge as mayordomo or take part in other important ways in the feasts and ceremonies.

People continue to visit El Pedimento. It draws many from far communities, speaking other languages, and many who return from the north. So do the Fridays of Lent, lending their Catholic disguise to the old market days and to the trade routes along the ancient paths. Now the markets carry goods advertised on television, over the radio, and by word of mouth from those who live outside the region or in the United States. In the old mercados, metates are offered for sale alongside CD players, and Norteño music is played along with local marimba, coastal *chilenas*, and Zapotec songs, while in New York City, Oaxaqueños sell flowers on the street.

At the Feast of San Pedro, women beautifully adorned in their Native attire dance to cumbias and local sones with the Negritos, as the orchestra performs on a stage with five-foot speakers. Later, as part of the enduring tradition, the men dance with the alligator, dressed as a bride, accompanied by the bass saxophone and the large band.

La Princesa, Huamelula, 1999

End Notes

THE PLACE AT THE EDGE OF THE SEA

1. Documents from the Archivo Municipal de Huatulco (AMH). These documents were located by a colleague and me where they had been forgotten in a warehouse when the municipal building was being remodeled. After sorting through the moldy leaflets, boxes, and debris left in this room, we found one packet wrapped in turquoise plastic. This packet held more than forty-nine original documents dating from 1500s to the 1900s and an index. The book mentioned was not among them, nor was the book of tributes and a few other sources. These were located later, after making several inquiries.

2. Several sources have been consulted in order to understand the etymology of the names in this region. Since this area is a juncture, where at least four to five languages have been used, not to mention the fact of dialectical differences between, for example, lowland and highland Zapotec and Chontal, a great deal of consideration has been given to each place name. The Nahuatl that was spoken in the area pre-dates a form spoken in other areas. In addition, each of the villages has its own name for a particular landmark, and some place names simply become obsolete after they have been abandoned for long periods.

3. AMH, doc. 3, 1539, fojas 7–8.

4. AMH, doc. 3, 1539, fojas 7–8; AMH, doc. 2, 1539, foja 13. Many indigenous villages in Oaxaca and elsewhere in México have old maps, or *lienzos*, that help determine the boundaries of the original settlements. Some of these maps are drawn on cloth (lienzo means linen or cloth), some on the bark paper made traditionally in México of *amate*, some on deerskin vellum. A few pre-date the Spanish Conquest. Most illustrate in abbreviated form the Native states and their *señoríos* or *cacicazgos*, their rulers or heads. Most of the *Relaciones* were accompanied by maps, but Huatulco's map is missing. A photograph of a lienzo was found with the 16th-century *fojas*, but it has not yet been deciphered, nor does anyone know what became of the original.

5. AMH, doc. 48, antes 45, *Titulación del Pueblo de Santa Maria, copia cotejada a maquina,* 1950. This collection of several notarized and sealed copies of documents, with different dates from the 1700s, consists of several petitions and claims related to the pirate raids, tributes, and delimitations of lands.

6. *"Casiques que estan retratados bajo de la Iglesia son los fundadores y pobladores de este pueblo como constara la pintura de la fundación antigua Hus ecli de celebramos esta escritura con graves . . . pena de mil pesos para la Caja Real del Rey Nuestro Señor el que maltrata a estos dos pueblos asi entregamos su posesión con todas las mojoneras y con escritura y título jurídico y Vista todos la republica de la cabecera de Huamelula juntamente con el casique don Juan de Zúñiga quien conquistó el pueblo cabecera de Huamelula que Yo dueño de Salinas de los Tunales de Máscalo Horiada y sus Salinas de todas las Salinas de hoy otro como las de Tunales . . . dicho Casique fué el que fundó el pueblo de San Miguel de Huatulco y el pueblo de Santa María de Huatulco como binieron los testigos y Gobernadores del pueblo de San Mateo de las Piñas quedaron de testigos de Vista de la posesión de los del pueblo de Huatulco."*

7. Francisco del Paso y Troncoso, *Papeles de la Nueva España: segunda serie geografía y estadistica,* tomo IV. Manuscritos de la Real Academia de la Historia de Madrid y del Archivo de Indias en Sevilla. Años 1579–1581 (Madrid, 1905), page 248. There is a more recent version of these *Relaciones,* edited by René Acuña: *Relaciones geográficas del siglo XVI: Antequera tomo primero.* (México: UNAM, 1984). However, it must be noted that the document from the AMH predates these inquiries by at least fifty years.

8. René Acuña, *Relaciones geográficas del siglo XVI,* pp. 188, 189, 203.

9. Daniel Hiernaux-Nicolas, *La geografía como metáfora de la libertad : Textos de Eliseo Reclus* (México: Centro de Investigacion Científica "Ing. Jorge L. Tamayo," 1999). The geographer Eliseo Reclus wrote in 1895: "The best port of the coast is the one of Huatulco, or Guatulco (Coatulco), that is to say, 'The place of the Great Serpent.' The mouth is about 600 meters wide. It allows access to the bay that is well-guarded from the winds, where large boats find depths of seven to sixteen meters, decreasing gradually towards the shoreline. On the elevation from the beach of the port is the villa of Crespón, a small village of fishermen who collect pearl oysters and *Purpúra* shells (*Aptisia depictans*). On one of the exterior promontories the abyss of the ocean is concentrated in caverns and breaks through a blowhole over fifty meters above the waves. One can see ancient Zapotec or Huabi (Huave) steps and remains of buildings on the esplanade of one of the nearby promontories. A now ruined city of a neighboring country was the capital of the Huabi nation, a colony of navigators that were supposedly from Perú and which has settled in one of the villages close by, Jalapa Marqués." Author's footnote attributed to J. W. von Muller, *Beitrag zur Geschichte, Statistik und Geologie von Mexiko.*

10. Manuel Martínez Grácida , *Catálogo etimológico de los nombres de los pueblos, haciendas y ranchos del Estado de Oaxaca* (Oaxaca: Imprenta del Estado en el Ex-obispado, 1883), p. 51.

11. Paso y Troncoso, *Papeles de la Nueva España*, p. 234.

12. Pedro de Pantoja was an old *poblador*, or early settler of New Spain. He acquired Cimatlan, Cacalotepec, and other areas close along the Pacific Coast in what is described as "Cortes' Pacific seaport." Cimatlan and Cacalotepec were retained as crown properties after 1533. Robert Himmerich y Valencia, *The Encomenderos of New Spain, 1521–1555* (Austin: University of Texas Press, 1996), p. 211.

13. Maximiliano Amador Lavariega, unpublished family document, 1987.

14. Peter Gerhard, *A Guide to the Historical Geography of New Spain*, revised edition (Norman: University of Oklahoma Press, 1993), p. 125.

15. Viola Waterhouse, "The Grammatical Structure of Oaxaca Chontal," in *International Journal of American Linguistics*, vol. 28, no. 2, April 1962 (Bloomington: Indiana University Research Center), pp. 5 and 105–117. Chontal is connected only to language in Honduras and to the old languages on the border of California and Arizona. The origin of the Chontal language remains a puzzle, with various conjectures and theories. To date, Viola Waterhouse has offered the best summary of the linguistic debate related to the Oaxacan Chontal language, which was previously classified as Mayan and Nahuatl. The Hokan relationship is attributed to Kroeber in 1915. While some call both coastal and mountain Chontal Tequistlateco, Waterhouse prefers to distinguish the Coastal Chontal dialect from the Tequistlateco mountain dialect. There are a number of other subclassifications of the language after Hokan, such as Macro Yuman and Coahuilan.

16. Francisco de Burgoa, *Geográfica descripción de la parte septentrional, del Polo Ártico de la América* (Oaxaca: Instituto Oaxaqueño de las Culturas, 1997). The ecclesiastic chroniclers reported that the Chontal "ate" one of the tribute collectors.

17. Huntington Library, HM 27 Portulano 1553, foja 5,7, 15; HM 25, Portolan 1550, fojas 4, 5, 12; HM 10, Portulano 30, VI.921, fojas 2, 3, 5. Portulano and Portolan are used by the Huntington Library.

18. *Des Herrn Thiery de Menonville Reife, mach Guaxaca in Neu Spanien.* Uberfecto vo. Bibliothefax Reichard. Leipzig, in der Gehgandfchen Buchandlung 1789. Treatise.

19. H. Harrington, *View of South America and México*, vol. 1 (1825), p. 113.

20. P. J. Bakewell, *Minería y sociedad en el México colonial:Zacatecas (1546–1700)* (México: Fondo de Cultura Económica, 1984), p. 104.

21. Paso y Troncoso, *Papeles de la Nueva España.*, page 26; Gerhard, *Guide to the Historical Geography of New Spain*, pp. 123–126.

22. Archivo General de la Nación (AGN) Mercedes, vol. 3, exp. 232, fs. 1–2, año 1550.

23. AGN Mercedes, vol. 3, exp. 663, año de 1551.

24. AGN Mercedes, vol. 41, exp. S/N, f. 88 (89), año 1554.

25. AGN Mercedes, vol. 41, exp. S/N, f. 88 (89), año de 1554.

26. Peter Gerhard, *Pirates on the West Coast of New Spain, 1575–1742* (Glendale: Arthur H. Clark, 1960), page 34–36. Gerhard also quotes from Francis Pretty, *The Admirable and Prosperous Voyage of the Worshipfull Master Thomas Cavendish*, in Richard Hakluyt, *Principal Navigations, Voyages, and Discoveries of the English Nation*, vol. III (London: Dent and Sons, 1600), p. 814.

27. Lavariega, unpublished family document. Extolling the virtues of the harbor at Huatulco, the deputy governor stated, "The storms that are likely to strike this coast are during the rainy season, some southeasters that saturate the Port and pass quickly; but they never endanger the ships that have good anchors and mooring lines."

28. AGN General de Parte, vol. 5, exp. 954, fs. 259, año de 1599.

29. Huntington Library, HM 918, *Derrotero general del Mar del Sur*, 1669, folios 6–20. HM 265 Hack, William, *A Description of the Sea Coasts in the South Sea of America* , 1684, fs. 1–6. HM 518 *Derrotero y noticias de las corrientes y vientos reynantes en las costas y los mares*, 1798, fs. 76–94.

30. Gerhard, *Pirates on the West Coast of New Spain, 1575–1742*, p. 101. Leandro Martínez Machuca of Huamelula suggests an alternative derivation of Pichilingue from coastal Chontal: "little yellow ducks" (*pichi* = little yellow and *lingi* = ducks). See also endnotes 29 and 30 from the chapter "Poblados."

31. AMH, doc. 24. *". . . por cuanto decimos a nosotros Naturales de este Pueblo Jurisdicción del Puerto de Huatulco, y decimos que no tenemos papeles ni mercedes, ni instrumentos, si tuviéramos presentamos ante Usted, que estamos nosotros muy pobres, y cuando entró el Inglés de nuestro pueblo nos llevó los papeles, nos quedamos sin instrumento ninguno, esto es lo que declaramos ante usted, que si usted nuestro Juez Privativo, y nos mira con ojos de piedad, y caridad que nos ampare a nosotros pobres naturales que somos tributarios del Rey Nuestro Señor que Dios guarde. . . ."*

32. AMH, doc. 48, antes 45, *Titulación del Pueblo de Santa Maria, copia cotejada a maquina, 1950.*

33. Wandering cattle were among the grievances cited by the people of Huatulco in the petition of 1702: "We ask and supplicate through our Dear Lord, the manner in which our work is carried out with the Spaniard whose name is Bartolome de la Torre who has a Hacienda of cattle that is very close to our village, about half a league from where he had his home and the corral for his cattle. It comes into our village and it does much harm. It eats our banana plants, our corn, and our cotton. Since we are poor and we do not have a way to make the tribute to the King, nor charity, and our obligation is to support our poor selves; this is what we declare. . . ." *". . . [P]edimos, y suplicamos por el Señor Dios la manera de nuestro trabajo lo que pasamos con un*

español, se llama Bartolomé de la Torre tenía una Hacienda de ganado mayor, está muy cerca de nuestro pueblo como media legua a donde lo tenía su casa, y su corral de ganado, nos entra a nuestro pueblo, nos hace mucho daño y come nuestro platanar y milpas y algodón, por que somos pobres, que no tenemos por donde sacar el tributo del Rey, y más limosna, y nuestra obligación para sustentarnos a nosotros pobres está lo que declaramos ante saber. Don Luis Eugenio de Valenzuela. Don Gregorio de Velásquez. Juan Martín." AMH, doc. 24.

34. AGN Mercedes, vol. 3, exp. 824–825, año de 1551, p. 179.

35. AGN General de Parte, vol. 5, exp. 954, f. 259, año 1599.

36 AGN Tierras, vol. 4, ff. 52 to 68, año 1723.

BAHÍAS / BAYS

1. Fernando de Alva Ixtlilxóchitl, *Obras Históricas*, tomo I–II (1898), edited by Edmundo O'Gorman (México: UNAM, 1975), p. 28.

2. Enrique Fernandez Dávila and Susana Gómez Serafín, *Arqueología de Huatulco, Oaxaca: Memoria de la primera temporada de campo del poryecto arqueológico Bahías de Huatulco* (Mexico: SEP-INAH, 1988).

3. AGN Mercedes, vols. 5–6, ff 102v., 281v; vol.5, f. 70v; vol.8, ff. 71, 251. Rolf Widmer, *Conquista y despertar de las costas de la Mar del Sur (1521–1684).* (México:Consejo Nacional Para La Cultura Y las Artes, 1990).

4. José Antonio Gay, *Historia de Oaxaca* (México: Editorial Porrúa "Sepan Cuantos," no. 373, 1990), p. 51, fn. 2.

From Manuel Martínez Gracida, Gay states: "Huatulco Santa María, municip., dist. de Pochutla. Cuauhtolco. Sig. En mex. Lugar donde se reverencía un madero. Etim. Cuahuitl, leño ó madero; toloa, inclinar la cabeza por reverencia; co, lugar de. Esta etimología se le da por la Cruz que allí, segun se dice, puso Santo Tomás; pero en el Libro de los Tributos, el geroglífico de Huatulco es una cabeza de águila de la cual sale una rama de árbol con una flor en la punta; circunstancia que me hace creer que el verdadero nombre es Cuauhtxochco, y en este caso significa En Arbol Florido Donde Estaba Una Aguila. Etim. Cuahuitl, árbol; cuauhtli, águila; xochitl, flor; co, en."

On p. 296, Gay cites Francisco de Burgoa, *Geográfica descripción.* This is what Burgoa records about the holy wooden cross: "Our Lord reserved [in Huatulco] the triumphal standard of his holy passion and death in one very outstanding and beautiful cross which is more than 1500 years of antiquity. Without understanding its highest mysteries, these gentiles adored the cross like a divine object, as a general office for the remedy of all their needs and as a general pharmacy for all their illnesses. Observing the notices and memoirs of the elders by computing their centuries and ages, they also saw its correspondence with the apostles, with the dress worn by the apostles, the long tunic, tightened with a mantle, the long hair and beard, embracing the cross. In awe of the wonder, they gathered at the beach to see

him, and he greeted them in a benevolent manner in their native tongue; and some days he showed them many things they did not understand; and the majority of days and nights he remained on his knees, kneeling and he ate very little and when he wanted to leave he told them with the sign [symbol] of all their healing, to venerate and respect it and that the time would come when the true God and Lord would become known."

5. Gay, *Historia de Oaxaca*, p. 51. Gay discusses Quetzalcoatl and says that historians compare him to the apostle Saint Thomas. He uses Veitia as a source for the etimology of Quauhlolco, composed from Quauhtli, meaning *madero* or wood; the verb *toloa*, to revere by bowing the head; and *co*, which means place: "place where the wood is adored": "Su verdadero nombre, según Veitia, es Quauhlolco, compuesto de Quauhtli, 'madero' del verbo toloa, que significa hacer reverencia bajando la cabeza, y so, que denota lugar. El todo quiere decir: "lugar donde se adora el madero."

6. Lavariega, unpublished family document.

7. HM 918, *Derrotero general del Mar Del Sur*, 1669, f. 14. HM 265 William Hack, *A Description of the Sea Coasts in the South Sea of America*, 1684, f. 4.

8. Paso y Troncoso, *Papeles de Nueva España*, p. 26.

9. Gerhard, *Pirates on the West Coast of New Spain*, and AMH doc. 24, 1700s to 1844. As Gerhard describes Cavendish's arrival: "Since he was reasonably sure that news of his presence had not yet reached México, Cavendish decided to follow Drake's example and raid the defenseless port of Guatulco. The English squadron anchored off the mouth of the Copalita River on August 5, and a pinnace was sent ahead with thirty men, arriving at Guatulco early the following morning. Although the port had further declined in importance since Drake's visit, it still had a few hundred inhabitants and a certain amount of local trade. Moreover, it was being used as a depot for Chinese merchandise brought around from Acapulco and illegally transshipped to Perú. Shortly before Cavendish's arrival, two Peruvian ships had called there and exchanged a large amount of silver for Chinese goods. Juan de Rengifo, the new *alcalde* [mayor], apparently profited from this contraband trade and consequently was quite pleased to see Cavendish's pinnace coming into the bay. The only other ship in port at the time was a fifty-ton bark loaded with cacao from Acajutla." Gerhard, *Pirates on the West Coast of New Spain*, p. 84. Gerhard also mentions Gay, *Historia de Oaxaca*, page 77, as well as Murguía, "Estadistica Antigua," fs. 192–193, and Francis Pretty, *The Admirable and Prosperous Voyage of the Worshipfull Master Thomas Candish*, p. 813.

10. Lavariega, unpublished family document. The story of the pirate's attempt to destroy the cross is mentioned in Gay, *Historia de Oaxaca*, t. 1, c. 16 : "This cross became famous since the time of Thomas Candisk [Gay's spelling for Cavendish] when he used without success his forces and strength to weaken and destroy the cross. From then on numerous people of authority and knowledge served as witnesses

and testified in what amounted to more than 1,000 folios, the oral tradition of the cross's remote and mysterious origin."

11. AMH doc. 14 Jose Justo Ziga, page 4, 1816–1831; doc. 6, *Un testimonio y documento de 1890, De la escritura de venta de derechos y acciones otorgada a favor del Sr. Hipólito Cruz, de una Fracción de terrenos por el Sr. Justo Ziga* doc. 15, *Un testimonio de la escritura del terreno del Bajo de Coyula, a favor del Sr. Apolonio Isidoro Manzano, 1850s*; doc. 24, 1844; doc. 34, *Un cuadro que contiene copia de escritura del Bajo de Coyula, 1868–1869*; doc. 36, *Un cuadro que contiene testimonio original del terreno del Bajo de Coyula el año de 1934*; doc. 45, *Legajo que contiene comprobante de pago, Bajose de Coyula y Arenal hasta el año 1946.*

12. Fernández's study mentions "plataformas habitacionales, casas habitacionales, acondicionamiento habitacional." Enrique Fernández Dávila and Susana Gómez Serafín, editors. *Arqueología de Huatulco, Oaxaca: Memoria de la primera temporada de campo del proyecto arqueológico Bahías de Huatulco* (México: Colección Científica, INAH, 1988).

13. AMH doc. 28, 1844; doc. 38, *Un testimonio original del terreno de "Bajo del Arenal," 1936*; doc. 39, *Un expediente de embargo llevada a efecto de los terrenos del Bajo de Arenal en el año 1936*; doc. 45, *Legajo que contiene importantes de pagos cubiertos de los "Bajos de Coyula y Arenal" hasta de 1946*; doc. 46, *Un sobre que contiene copias de revaluo del Bajo del Arenal, 1944.*

14. AMH doc. 3, 1539; doc. 48, 1950.

15. Gary M. Feinman and Linda M. Nicholas, "*Especialización artesanal en Ejutla prehispánico,*" in *Cuadernos del Sur,* vol. 3, no. 10 (Mayo–Agosto 1995), pp.37–57. See also the article "Art in Shell of the Ancient Americans" by William Henry Holmes, republished as *El arte de la concha entre los antiguos Americanos,* translated by Lourdes Suárez Diez and Rufina Bórquez de la Fuente (INAH, Serie Arqueología, México, 1997).

16. Miguel Covarrubias, *México South: The Isthmus of Tehuantepec* (London: KEPI, 1946), pp. 66–67.

17. Pedro Carrasco, *Pagan Rituals and Beliefs Among the Chontal Indians of Oaxaca, México,* in *Anthropological Records,* vol. 20, no. 3, p. 110.

18. AMH index related to doc. 12, *Un testimonio de la escritura de venta del terreno denominado 'Chahuey.'*

19. Peter Gerhard, *A Guide to the Historical Geography of New Spain,* p. 125. Regarding Huatulco generally, Gerhard states: "The natives here began to disappear very soon after the Conquest. The greatest loss occurred before 1550, but later plagues took many lives in 1566–7, 1576–7, and 1737–8. The number of native people paying tributes is estimated at 3,000 in 1550, 2,000 in 1570, and only 385 in 1646 (Cook and Borah, 1971–9, III, pp.68–9)."

20. Arrocito gets its name from the tiny white shells, the size of grains of rice, that cover the beach.

21. See endnote 4 in the chapter "The Place at the Edge of the Sea."

22. Rolf Widmer, *Conquista y despertar de las costas de la Mar del Sur (1521–1684),* (México: Consejo Nacional para la Cultura y las Artes, 1990).

23. Rolf Widmer, *Conquista y despertar de las costas de la Mar del Sur (1521–1684).*

24. Huntington Library, HM 918, *Derrotero general del Mar del Sur,* 1669, folios 6–20. HM 265 Hack, William, *A Description of the Sea Coasts in the South Sea of America ,* 1684, fs. 1–6.

25. Sara de Leon, who works at the Instituto Nacional Indigenista in Huamelula, has spent many years there. In the 1990s she published four small monographs for the Chontal community—"Lo que dicen los Abuelos"—based on interviews with some of the elders from the region. They are scarce, and I saw them once in 2001.

RÍOS / RIVERS

1. Unpublished document, INAH, Oaxaca, 1999.

2. AMH doc. 4 is a document from 1837 and 1844 stating that the lands of Coyula belonged to Huatulco, but that they were leased to Pochutla on the condition that the boundaries would be respected in order to avoid any damage to the lands of Huatulco. Decree 52, regarding laws pertaining to those who have cattle in 1844 to 1845, is annexed.

3. Antonio Peñafiel, *Nomenclatura Geográfica de México: Etimologías de los Nombres de Lugar, Correspondientes A Los Principales Idiomas Que Se Hablan En La República* (México: Oficina Topográfica de la Secretaría de Fomento, 1897).

4. Peter Gerhard, *A Guide to the Historical Geography of New Spain,* p. 123

MONTES / MOUNTAINS

1. Peter Gerhard, *A Guide to the Historical Geography of New Spain.* Also René Acuña, *Relaciones geográficas del siglo xvi,* August 29, 1579, pp. 24–28.

2. AMH doc. 3.

3. AMH doc. 2, *Un libro sobre quejas que hicieron los de San Mateo Piñas por despojo que hicieron los de Huatulco en los cerros de 'Llano Juarez,' Platanar*; doc. 7, *'Llano Juárez' Hipolito Cruz—Petición que hizo el sr. Hipolito Cruz de una fracción de terrenos conocido en el nombre de 'Llano Juarez'*; doc. 17, *Un libro que contiene litigios que tenían pendientes Huatulco con San Mateo Piñas por el cerro de 'Llano Chaca, Llano Juárez.'*

POBLADOS / VILLAGES

1. Maximiliano Amador Lavariega, unpublished family document, 1987.

2. Higinia Alcántara Mijangos talked about the origins of other place names, as well: "There is Arroyo Costoche. The *costoche* is an animal smaller than a dog. Here the people believe that when the costoche comes close to the town, it's coming to announce that someone will soon die. And we believe that when the costoche cries at the edge of the town, it coincides with a death. They also say that when the owl sings it announces something. That's why they call it the animal of bad omens. Now then, there are many coincidences.

"At the Cerro Montoso, they called it this because before it was hard to enter. The stone trees are there, they call them stone trees because the wood is very hard and it takes years for them to grow."

3. The names of rivers, like the names of other landmarks, change over time and from village to village. Speaking in Santa María Huatulco, don Ignacio García said, "The river that is born in this place is called Benito Juárez. We called it Río Retil, but here we call it Río Cruz. Where it springs, higher up to the side of Cuajiniquil is the corozal palm (cohune palm), and there they call it the Corozal River. Once it descends right through the town of Benito Juárez, they call it the Río Sal, but here it has another name, they call it Río Cruz, because here it forms a cross with the Magdalena River. Then it descends and empties at Coyula. There, where the bridge fell during the hurricanes, is where the Cruz River and the Magdalena River meet. The Magdalena River gets its name from Magdalena because its source is in a small town known as Santa María Magdalena. . . .

"Cuajinicuil is here [gesturing]. They are people of Huatulco. Cuajinicuil is also the name of the river. Xuchitl is also a river. All these rivers empty at Arenal. Arenal changed greatly. There were many alligators, egrets, a bird known as the *piyusco* that we would eat. There were other birds known as *perfectas*, the brown heron. There were other large animals known as *tacuares*. They screamed at nighttime.

"The old ones would say that in the past there were many coyotes. The coyotes would get the turtle nests and eat the eggs. In those days we didn't eat turtle eggs, and they were plentiful. But the coyotes would seize the nests, and that's why it is called playa El Coyote. They say that San Agustín got its name from a man who lived there by himself. His last name was Agustín. The name caught. And there is Boca Vieja (Old Mouth), because this is the mouth where the rivers empty in Coyula. There is another beach they call Iztapa, because there was a very large salt lagoon, but they no longer work it. It is part of Huatulco. . . .

"Huatulco has that name because, supposedly, it had so much water. My grandmother told me that this is why they gave it the name of Aguatulco. I asked my grandmother. It is like the name Pochutla, because it has many pochote trees. There are so many ceibas, especially up above where the plantations are located.

"She told me that Hacienda Vieja was an established place. There were parts where the old hacienda was established. Pueblo Viejo did not have enough water then, as is the case presently. The creek is called Todos Santos. There is Las Pozas [The Wells] because this is the watering hole where people would stop overnight, on the way to Santa Cruz for the feast days.

"Agua Hedionda [Stinking Water] is sulfured water. There are many people who know that it is a remedy. They go there to put their feet in the water, to heal wounds. They say that the sulfured waters cure. It just has such a foul smell."

4. Cástulo García García, *Breve Historia de San Mateo Piñas*. (Oaxaca: published by the author, 1987).

5. On ancient religious beliefs, don Cástulo added, "[T]he most curious thing is that they knew how to transport themselves to other dimensions. Using the *teponatzli*, the drum, they received energy from the earth, and through the *chirimiya* [flute], they would come in contact with the cosmic energy. So they would meditate and reach other dimensions. It was a very beautiful ceremony. And here there has been a misunderstanding of our ancestors, because it has been said that the heart must be given to God.

"It was symbolic language, that is to say, for example, the masons use their left foot forward before the right because the heart is on the left side, and it is first offered to everyone from the left, love, affection. So this was what was to be given to God, love and affection to God, but they did it physically. They prepared a young maiden and took out her heart to give it, in a physical sense. This is one of the things about which Hernán Cortés reproached Moctezuma. On the other hand, they [the Spaniards] killed for ambition and to rob us."

6. Don Cástulo made the point that Oaxaca is not the only place to research Viceregal titles. "In the case of San Miguel del Puerto, it seems that San Miguel's jurisdiction came all the way down to Santa Cruz. But they have no document, so they can't claim their rights. Nevertheless, this document exists in Spain. There must be one that exists there. When they first gave it, it must have been around 1706, but they didn't get their title until around 1744, and they didn't get possession until around 1751."

7. "[In] San Carlos Yautepec, when a Zapotec went by, the Chontales would kill him. They had an oven. They say they still have those ovens where they would throw him in out of anger because they had so much rage against the Zapotecs." Cástulo García García, conversation with author.

8. "This is where the legend of the princess Donaji comes into play. The Zapotec princess Donaji married the Mixtec prince, and they had their palace close to Monte Alban. They thought this would placate

both groups, but this did not happen, because the Zapotec king attempted an assault against his son-in-law's people. The princess finds out, and she tells her father to be on guard, because the Mixtecs are about to do the same to his people. He takes her advice, and when they arrive the Mixtec king realizes that it is his daughter-in-law who has warned her father. When the Mixtec king returns, he orders her head cut off. It rolls down a precipice and falls into the Atoyac River.

"As the years pass, there's a Spanish poet writing and passing along the river's edge, and he finds a lovely rosebush. He makes the attempt to take the rosebush to plant in his home. As he digs through the dirt and sand, he finds the princess's head intact with the roots. It's the symbol the marimba has in the City of Oaxaca, surrounded by laurels. This is where this legend is from." Castúlo García García, conversation with author.

9. AMH, doc. 4, 1837–1844

10. However, the Lavariega family history notes: "[Don C. Lavariega] was the principal informant of Maximilian Amador, the priest–author of the legends and traditions of Pochutla, [written in] 1925. Another informant was Señora Concepción García, an elder who declares that she was thirteen years of age when the ex-insurgent Vicente Guerrero was apprehended in 1831."

11. Enrique Fernández Dávila and Susana Gómez Serafín, *Arqueología de Huatulco, Oaxaca.*

12. Lavariega, unpublished family document, 1987.

13. Pedro Carrasco, *Pagan Rituals and Beliefs Among the Chontal Indians of Oaxaca, México*, p. 110.

14. Robert Himmerich y Valencia, *The Encomenderos of New Spain: 1521–1555*, pp. 128 and 166–167; and Peter Gerhard, *A Guide to the Historical Geography of New Spain*, p. 124. Gerhard says that Astata was "held from 1528" by Juan Bello; Himmerich states that Bello was tried by the Inquisition in 1527.

15. Mazatan is the spelling used in the region for the Morro Mazatan, rather than Mazatlan, as it is used for the city in the state of Sinaloa, México.

16. Peter Gerhard, *A Guide to the Historical Geography of New Spain*, p. 125.

17. Viola Waterhouse, "The Grammatical Structure of Oaxaca Chontal."

18. Charles Brasseur de Bourbourg, *Viaje por el istmo de Tehuantepec*, (México: Secretaria de Educación Pública, 1984).

19. Sara de Leon, *"Lo que dicen los Abuelos,"* 1993.

20. Antonio Peñafiel, *Nomenclatura Geográfica de México;* Alonso De Molina, *Vocabulario en Lengua Castellana y Mexicana y Mexicana Castellana* (México: Biblioteca Porrúa, 2001); and Ruben Leyton Ovando, *Huamelula: Un Pueblo Chontal de la Costa de Oaxaca.* (Jalapa: Universidad Veracruzana, unpublished thesis, 1972), p. 23.

21. Antonio Peñafiel, *Nomenclatura Geográfica de México;* Alonso De Molina, *Vocabulario en Lengua Castellana y Mexicana y Mexicana Castellana;* and Ruben Leyton Ovando, *Huamelula: Un Pueblo Chontal de la Costa de Oaxaca.*

22. Jesús Avendaño Hernández, *Astata, Lugar de la Garza* (Oaxaca City: published by the author, 2001).

23. Lyle Campbell, *American Indian Languages: The Historical Linguistics of Native America*. Oxford Studies of Anthropological Linguistics (Cambridge: Oxford University Press, 1997); Lyle Campbell, *Historical Linguistics* (Cambridge: MIT Press, 2000); and Shirley Silver and Will K. Miller, *American Indian Languages: Cultural and Social Contexts* (Tucson: University of Arizona Press, 1997).

24. Peter Gerhard, *A Guide to the Historical Geography of New Spain*, p. 124; Robert Himmerich y Valencia, *The Encomenderos of New Spain*, p. 174.

25. Peter Gerhard, *A Guide to the Historical Geography of New Spain*, p. 124

26. AGN Tierras 192, exp. 7, 25 fojas, año de 1702.

27. Francisco de Burgoa, *Palestra historial de virtudes y exemplares apostólicos;* Juan de Torquemada, *Monarquía Indiana*, vol. 1–7 (México: UNAM, 1975–83); Francisco del Paso y Troncoso, *Papeles de la Nueva España.*

28. Pedro Carrasco, "Pagan Rituals and Beliefs Among the Chontal Indians of Oaxaca, México," in *Anthropological Records*, vol. 20, no. 3 (May 27, 1960), pp. 87–117. According to his article, Carrasco visited the Chontal area in the mountains only once. But he conducted an interview with a Chontal man whom he had met earlier and went to see him at the Muséo Nacional in Mexico City in 1951.

29. Engel Sluiter, "The Word Pechelingue: Its Derivation and Meaning," in *The Hispanic American Historical Review* (November 1944), pp. 683–699. Sluiter makes reference to the fact that the play *Marta la Piadosa* (Martha the Pious) by Tirso de Molina (ca. 1584?–1648) mentions the "moros y pechelingues." In another passage, Sluiter quotes in Portuguese that in Algiers the name for pirates was Turcos (pp. 691 and 694). It appears that the few Spanish colonists or priests from this period influenced the names that the Native people of Huamelula gave to the pirates and other characters, based on what was popular at the time.

30. Engel Sluiter, "The Word Pechelingue: Its Derivation and Meaning." Sluiter writes: ". . . towards the close of the 17th century, the

meaning of the word expands. In his *Historical Memoir of Pimería Alta,* Eusebio Kino, the famous Jesuit of Northwest México, writes: '. . . we set out in the South Sea in November, 1685, by order of his Excellency, with two of the ships of California to meet and warn and rescue the China galleon from the hostile pirates, for the *Pichilingües* with many pirogues were lying in wait for it, to rob it, in the port of Navidad.' Here the term is used synonymously with 'pirates,' irrespective of nationality. This broad meaning is even more clearly illustrated by Miguel Venegas in the 1757 imprint of his *Noticia de la California.* Speaking of the capture of one of Juan Iturbi's pearl-fishing vessels by Spilbergen in 1615, Venegas says: '*Apresaronle uno de los Navios los Pyratas Europeos, bien celebrados en America con el nombre de Pichilingües, que no sin desdoro de nuestro poder infestaban el Mar del Sur. . . .' Pichilingüe* is now fully synonymous with pirate, corsair, filibuster, buccaneer, scum of the sea." Kino, p. 693.

31. Miguel Covarrubias, *México South: The Isthmus of Tehuantepec.* Covarrubias reported at the beginning of the 20th century that the oldest women took pride in wearing this cloth, no matter what the stench might be.

32. Zelia Nuttall, "A Curious Survival in Mexico of the Use of the Purpura Shell-Fish for Dyeing," in *Putnam Anniversary Volume: Anthropological Essays* (New York: G. E. Stechert, 1909), pp. 367–84. Nuttall interviewed the people of Huamelula who had knowledge about the purple skirts that she said were named "*de caracolillo*," "dyed with Purpura."

33. See John Bierhorst, *History and Mythology of the Aztecs: The Codex Chimalpopoca.* (Tucson: University of Arizona Press, 1992).

34. Peter Gerhard, *A Guide to the Historical Geography of New Spain,* p. 125. "The numbers were not great, but by 1699 Tonameca was a predominantly Negroid settlement, and mulattoes were scattered along the coast as far as Astatla and Guamelula. The 1786 census has 52.5 mulatto tributaries in the jurisdiction, while that of 1789 shows 219 individual mulattoes. In addition, there was a sprinkling of Spaniards, mestizos, Filipinos ('chinos'), and Peruvians ('peruleros'), a thoroughly mixed-up racial situation."

35. Compare with Jesús Jáuregui y Carlo Bonfiglioli, *Las Danzas de Conquista I.México Contemporaneo* (México: CONACULTA, 1996). The authors analyze contemporary *danzas de conquista* and discuss other authors, such as Ricard, Warman, and Brisset, who have looked at similar genres of "theatrical" indoctrination.

36. This quotation was taken from an e-mail reference, "Learning to Read Mixtec Codices" on the Foundation for the Advancement of Mesoamerican Studies Website, after personal communication with John Pohl. What first caught my attention was John M. D. Pohl, "Mexican Codices, Maps and Lienzos as Social Contracts" in *Writing Without Words: Alternative Literacies in Mesoamerica and the Andes,* Elizabeth Hill Boone and Walter Mignolo, editors, (North Carolina: Duke University Press, 1994), p. 141.

37. Leandro Martínez Machuca, *Cuentos y Leyendas Chontales* (San Pedro Huamelula: published by the author, 1998), pp. 38–39. In this book of 89 pages, don Leandro Martínez Machuca has some of the most important Chontal stories collected from his parents and other elders. Martínez Machuca now lives in Mexico City.

38. See John Bierhorst, *History and Mythology of the Aztecs,* p. 147, 77:16 and fn. 23. The author emphasizes his disagreement with the tradition that Cipactonal is the male, Oxomoco the female (FC 4:4:6: Oxomoco cioatl . . . auh in Cipactonal oquijchtli).

EL ENCANTO DEL NORTE / THE ENCHANTMENT OF THE NORTH

1. Carol Zabin et al. *Mixtec Migrants in California Agriculture: A New Cycle of Poverty,* California Institute for Rural Studies, Publication #009.

2. Donald L.Brockington, María Jorrín, and Robert Long. *The Oaxaca Coast Project Reports,* part I (Nashville: Vanderbilt University Publications in Anthropology, 1974); and Donald L. Brockington and J. Robert Long, *The Oaxaca Coast Project Reports,* part II (Nashville: Vanderbilt University Publications in Anthropology, 1974).

3. Ferdinand Anders, Maarten Jansen, and Luis Reyes García, *Crónica Mixteca: El rey 8 Venado, Garra de Jaguar, y la dinastía de Teozacualco-Zaachila, libro explicativo del llamado Códice Zouche-Nuttall* (México: Fondo de Cultura Económica, 1992).

4. Heather Harris. Harris's work touches on the persistence of verbal art in the telling of Ice Age origins and migrations. Here we may not be traveling so far in space, but we are certainly traveling in time.

5. Gaspar Rivera-Salgado, "Mixtec Activism in Oaxacalifornia: Transborder Grassroots Political Strategies," in *American Behavioral Scientist* (vol. 42, no. 9, June–July 1999) pp. 1439–1458.

Bibliography

Acevedo, María Luisa, et al. "Chontales," in Etnografía y educación: El estado de Oaxaca. Oaxaca: Colección Científica.

Acuña, René. Relaciones Geográficas del siglo XVI: Antequera, tomo primero. México: Universidad Nacional Autónoma de México, 1984.

Aguirre Beltrán, Gonzalo. La población negra de México: Estudio etnohistoria. México: Fondo de Cultura Económica, 1972.

Archivo General de la Nación, UNAM. Corsarios Franceses e Ingleses en la Inquisición de la Nueva España. México: Imprenta Universitaria, 1945.

Al-Shimas, Kamar. The Mexican Southland: An Account of the Author's Wanderings upon, and of the Plants, Animals, People, Commerce, and Industries of the Isthmus of Tehuantepec. Indiana: Benton Review Shop, 1922.

Álvarez Martínez, Félix. Galeón de Acapulco: El viaje de la Misericordia de Dios. Madrid: Gráficas Andemi, S.L.

Alzate y Ramírez, José Antonio de. (1737–90). Memoria sobre la naturaleza, cultivo y beneficio de la grana. México: AGNM, 1981.

Anders, Ferdinand, Maarten Jansen, and Luis Reyes García. Crónica Mixteca: El rey 8 Venado, Garra de Jaguar, y la dinastía de Teozacualco-Zaachila, libro explicativo del llamado Códice Zouche-Nuttall. México: Fondo de Cultura Económica, 1992.

Anders, Ferdinand, Maarten Jansen, and Luis Reyes García. Los templos del cielo y de la oscuridad: Oraculos y liturgia, libro explicativo del llamado Códice Borgia. México: Fondo de Cultural Económica, 1993.

Avendaño Hernández, Jesús. Astata: Lugar de la garza. México, 2001.

Aveni, Anthony F., and Horst Hartung. "Archeoastronomy and Dynastic History at Tikal," in Proceedings: 46 International Congress of Americanists: New Directions in American Archaeoastronomy, Anthony F. Aveni, editor. BAR International Series 454, 1988, pages 1–17.

Barabas, Alicia M., and Miguel A. Bartolomé, editors. Configuraciones étnicas en Oaxaca: Perspectivas etnográficas para las autonomías. vol. I, II. México: INAH, INI, 1999.

Bartolomé, Miguel Alberto, y Alicia Mabel Barabas, Tierra de la palabra. Historia y etnografía de los chatinos de Oaxaca. México: INAH, 1982.

Bartolomé, Miguel, y Alicia Mabel Barabas. La pluralidad en peligro: procesos de transfiguración y extinción cultural en Oaxaca (chochos, chontales ixcatecos y zoques). México: Serie Antropología INAH, INI, 1996.

Basauri, Carlos. Población indígena de México. Etnografía. Oaxaca: CNCA/INI, 1990.

Beletsky, Les. Tropical México: The Cancún Region, Yucatán Península, Oaxaca, Chiapas, and Tabasco. New York: Academic Press, 1999.

Belmar, Francisco. Estudio del chontal. Oaxaca, 1900.

Berlin-Newbart, Heinrich. Fragmentos desconocidos del codice de Yanhuitlan y otras investigaciones mixtecas. México: 1947.

Berry, Charles F., The Reform in Oaxaca, 1856–1876: A Microhistory of the Liberal Revolution. Lincoln: University of Nebraska Press, 1981.

Blanton, Richard E., Gary M. Feinman, Stephen A. Kowalewski, and Linda M. Nicholas. Ancient Oaxaca: The Monte Albán State. Cambridge: Cambridge University Press, 1999.

Borah, Woodrow, Comercio y navegación entre México y Perú en el siglo XVI. México: IMCE, 1975.

Brasseur de Bourbourg, Abbot Charles (1814–74). Viaje por el istmo de Tehuantepec. México: Secretaría de Educación Pública, 1984.

Bricker, Victoria. "The Relationship between the Venus Table and an Almanac in the Dresden Codex," in Proceedings: 46 International Congress of Americanists: New Directions in American Archaeoastronomy, Anthony F. Aveni, editor. BAR International Series 454, 1988, pages 81–105.

Brockington, Donald L., María Jorrín, and J. Robert Long, editors. *The Oaxaca Coast Project Reports*, parts I, II. Nashville: Vanderbilt University Publications in Anthropology, no.8, 1974.

Brockington, Donald Leslie. *The Archaeological Sequence from Sipolite, Oaxaca, México*. Madison: Society for American Archaeology and the University of Wisconsin Press, 1966.

Brockington, Lolita Gutiérrez. *The Leverage of Labor: Managing the Cortés Hacienda in Tehuantepec, 1588–1688*. North Carolina: Duke University Press, 1989.

Burgoa, Francisco de (1605–81). *Palestra historial de virtudes y exemplares apostólicos*. México: Impresa del Museo Nacional, 1903–04 (original 1670).

Burgoa, Francisco de. (1605–81). *Geográfica descripción*. México: Talleres Gráficos de la Nación, 1934.

Bustamante, Carlos María de (1774–48). *Memoria estadística de Oaxaca y descripción del Valle del mismo nombre. Extractada de la que en grande trabajó José Murguía y Galardi*. México: Secretaría de Patrimonio Nacional, 1963.

Caballero López, Lamberto. *Proezas de Cosijopii, el rey tehuano*. Oaxaca, México: Gobierno del Estado, Instituto Oaxaqueño de las Cultura, Casa de la Cultura Oaxaqueña, 1994.

Campbell, Howard, Leigh Binford, Miguel Bartolomé, and Alicia Barabas. *Zapotec Struggles: Histories, Politics, and Representation from Juchitán, Oaxaca*. Washington: Smithsonian Institution Press, 1993.

Censo general de población 1900 estado de Oaxaca, 3 vols. México: Dirección General de Estadística.

Chassen-López, Francie R. "Cheaper than Machines: Women and Agriculture in Porfirian Oaxaca, 1880–1911," in *Women of the Mexican Countryside 1850–1990*, Heather Fowler-Salamini and Mary Kay Vaughn, editors. Tucson: University of Arizona Press, 1994.

Coatsworth, John, "Anotaciones sobre la producción de alimentos en el porfiriato," in *Historia Mexicana*, vol. 25, no.2, 1976.

Cook, Scott, and Martin Diskin, editors. *Markets in Oaxaca*. Austin: University of Texas Press, 1976.

Corbett, Jack, et al., editors. *Migración y Etnicidad en Oaxaca*. Nashville: Vanderbilt University Publications in Anthropology, no. 43, 1992.

Cortés, Hernán. *Letters from México*, edited and translated by Anthony Pagden. New Haven: Yale University Press, 1986.

Cortés, Hernando. *Five Letters: 1519–1526*. New York: Norton, 1929.

Covarrubias, Miguel. *México South: The Isthmus of Tehuantepec*. London: KEPI Limited, 1946.

Cruz, Wilfrid C. *El Tonalamatl Zapoteco*. Oaxaca: Imprenta del Gobierno de Oaxaca, 1935.

Dampier, William. *A New Voyage Round the World*. London: Argonaut, 1927.

del Paso y Troncoso, Francisco. *Epistolario de Nueva España (1505–1815)*. México: Antigua Librería Robredo, 1939.

del Paso y Troncoso, Francisco, *Papeles de Nueva España*. Madrid: Rivadaneyra, 1905.

del Paso y Troncoso, Francisco. *Xustlahuacan: Relaciones del siglo XVIII relativas a Oaxaca*. México: Biblioteca de Historiadores Mexicanos, Vargas Rea, 1950.

del Paso y Troncoso, D. Francisco, y D. Luís González Obregón. *Colección de gramáticas de la lengua mexicana histórica y lingüística*. México: Museo Nacional de México, 1904.

Diskin, Martín, and Scott Cook. *Mercados de Oaxaca*. México: INI, 1989.

Donkin, R. A. *Spanish Red: An Ethnogeographical Study of Cochineal and the Opunta Cactus*. Philadelphia: The American Philosophical Society, vol. 67, part 5, 1977.

Esparza, Manuel. "Los proyectos de los liberales en Oaxaca (1856–1910)," in *Historia de la cuestión agraria mexicana*, vol. 1, no. 288.

Exchange of notes between China and México embodying an agreement for the provisional modification of the Sino-Mexican treaty of 1899. Peking: 1921.

"Feasibility Study on Manufacture of Tamarind Seed Starch in Dandakaranya Region." Hyderabad, India: Small Industry Extension Training Institute, 1971.

Fernández Dávila, Enrique, and Susana Gómez Serafín, editors. *Arqueología de Huatulco, Oaxaca: Memoria de la primera temporada de campo del proyecto arqueológico Bahías de Huatulco*. México: Colección Científica, INAH, 1988.

Feinman, Gary M., and Linda M. Nicholas. "Especialización artesanal en Ejutla prehispánico," in *Cuadernos del Sur*, vol. 3, no. 10, Mayo–Agosto 1995, pp.37–57.

Flannery, Kent V., and Joyce Marcus. *The Cloud People: Divergent Evolution of the Zapotec and Mixtec Civilizations*. New York: Academic Press, 1983.

Fowler-Salamini, Heather, and Mary Kay Vaughn, editors. *Women of the Mexican Countryside, 1850–1990*. Tucson: University of Arizona Press, 1994.

Funnell, William. *A Voyage Round the World*. London: Botham, 1707.

Galarza, Joaquín. *Estudios de escritura indigena tradicional (Azteca–Nahuatl): Manuscritos indígenas tradicionales*, vol. I, México: Archivo General de la Nación, 1979.

Galvano, Antonio. *The Discoveries of the World, from their First Original* unto the Year of Our Lord 1555, by Antonio Galvano, Governor of Ternate. Corrected, Quoted and Published in England, by Richard Hakluyt, (1601). London: Cambridge University Press, 1969.

García García, Cástulo. *Breve historia de San Mateo Piñas.* Oaxaca: 1987.

Gay, José Antonio. *Historia de Oaxaca.* México: 1881.

Gay, José Antonio. *Historia de Oaxaca,* 2 vols. México: 1950.

Gay, José Antonio. *Historia de Oaxaca.* "Sepan Cuantos," no. 373. México: Editorial Porrua, 1990.

Gerber, Frederick H. *Indigo and the Antiquity of Dyeing.* Florida: Frederick H. Gerber, 1977.

Gerber, Frederick H. *Cochineal and the Insect Dyes.* Florida: Frederick H. Gerber, 1978.

Gerhard, Peter. *Pirates on the West Coast of New Spain 1575–1742.* California: Arthur H. Clark, 1960.

Gerhard, Peter. *The Southeast Frontier of New Spain.* Princeton: Princeton University, 1980.

Gerhard, Peter. *The North Frontier of New Spain.* Princeton: Princeton University, 1982.

Gerhard, Peter. *A Guide to the Historical Geography of New Spain.* Norman: University of Oklahoma, 1993

Gerhard, Peter, and Howard E. Gulick. *Lower California Guidebook: A Descriptive Traveler's Guide.* Glendale: Arthur H. Clark, 1964.

Gibson, Charles. *The Aztecs Under Spanish Rule: A History of the Indians of the Valley of México, 1519–1810.* Stanford: Stanford University Press, 1964.

González Navarro, Moisés. "Indio y propiedad en Oaxaca," in *Historia Mexicana,* vol. 8, no. 2, 1958, pages 176–78.

Hernández Díaz, Jorge. "Mujeres chatinas, matrimonios y trabajo," in *Las mujeres en el campo,* edited by Josefina Aranda. Oaxaca: Instituto de Investigaciones Sociológicas de la Universidad Autónoma Benito Juárez, 1988.

Hiernaux-Nicolas, Daniel. *La geografía como metáfora de la libertad: Textos de Eliseo Reclus.* México: Centro de Investigacion Científica "Ing. Jorge L. Tamayo," 1999.

Himmerich y Valencia, Robert. *The Encomenderos of New Spain, 1521–1555.* Austin: University of Texas Press, 1991.

Humboldt, Alejandro de. *Ensayo politico sobre el reino de la Nueva España,* tomo I–V. México: Editorial Pedro Robredo, 1941.

Humboldt, Alejandro de. *Ensayo politico sobre el reino de la Nueva España.* México: Editorial Porrua, 1984.

Icaza, Francisco. *Diccionario autobiográfico de conquistadores y pobladores de Nueva España.* Guadalajara: A. Levy, 1969.

Inéz Davila, José. *Amparo promovido por el sr. lic. D. José Inés Dávila apoderado de la sra. doña Consuelo Cruz de Ruíz, contra actos de la 2a sala del Tribunal Superior de Justicia de Oaxaca.* México: Serralde, 1910.

Ixtlilxóchitl, Fernando de Alva, *Obras Históricas,* tomo I–II, edited by Edmundo O'Gorman. México: UNAM, 1975.

Ixtlilxóchitl, Fernando de Alva. *Nezahualcóyotl Acolmiztli, 1402–1472,* selection of texts and prologue by Emundo O'Gorman. México: Gobierno del Estado de México, 1972.

Jáuregui, Jesús y Carlo Bonfiglioli. *Las danzas de conquista 1: México contemporáneo.* México: Consejo Nacional Para La Cultura Y Las Artes, Fondo de Cultura Económica, 1996.

Karttunen, Frances. *An Analytical Dictionary of Nahuatl.* Norman: University of Oklahoma Press, 1983.

Krauze, Enrique. *Místico de la autoridad Porfirio Díaz.* México: Fondo de Cultura Económica, 1987.

Krofges, Peter C. *El lienzo de Tecciztlan y Tequatepec: Análisis e interpretación de un documento histórico-cartográfico de la Chontalpa de Oaxaca.* Hamburg: Universidad de Hamburgo, 1997 (unpublished thesis).

León-Portilla, Miguel, and Earl Shorris. *In the Language of Kings: Mesoamerican Literature, Pre-Columbian to the Present.* New York: Norton, 2001.

León-Portilla, Miguel. *Aztec Thought and Culture: A Study of the Ancient Nahuatl Mind.* Norman: University of Oklahoma Press, 1963.

León-Portilla, Miguel. *Los antiguos Mexicanos a través de sus crónicas y cantares.* México: Fondo de Cultura Económica, 1961.

Leyton Ovando, Rubén. *Huamelula, un pueblo chontal de la Costa de Oaxaca.* Jalapa, Veracruz: Universidad Veracruzana, 1972 (unpublished thesis).

Lockhart, James. *The Nahuas After the Conquest.* Stanford: Stanford University Press, 1992.

López-Austin, Alfredo. *Tamoanchan y Tlalocan.* México: Fondo de Cultura Económica, 1994.

"Las Bahías de Huatulco," in "Costa de Oaxaca, México." Library of Congress, MLCS 91/06901 (brochure).

Ma, Huan. *Ying-yai Sheng-lan: The Overall Survey of the Ocean's Shores, 1433.* London: Hakluyt Society Press, 1970.

Martínez Gracida, Manuel. *Catálogo etimológico de los nombres de los pueblos.* Oaxaca: Imprenta del Estado en el Ex-Obispado, dirigida por I. Candiani, 1883.

Martínez Gracida, Manuel. *El rey Cosijoeza y su familia*. México: Oficina Tipográfica Secretaría de Fomento, 1888.

Martínez Gracida, Manuel, *Historia Antigua de la Chontalpa Oaxaqueña*. Oaxaca: Imprenta del Gobierno Federal, 1910.

Mendez Martínez, Cuauhtemoc. *San Miguel del Puerto a través de la historia: Recopilación del autor.* n.d. (unpublished document).

Mejía Sánchez, Ernesto. *Inquisición sobre Oaxaca y otros textos*. México: Bibliófilos Oaxaqueños, 1969.

Molina, Alonso de, *Vocabulario de la Lengua Mexicana*. Leipzig: Teubner, 1880 (1904).

Molina, Alonso de, *Vocabulario en Lengua Castellana y Mexicana*. México: Editorial Porrúa, 2001.

Motolinía, Tomás, *Memoriales*. México: Editorial Porrua, 1984.

Motolinía, Tomás, *Historia de los indios de la Nueva España*. México: Editorial Porrua, 1984.

Motolinía, Toribio de Benavente (d. ca. 1565). *Memoriales o libro de las cosas de la Nueva España y de los naturales de ella*, edición preparada por Edmundo O'Gorman. México: UNAM, 1971.

Motolinía, Toribio de Paredes. *Relación de los ritos antiguos, idolatrías y sacrificios de los Indios de la Nueva España, y de la maravillosa conversión que Dios en ellos ha obrado*. México: Primera Edición Facsimilar, 1979.

Nolasco Armas, Margarita. *Oaxaca indígena: Problemas de aculturación en el estado de Oaxaca y subáreas culturales*. Oaxaca: Instituto de Investigación e Integración Social del Estado de Oaxaca, 1972.

Nuttall, Zelia, "A curious survival in Mexico of the use of the purpura shell-fish for dyeing," in *Anthropological Essays*. New York: G. E. Stechert, 1909, pp. 367–84.

Nuttall, Zelia, editor and translator. *New Light on Drake: A Collection of Documents Relating to His Voyages of Circumnavigation, 1577–1580*. London: Hakluyt Society, 1914.

Orozco, Gilberto. *Tradiciones y leyendas del Istmo de Tehuantepec*. México: Revista Musical Mexicana, 1946.

Paddock, John. *Lord 5 Flower's Family: Rulers of Zaachila and Cuilapan*. Nashville: Vanderbilt University Publications in Anthropology, no.29, 1983

Peñafiel, Antonio. *Nomenclatura geográfica de México: Etimologías de los nombres de lugar*. México: Oficina Tipográfica de la Secretaría de Fomento, 1897

Peñafiel, Antonio. *Nombres geográficos de México: Catálogo alfabético de los nombres de lugar pertenecientes al idioma "Náhuatl."* México: Oficina Tipográfica de la Secretaría de Fomento, 1885.

Peterson, Roger Tory, and Edward L. Chalif. *A Field Guide to Mexican Birds: México, Guatemala, Belize and El Salvador*. New York: Houghton Mifflin Company, 1973.

Pickett, Velma, et al. *Castellano–Zapoteco, Zapoteco–Castellano: Dialecto del zapoteco del Istmo*, Serie de Vocabularios Indigenas Mariano Silva y Aceves, no. 3. México: Instituto Lingüístico de Verano, SEP, 1959

Piña Lujan, Ignacio. *La grana o cochinilla del nopal*. México: Laboratorios Nacionales de Fomento Industrial, 1977.

Pretty, Francis. *The Admirable and Prosperous Voyage of the Worshipfull Master Thomas Cavendish*, in Richard Hakluyt, *Principal Navigations, Voyages, and Discoveries of the English Nation*, vol. III. London: Dent and Sons, 1600.

Reko, Blas Pablo. *Mito botánica Zapoteca*. México: Academia Nacional de Ciencias "Antonio Alzate," 1945.

Rojas, Basilio. *Efemerides oaxaqueñas*. México: 1962 (original 1911)

Romero Frizzi, María de los Angeles. *Lecturas históricas del estado de Oaxaca: Época colonial*. México: INAH, 1986.

Rubio Sánchez, Manuel. *Historial del cultivo de la grana o cochinilla en Guatemala*. Guatemala: Tipográfica Nacional, 1994.

Sahagún, Bernardino de, *Historia de las cosas de la Nueva España*, tomo 1–2. México: Consejo Nacional para la Cultura y las Artes, Alianza Editorial Mexicana, 1989.

Sahagún, Bernardino de, *Historia general de las cosas de Nueva España*. México: Imprenta del Ciudadano Alejandro Valdés, 1829

Santibañez Miguel, Tito. *Como hacemos el cultivo de la grana cochinilla*. Oaxaca, México: Instituto Tecnológico Agropecuario de Oaxaca, Casa de la Cultura Oaxaqueña, 1992.

Sarabio Viejo, María Justina. *La grana y el añil: Técnicas tintóreas en México y América Central*. Sevilla: Publicaciones de estudios Hispano-Americanos de Sevilla, 1994.

Shroeder, Susan, Stephanie Wood, and Robert Haskett, editors. *Indian Women of Early México*. Norman: University of Oklahoma Press, 1997.

Sluiter, Engel. "The Word *Pechelingue*: Its Derivation and Meaning," in *The Hispanic American Historical Review*, November 1944, pages 683–89.

Small Industry Extension Training Institute. *Feasibility study on manufacture of tamarind seed starch in Dandakaranya region*. Hyderabad, India: Small Industry Extension Training Institute 1971.

Spielbergen, Joris Van. *The East and West Indian Mirror, Being an Account of Joris van Spielbergen's Voyage Round the World (1614–1617)*. London: Hakluyt Society, 1906.

Stiller, Dankwart, and Detlef Katenkamp. *Histochemistry of amyloid: General considerations, light microscopical and ultrastructural examinations.* Jena: Fischer VEB, 1975.

Taylor, William B. *Landlord and Peasant in Colonial Oaxaca.* Stanford: Stanford University Press, 1972

Thiery de Menonville, Nicolas Joseph (1739–80). *Traite de la culture du nopal et de la éducation de la cochenille dans les colonies francaises de l'Amerique, précéde d'un voyage à Oaxaca.* Paris: Dellalain, 1787.

Thiery de Menonville, Nicolas Joseph. *Des herrn Thiery de Menonville Reise nach Guaxaca in Neu-Spanien.* Leipzig: Weygand, 1789.

Thomas, David Hurst. *Archeological and Historical Perspectives on the Spanish Borderlands West,* vol. 1. Washington: Smithsonian Institution Press, 1989.

Tibón, Gutierre. *Pinotepa Nacional: Mixtecos, negros y triques.* México: Universidad Nacional Autónoma de México, 1961 (original 1905).

Tibón, Gutierre. *Aventuras en México, 1937–1983.* México: Editorial Diana, 1983.

Tichy, Franz. "Measurement of Angles in Mesoamerica: Necessity and Possibility," in *Proceedings: 46 International Congress of Americanists: New Directions in American Archaeoastronomy,* Anthony F. Aveni, editor. BAR International Series 454, 1988, pages 105–21.

Torquemada, Juan de. *Monarquía Indiana,* vol. 1–7. México: UNAM, 1975–83.

Turner, John Kenneth. *Barbarous México.* Austin: University of Texas Press, 1969.

Vera-Cruz y Oaxaca en 1798. México: Vargas Rea, 1946.

Villa Rojas, Alfonso. "Los Chontales," in *Handbook of Middle American Indians, vol.7.* Austin: University of Texas Press, 1969, pages 244–75.

Villalobos, Samuel. "Doña Juana C. Romero, Benefactora de Teuantepec. Discurso del Dr. Samuel Villalobos," in *Ex-Alumnos,* Abril 30, 1954.

Waterhouse, Viola Grace. *The Grammatical Structure of Oaxaca Chontal.* Bloomington: Indiana University Research Center in Anthropology, Folklore, and Linguistics, 1962.

Weitlander, Roberto J., "Notas de los informes de Weitlaner" (unpublished). México: INAH, Convento del Carmen, 1967.

Weitlaner, Roberto J., and Marlene Aguayo A. "Consejo de planeación e instalación del Museo Nacional de Antropología: Los chontales, estado de Oaxaca." México: INAH, 1962 (unpublished document).

Whitecotton, Joseph W., and Judith Bradley Whitecotton. *Vocabulario Zapoteco–Castellano.* Nashville: Vanderbilt University Publications in Anthropology, no. 45, 1993.

Widmer, Rolf. *Conquista y despertar de las costas de la Mar del Sur (1521–1684).* México: Consejo Nacional para la Cultura y las Artes, 1990.

Williams, J. J. *The Isthmus of Tehuantepec: Being the Results of a Survey for a Railroad to Connect the Atlantic and Pacific Oceans, Made by the Scientific Commission.* New York: D. Appleton & Company, 1852.

Widmer, Rolf. *Conquista y despertar de las costas de la Mar del Sur, 1521 1684.* México: CONACULTA, 1990.

Young, M. Jane. "Directionality as a Conceptual Model for Zuni Expressive Behavior," in *Proceedings: 46 International Congress of Americanists: New Directions in American Archaeoastronomy,* Anthony F. Aveni, editor. BAR International Series 454, 1988, pages 171–83.

Yuste López, Carmen, *El comercio de la Nueva España con Filipinas, 1590–1785.* México: INAH, 1984.

Yuste, Carmen, et al. *El galeón del Pacífico: Acapulco–Manila 1565–1815.* México: Gobierno Constitucional del Estado de Guerrero, 1992.

Zárate Morán, Roberto. "El Corozal, un sitio arqueológico en la costa del Pacífico de Oaxaca," in *Cuadernos del Sur,* vol. 3, no. 10. Mayo–Agosto 1995, pages 9–36.

Index

A

abalone, 30
Acapulco, 22, 45
agriculture, 21, 45; Baja California, 168–69; Bajos de Coyula, 45; Bajos del Arenal, 49–51, 52–53; Cacaluta, 52–53; California, 172; El Pedimento region, 40; Paso de los Robles, 119; Punta Arena, 57; ritual observances, 144–47; San Isidro Chacalapa, 124, 125, 126; San Mateo Piñas, 106–7, 111; Santa María Huatulco, 93–94, 102–3
Aguatulco, 19
Aguatusco, 19
Alcántara Mijangos, Higinia, 27–28, 93–94
alligators, 42, 55, 119, 122; in Feast of San Pedro, 152, 162, 163, 164, 165
Alotepec, San Juan, 21
Alva Itlilxochitl, Fernando de, 27, 37–38, 167
Alvarado, Pedro de, 20, 155
Amador, Maximiliano, 93
Anders, Ferdinand, 176
archeological research, 16, 27, 51, 117
architecture and construction, 52, 64, 76, 127, 129–30, 169; Santa María Huatulco, 101–2, 103
Arenal, Bajos del, 45, 49–52
Arista, Lucino, 38, 49–52

B

Arrocito, 55–56
Astata, 18, 21, 22, 25, 124, 126–35, 141, 158
Avendaño, Abacuc Luis, 55
Avendaño, Ana Luz, 101
Avendaño, Beto, 100–101
Avendaño, Jesùs, 18
Aymoo, 165
Aztecs. See Mexica

Baja California, 17, 167–70
Baldes, Juan, 25
Barbas, Gaspar de, 23
Barra de la Cruz, 59–61
Bello, Juan, 127–28, 155
Benito Juárez, 84–91, 110–11
birds, 21, 40, 75, 78, 115, 124–25
Bocana, La, 64–65
Boquerón, El, 136, 137
boundaries. See land boundaries and ownership
Brockington, Donald Leslie, 16
Burgoa, Francisco de, 20
Bustamante, Anastasio, 30

C

Cacalotepec. See Cacaluta
Cacaluta, 26, 37, 52–55, 56
cacao, 22, 114
caracol (caracolillo). See dyes/dyeing: Purpúra pansa
Cárdenas, Lázaro, 78
Cárdenas, Pablo, 45
Carrancistas, 86, 87, 88
Carrasco, Pedro, 121

Cavendish, Thomas, 23, 30–34
ceiba tree, 27–28, 30, 75, 94, 105
Cerro Chino, 116
Cerro Culeco, 118
Cerro Espina, 106
Cerro Huatulco, 84, 96, 117
Cerro Leon, 25, 111
Cerro Limoncito, 117
Cerro Lobo, 72–73, 81
Cerro Sombrero (Macahuite, Cimmarón), 117
Cervantes, Artemio, 57
Cervantes Dominguez, Nestora, 35
Chahue, Bahía, 55
chapopote, 30
Chichimecas, 20, 27, 176
Chontales, 27, 48, 51, 57, 64, 105, 112, 121, 122, 126; Astata region, 129, 132; Feast of San Pedro rituals, 154–65; feasts and celebrations, 60; history, 138–40; language, 21, 40, 73, 132, 138–39; religious practices, 140–48; San Pedro Huamelula region, 136–65; during Spanish Conquest, 21–22; symbols of wealth, 154
church records, 16; San Pedro Huamelula, 148–50
Cimatlan. See Zimatan
Cipactonal, 165
climate, 37–39, 40, 55; Baja California, 167; Bajos de Coyula, 40–41; Bajos del Arenal,

50–52; see also hurricanes
clothing, 16, 21, 55, 90, 94, 109, 122, 131; for Feast of San Pedro, 151–52, 154–55
Coatepetl, 20
Coatulco, 20
cochineal, 21, 25, 111
Codex Chimalpopoca, 156
Codex Colombino, 176
Codex Zouche-Nuttall, 154, 158–59, 176
coffee, 58, 73, 75–78, 81, 104, 105, 106–7, 110, 111
copal, 64, 99, 114; see also incense
Copalita, Río, 16, 17, 63–65, 75, 97
coquitos, 40
corn (maize), 23, 53, 109, 175
Cortés, Hernán, 18, 19, 22–23, 111, 156
Cortés, Martín, 127
Covarrubias, Miguel, 51
Coyula, Bajos de, 40–49, 107
Coyula, Río, 16, 23, 41, 42, 45
coyul palm, 40
crow(s), 52, 53
Crucecita, 61, 104; see also Santa Cruz
Cruz, Albino, 57
Cruz del Monte, 38–40, 86, 91; see also El Pedimento
Cruz Martínez, Edmundo, 27, 28–29, 36–37, 40, 55
Cuajinicuil, 38, 81–82, 88
Cuauhtemoc, 50, 51, 52
Cuauhtxochco, 20

D

decorative arts, 8, 9, 51, 151–52; body ornament, 71; see also clothing
derrotero(s), 23, 24, 30, 57, 138
Día de los Muertos, 37, 82, 83, 93, 97–101, 103, 105, 132; see also Todos Santos
Díez de Miranda, Gutierre, 73
Drake, Francis, 23, 30
dyes/dyeing, 55, 57, 58, 70, 122, 154; cochineal, 21, 25, 88; Purpúra pansa, 22, 29, 36, 37, 40, 51, 55–56, 71

E

8 Deer, 117, 176
encantos, 17, 38, 58, 63, 106; Astata region, 127–29, 132, 176; Benito Juárez, 84, 85–86; Cerro Huatulco, 84, 96; Erradura, 105–106; Feast of San Pedro, 151; meaning and significance of, 17; Paso de los Robles region, 118–119, 122–24; El Pedimento, 38–40; Piedro de Moros, 113, 115; San Mateo Piñas, 109–10; San Miguel del Puerto, 75–76; San Pedro Huamelula region, 136, 148, 171; Santa María Huatulco, 96; similarities among, 175–76; Tangolunda, 58; Xadani, 73, 75; Yuviaga, 76
environment: Bahía Chahue, 55; Bahía de Santa Cruz, 27–28, 36–38; Baja California, 167; Bajos de Coyula, 40–42; Barra de la Cruz, 58–59, 60; La Bocana, 64; Paso de los Robles region, 122; El Pedimento, 38; Piedro de Moros, 113–15; San Isidro Chacalapa, 125, 126; San Miguel del Puerto, 75, 76; tourism, effects of, 39, 50, 55, 58, 60
Erradura, 104–06
Escamilla, Agustín, 171
Escamilla Zarate, María, 118–19, 136–38, 139

F

feathers, 21
Filipino immigrants, 25

fish and seafood, 29–30, 40, 51, 54, 62, 63, 116, 122, 125, 130; Bahia de Santa Cruz, 28–29, 34, 35–37, 43; Baja California, 167–68; Barra del Arenal, 50–51; hatchery, 54, 60
foodstuffs, 15–16, 35, 40, 41, 45, 47, 56–57, 66, 67–69, 79, 82, 101, 108, 115; for Feast of San Pedro, 152; mole, 133–34; for Todos Santos, 132, 133–36.
fundador, 143, 145–46

G

Gabriel, Rogelio, 82–84
Gabriel de Pantoja, Gabriel, 21
Gabriel García, Nicolas, 83
Gabriel Lavariega, Catarino, 83
García, Ignacio (Tío Nacho), 10, 34, 55, 75, 88, 96–97, 99, 104–05, 113
García, Irineo, 66–67
García, José A., 115, 116
García, Luciana, 66–67
García, Luis Reyes, 176
García, María, 114 15
García, Pedro, 19
García, Soledad, 100, 104–06
García, Soledad "Chole", 86–87
García, Ulidio, 86
García García, Cástulo, 18, 63, 107, 108–13, 139
Gay, Antonio, 20
Gerhard, Peter, 16, 22, 129
Gómez, Esperanza, 67
Gómez, Victoriano, 67
González, Susana, 45
González de Avila, Gil, 127
Guamelula. See Huamelula
guanacastle (guanacaste) tree, 27–28, 39, 44, 50
Guatulco. See Huatulco
Guelaguetza, 170, 171
Guerrero, Vincent, 30
Guinea, Diego de, 25

H

Hack, William, 23, 24
Harris, Heather, 176
healing practices, 49, 57, 67, 114
historical records, 16, 18–21, 24, 25, 117
Holy Cross of Huatulco, 28, 32–34, 94
Holy Week observances, 142–44

Honduras, 22, 112
Huamelula, 19, 21, 22, 25, 118, 119, 138, 167, 170–72, 174, 176–77; see also San Pedro Huamelula
Huatulco, 18, 19, 20, 21–22, 27, 30, 33, 38, 42, 45, 47, 79, 81, 83, 84, 88–89, 93–95, 110, 174, 176–177
Huatulco, Río, 38, 41, 45, 97
Huave, 17, 20, 38, 63, 136, 156
hurricanes, 38, 40, 78, 81–82, 90, 101, 104, 109

I

identity, cultural, 16–17, 25, 169, 170, 172, 174, 177
incense, 64, 99, 146, 162

J

jamaica (hibiscus), 101–02
Jansen, Maarten, 176
Jauna de Agua, 146, 148
Juánez Sanchez, Eme, 106–08

L

Lachimii, José, 154, 160
Laguna Culeca, 118, 121, 123, 124
land boundaries and ownership, 15, 16–17, 19, 25, 45, 47, 175; Arenal, 41–45; Bahía de Santa Cruz, 29; Benito Juárez, 84, 86, 88–89, 91, 110–11; Cerro Huatulco, 84; Coyula, 41–46, 65, 107; expropriation, 17, 47, 64–65, 78; Feast of San Pedro rituals, 159, 163, 165; La Bocana/Río Copalita region, 64–65; Paso de los Robles, 118–19; Piedro de Moros, 115–16; Pochutla, 42, 45, 65, 106, 107, 110; San Mateo Piñas, 25, 41, 81, 84, 86, 88–89, 91, 98, 110–11; San Miguel del Puerto, 79–80; San Pedro Huamelula, 141; Santa Maria Huatulco, 25, 41–46, 47, 79–80, 81–82, 84, 86, 88–89, 91, 97–98, 101, 106, 107, 110–11
language, 20, 51, 55, 90–91, 108–9; Benito Juárez, 84; Chontal, 138–39; El Pedimento area, 40; in Feast of San Pedro, 154; historical

evolution, 112; place names, 19, 20, 25, 27, 64, 82, 91, 94, 111–12, 122, 126, 138; prohibitions against dialect, 132
Laro Franco, Victoria, 94
Lavariega, Luciano, 115 16
Lavariega, Marcelina, 116, 117, 118
Lavariega, Maximiliano de, 30, 93, 113, 117
Lavariega, Silverio, 93, 116, 117–18, 167–68
Lavariega family, 20, 22, 32, 113, 115, 116
Lizama, Piedad, 105
López Ramírez, Hector, 159
Los Angeles, 170, 171
Los Loxicha, 111

M

Maguey, El, 30
Manzano, Angel, 45
Manzano, Concepción, 116
Manzano Ramírez, Andres, 47
maps, 12–13, 23, 24, 56
Mareños, 156, 157, 162, 163
Martínez, Abel, 58
Martínez, Francisco, 58–59
Martínez, Gorgonio, 115, 116
Martínez García, Filomeno, 86, 90–91
Martínez Grácida, Manuel, 20
Martínez Machuca, Leandro, 163
Maura, doña, 87–88
Maya, 8, 37, 126, 138, 168
Maya Chontal, 139
Mazatan, 21, 129
medicinal plants, 49, 57, 67, 114–15, 132
Méndez, Cuauhtemoc, 18, 80
Méndez family of Cuajinicuil, 81–82, 83
Mendoza, Antonio de, 22
Menonville, Thiery de, 21
Mexica, 20, 75, 109, 120
migration, 17, 54, 58, 60, 167, 169, 172–73, 176–77; into Huatulco, 25, 173; motivation behind, 54, 173–74
Mijangos, Virginia, 28, 94–96
mining, 22, 25, 117
Mixtec, 9, 27, 51, 55–56, 94, 113, 116, 117, 158–59, 176; in California, 15, 172–73; dyeing practices, 55–56
Moctezuma, 20, 156

Moctezuma, 20, 156
Morales, Hugo, 172
Muhú, 152–56, 159–63
Muliatas, 155, 162

N

Nahua, 20, 25, 27, 53, 70, 82, 91, 94, 120, 126, 138, 139, 154, 167, 175
Narvaez, Isidoro, 10, 61, 65
Nuttall, Zelia, 154, 158–59

O

Oaxaca City, 16, 18, 21, 33, 35, 36, 38, 104, 118, 122, 136, 138
Olea Lavariega, Albano, 115
Olea Lavariega, Gabriel, 115
Olmedo Lavariega, Artemia, 46–47
Ortíz, Albino, 57
Ortíz, Genaro, 93–94
Ortiz, José (Tío), 41–47, 93
Ortíz Lopez, Araceli, 93

P

Panama, 154
Paso Ancho, 106
Paso de los Robles, 118–25
Pechilingües. See Pichilingües
Pedimento, El, 27, 29, 34, 38–40, 86, 173
Peláez de Barrio, Juan, 20
Peralta, Beto, 111
Peralta Gabriel, Filiberto, 88–89
Pérez, Domingo, 19
Perú, 22
Pichilingües, 23, 152, 154–56, 158–60, 162, 167; see also pirates
Piedro de Moros, 112, 113–18
pineapples, 110
Piñon, Celia, 127–35, 141, 143–44
Piñon, Eloy, 130, 131
pirates, 19, 22, 23, 30–33, 113, 167; see also Pichilingües
Pluma Hidalgo, 104
pochote tree, 20, 27–28
Pochutla, 16, 25, 42, 65, 97; see also land boundaries and ownership
Pohl, John, 158–59
primordial title, 16, 18–19
Punta Arena, 57

Q

Quetzalcoatl, 20, 27, 28, 37, 79, 93 167, 176

R

Ramírez, Ambrosio, 42
Relaciones, 19–20, 30, 55, 150
Rey, Valentin, 140, 141
Ricárdez, Beto, 118–21, 122–25, 146
Ricárdez, Flora, 61
Ríos, Ariana, 68
rituals and festivals: agricultural, 145–48; in Bahía de Santa Cruz area, 34–35; Chontal feasts and celebrations, 60; Christmas in Barra de la Cruz, 59–61; Feast of San Pedro, 23, 150–65; Gue-laguetza, 170; Lenten, 34–36, 40, 86, 121, 128; of ancient peoples, 18, 19, 29, 109, 120; San Miguel del Puerto, 76, 78–79; significance of, 16; wedding, 67–69, 109; see also Día de los Muertos, El Pedimento, Holy Week, Todos Santos
Robles Alegría, Juana, 118, 171
Robles, Martín, 119

S

salt, 19, 22, 35, 38, 50, 121, 141
San Agustín, Bay of, 50
Sánchez, Ernestina, 107, 108
Sánchez, Manuel, 107
San Isidro Chacalapa, 119, 125–26
San Mateo Piñas, 19, 25, 63, 106–13; see also land boundaries and ownership
San Miguel de Huatulco, 19, 55
San Miguel del Puerto, 55, 63, 64, 73, 75–81, 97
San Pedro Huamelula, 18, 136–50; see also rituals and festivals; Feast of San Pedro
Santa Cruz, Bahia de, 27–38; environment, 28, 29, 36–38; fishing industry, 36–37, 42; pirate activity, 30–32; see also Holy Cross of Huatulco
Santa María Huamelula, 141
Santa María Huatulco, 16,
93–103, 104; founding, 93, 94–95; historical development, 18–23, 25; Lenten feast, 35; recent development, 101–02, 104; see also Día de los Muertos; land boundaries and ownership
Seco, Río, 66–69, 70
Simeón Martínez, Gil, 168–69
Simón, Juan de, 19
slaves, 20, 22–23, 24, 114, 156, 162
snake(s), 20, 73, 76, 132
Sonoma Valley, California, 172–73
Spanish Conquest, 15–16, 19, 28, 109
spiritual life, 18, 63, 67; ancient practices, 109; Astata region, 127–29, 132; beliefs about the dead, 105; Chontal religion, 144; founding of Santa Maria Huatulco, 94–95; nagualismo (nagual), 63, 67; newer religions, 100; Paso de los Robles region, 122–24; preparation of altares, 82, 83; San Pedro Huamelula, 141, 144–48; see also encan-tos; rituals and festivals
sugar, 15–16, 21–22

T

Tangolunda, 57–59, 60, 130
Tehuantepec, Isthmus of, 15, 22, 27, 37, 63, 112, 119, 136, 151–52, 174
terral, 37
Todos Santos, 37, 132–35
Toltecs, 27, 38, 167, 176
Tómas, Santo, 28, 94, 104–06
Tonameca, 109
Tonantzin, 109
Tonatiuh, 20
Torre, Bartolome de la, 23
Torrencín, Aladino, 154, 160
Torres Ramírez, Baldomero, 115
tourism, 17, 57, 64, 91, 130, 174; Bahía de Santa Cruz, 29; Baja California, 167, 170; Bajos del Arenal, 52; El Pedimento region, 38, 40; environmen-tal effects, 38, 40, 58, 60; La Bocana, 64, 65; Tangolunda, 57–58, 59
trade, 15–16, 20, 21, 23, 51, 112–13, 121–122; salt, 121–22; shells, 49, 113
Tututepec, 20, 27, 117, 176
turtles, 40, 53, 67, 122

U

United States: California, 170–73; Colorado, 58; New Jersey, 174–75; Texas, 54

V

Vásquez, Abdías, 46
Vásquez, Pancho, 41, 42
Virgen del Rosario, 140–43, 148–49

W

Waterhouse, Viola, 132, 172
wheat, 15–16

X

Xadani, 25, 70, 73–75
Xuchitl, 38, 82–84, 85

Y

Yerba Buena, 29
Yuviaga, Río, 76

Z

Zapotec, 25, 27, 29, 77, 85, 94, 107, 108, 111, 112, 139, 173
Zárate, Elizabeth, 138, 141
Zárate, Jaime, 162
Zárate, Leticia, 170–72
Zárate, Manuel, 136–38, 145–46
Ziga, José Jesus, 45
Ziga, Justo, 45, 116
Ziga, Leonorio, 47
Ziga, Lucía, 45
Ziga, Nereo, 27, 45–46, 50, 71
Ziga, Peralta, 45
Ziga Manzano, José, 47
Zimatan, 69–71